Does Your Broker Owe You MONEY?

Does Your Broker Owe You MONEY?

*If You've Lost Money in the Market
and It's Your Broker's Fault — You Can Get It Back*

DANIEL R. SOLIN

A PERIGEE BOOK

A PERIGEE BOOK
Published by the Penguin Group
Penguin Group (USA) Inc.
375 Hudson Street, New York, New York 10014, USA
Penguin Group (Canada), 90 Eglinton Avenue East, Suite 700, Toronto, Ontario M4P 2Y3, Canada
(a division of Pearson Penguin Canada Inc.)
Penguin Books Ltd., 80 Strand, London WC2R 0RL, England
Penguin Group Ireland, 25 St. Stephen's Green, Dublin 2, Ireland (a division of Penguin Books Ltd.)
Penguin Group (Australia), 250 Camberwell Road, Camberwell, Victoria 3124, Australia
(a division of Pearson Australia Group Pty. Ltd.)
Penguin Books India Pvt. Ltd., 11 Community Centre, Panchsheel Park, New Delhi—110 017, India
Penguin Group (NZ), Cnr. Airborne and Rosedale Roads, Albany, Auckland 1310, New Zealand
(a division of Pearson New Zealand Ltd.)
Penguin Books (South Africa) (Pty.) Ltd., 24 Sturdee Avenue, Rosebank, Johannesburg 2196,
South Africa

Penguin Books Ltd., Registered Offices: 80 Strand, London WC2R 0RL, England .

While the author has made every effort to provide accurate telephone numbers and Internet addresses
at the time of publication, neither the publisher nor the author assumes any responsibility for errors, or
for changes that occur after publication. Further, the publisher does not have any control over and does
not assume any responsibility for author or third-party websites or their content.

PRINTING HISTORY
Alpha trade paperback edition / 2002
Silvercloud trade paperback edition / 2004
Perigee trade paperback edition / November 2006

Library of Congress Cataloging-in-Publication Data

Solin, Daniel R.
    Does your broker owe you money : if you've lost money in the market and it's your broker's fault—
you can get it back / Daniel R. Solin.
        p. cm.
    Originally published: 2nd. Bonita Springs, Fla. : Silver Cloud, c2004.
    Includes bibliographical references and index.
    ISBN 0-399-53336-2
    1. Stockbrokers.   2. Securities.   3. Fraud.   I. Title.
    HG4621.S675 2006
    332.6'2—dc22
                                                                    2006050712

PRINTED IN THE UNITED STATES OF AMERICA

10   9   8   7   6   5   4   3   2

PUBLISHER'S NOTE: This publication is designed to provide accurate and authoritative information
in regard to the subject matter covered. It is sold with the understanding that the publisher is not
engaged in rendering legal, accounting, or other professional services. If you require legal advice or
other expert assistance, you should seek the services of a competent professional. Continued on page
275.

Most Perigee Books are available at special quantity discounts for bulk purchases for sales promotions,
premiums, fund-raising, or educational use. Special books, or book excerpts, can also be created to fit
specific needs. For details, write: Special Markets, The Berkley Publishing Group, 375 Hudson Street,
New York, New York 10014.

To all investors.
You deserve far more than you have been receiving.
I hope that this book helps you reach your investment goals.

Acknowledgments

This third edition of this book could not have been written without the assistance of Jon Zonderman, who was so instrumental in the previous versions. I continue to be very fortunate to have the benefit of his extraordinary talent.

My sincere thanks to John Duff at Perigee Books for his support and insight.

My designer, Meghan McPhail, dealt with conflicting input from many sources and still succeeded in producing a cover and interior design that greatly added to the quality of the final product.

My daughter, Sabrina Weill, a talented author, again provided countless hours of assistance that contributed immensely to the overall tone and readability of the book. She did so with endless patience and tolerance.

My wife, Patricia Solin, sets an example of kindness, decency, and genuine concern for the lives of others, which is a daily inspiration to me and a reminder of how fortunate I am to be married to her.

Contents

What's New?

I wrote the first edition of this book in the spring of 2002 and updated it in early 2004. In 2003, eleven brokerage firms alleged to have hyped the stocks of their investment-banking clients in reports authored by their much-touted analysts reached a global settlement of the disturbing charges against them. Under this agreement, the firms paid $1.4 billion in fines, penalties, and restitution.

These firms were the leaders of the brokerage industry: Bear Stearns; Citigroup/Salomon Smith Barney; Credit Suisse First Boston; Deutsche Bank Securities; Goldman Sachs; J.P. Morgan Securities; Lehman Brothers; Morgan Stanley; Thomas Weisel Partners; UBS Securities; and US Bancorp Piper Jaffray. Merrill Lynch settled separately, and its "star" analyst, Henry Blodget, also contributed $4 million to the settlement.

Commenting on his investigation, New York Attorney General Eliot Spitzer didn't mince words:

It struck us as being a fundamental dishonesty, a fundamental problem that cut to the core of the lack of integrity on Wall Street.

So, what has changed? Has the securities industry reformed in any meaningful way? Unfortunately, it is still business as usual.

Many of the firms involved in the analyst scandal have continued to engage in unlawful practices. The significant fines they were assessed are apparently an acceptable cost of doing business. Here are some of the more notable recent examples of their bad behavior:

■ In May 2005, Citigroup Global Markets and Smith Barney Fund Management paid a whopping $208 million to settle charges that it misrepresented material facts when it recommended to the boards of certain mutual funds that they change from using a third-party transfer agent to a transfer agent that was a Citigroup affiliate;

■ Citigroup's wrongful conduct was not limited to activities in this country. In June 2005, it was fined $23.3 million by the United Kingdom's Financial Services Authority for dumping a "larger than usual number" of eurozone bonds on the market, forcing prices down, in violation of market rules.

■ In March 2005, Merrill Lynch paid a $13.5 million fine levied by New Jersey and Connecticut relating to improper "market timing" of mutual funds.

■ In June 2005, Morgan Stanley was fined $2.65 million for selling shares in an initial public stock offering it managed while the shares were still within the "lock-up" period. J.P. Morgan Chase & Co. and Goldman Sachs paid lesser fines for similar violations.

■ In November 2005 the New York Stock Exchange fined Lehman Brothers $500,000 for failing to supervise a trading strategy pegged to the closing price of a stock that gave it a profit while potentially harming its customers.

■ In January 2006, UBS was fined $54 million by the NYSE for engaging in market-timing involving mutual funds.

The mandatory arbitration system, which requires that investors who have been harmed by misconduct committed by their brokers submit their claims to industry-administered arbitration, has also come under heavy fire in the last couple of years. In testimony before the U.S. House Subcommittee on Capital Markets, Insurance, and Government-Sponsored Enterprises, held March 17, 2005 (at which I also testified), William Galvin, the respected Secretary of the Commonwealth of Massachusetts, stated his views on this system:

. . . what we have in America today is an industry-sponsored damage containment and control program masquerading as a juridical proceeding.

I could not agree more. This system is a national disgrace.

How has all of this affected brokerage firms' profits? They have gone up to record levels! Bear Stearns, which paid a $250 million fine to settle its part of a mutual-fund-trading scandal, reported record fourth-quarter earnings for 2005. The firm's profits rose 15 percent, to $407 million. Goldman Sachs, Lehman, Morgan Stanley, and Merrill Lynch also had banner years.

And what about the investors they serve? While the long-term average return of the stock market is 10.4 percent, relatively few investors actually achieved those returns, or anything close. Historically, fund investors underperform the average returns of the mutual funds in which they invest by as much as 75 percent. Why? Because gullible investors, egged on by their brokers, continue to chase "hot" funds with disastrous consequences, while ignoring the overwhelming research indicating that attempting to "beat the markets" is a fool's errand.

My core message is unchanged: For the vast majority of investors, using brokers or advisors who attempt to beat the markets is the first step to becoming a victim of broker misconduct. As I explain in my new book, *The Smartest Investment Book You'll Ever Read*, investors can invest easily themselves, without a broker or advisor, using no more than three mutual funds purchased directly from one of a number of major fund families. Doing this, they are likely to beat the returns of 95 percent of all professionally managed money, based upon historical data.

However, for the many victims of brokers or advisors whose have suffered losses due to irresponsible and indefensible advice given by these "investment professionals," there is the possibility of getting your money back, as long as you understand the system and know how to maneuver within it.

My wish for you is twofold: I hope that you are successful in recovering your losses if they were caused through the negligence or incompetence of your broker or advisor. And I also hope that you learn how to avoid the insidious system that has victimized so many of its clients in the past, and will surely continue to do so in the future.

1

Your Broker Just Might Owe You Money

My phone rings off the hook.

A retired man has lost $400,000 (about 30 percent of his nest egg) and determined that he and his wife will run out of money. He had placed his investment portfolio with a stockbroker and told the broker it needed to generate income. Instead, the broker invested the man's money in risky stocks. When this man came to see me for the first time, he insisted we meet in the lobby; he was afraid that if he came up to my fourth-floor office he would be tempted to jump off the balcony.

A well-known investment advisor who had full discretionary authority to make investments for a law firm's pension plan has gutted it. The advisor routinely traded for his own account ahead of the trades he made for clients—an illegal practice called frontrunning.

That is, the advisor selected thinly traded stocks (stocks that don't trade very frequently and that are therefore not very liquid), where he could move the price up or down by the volume of trades he placed for his clients. He then purchased these stocks for his own account several days before buying them for clients. Immediately after buying the stocks for clients, and thus driving the price up, the advisor sold out of his investment positions. The advisor's profits were both large and predictable.

His clients were not so fortunate; they suffered significant losses. But after an arbitration claim was filed and this practice was uncovered, the investment advisor quickly settled the case.

A widow's life savings, including the proceeds from her late husband's life insurance, has been reduced by 40 percent by a broker who "traded" mutual funds. The broker had convinced her that she had a well-diversified portfolio, even though she was fully invested in stocks and stock funds, with a significant portion of her portfolio in technology companies and tech-heavy funds. By trading mutual funds, the broker was able to significantly increase his commissions. She calls me in tears almost every day, waiting for her arbitration hearing and worrying about the outcome.

Another investor bought stock from a high-pressure telephone-sales "boiler room" brokerage firm. The stock, in a small company with few assets, was manipulated by the brokerage house and organized crime members and eventually crashed. The investor lost everything he put into the stock. The brokerage firm has closed. A broker employed by the brokerage firm has pled guilty to federal fraud charges and is in prison. We filed arbitration claims against both the brokerage firm and the major Wall Street firm that cleared trades for the small company.

All of these people are my clients.

If I could get these cases before a jury, I could recover their money for them. But I can't. These people, like all average American investors, are bound by the mandatory arbitration clause they signed when they opened their accounts with brokerage firms. We are stuck with a tribunal appointed by an industry organization that will have at least one "industry" representative on it. We will be lucky to get a fraction of what they are owed.

Some of my clients have been victims of outright fraud by stockbrokers and investment advisors who have committed illegal acts.

Others have been victims of the myriad conflicts in the relationship between brokers and their clients. These conflicts include the way brokers earn their living, through commissions on sales of stocks, bonds, and mutual funds (and the annuity-like "trailing commissions" on many mutual fund sales); the way brokerage houses earn their profits, increasingly through underwriting stock offerings for companies; the way brokerage house analysts work, by touting stocks in order to generate underwriting and other investment banking fees; and even by the way mutual funds and brokers who sell them put their interests and sometimes the interests of a few wealthy investors ahead of those of average investors like you, by allowing them to trade after the market has closed.

Finally, my clients have been victims of the advertising barrage from brokerage firms. They have been led to believe that by putting their trust into a stockbroker, and by using one particular brokerage firm or another, they can consistently "beat the market" by picking "mispriced" stocks, timing the market, and trading aggressively.

The major U.S. stock market averages (the Dow Jones Industrial Average, the Nasdaq market average, and the Standard & Poor's 500 index) all peaked in March and April of 2000, ending one of the longest bull runs in history. Between then and the end of 2002, these averages all declined the requisite 20 percent that defines a bear market, with the Nasdaq in a free fall of almost 80 percent before beginning to recover. Over that period, American investors lost over $7 trillion in stock-market wealth.

During this decline, many brokerage house analysts touted each new market decline as a "buying opportunity." What really was going on was the end of a financial asset bubble. During this time period, except for those who were consistently selling the market short (not a technique used by many average investors), pretty much everyone was losing money.

Whether your portfolio gained or lost money in the last 10 years, you have possibly—maybe even probably—been victimized by either blatant or subtle broker misdeeds. Yet few investors challenge their brokers by submitting a claim to arbitration. Of the more than 40 million Americans who have investment accounts with brokers or investment advisors, fewer than 9,000 filed arbitration claims in 2002, and that was a record-setting year. In 2005, the number of cases filed with NASD dropped to just 6,074.

If investors knew the truth about how the brokerage industry works, and the truth about their rights to recover their losses through arbitration, this number would be closer to 6 million than 6,000. Most investors don't know that they have recourse to try to recover losses when their rights have been violated and their trust broken. Even more don't know how to evaluate whether or not they have a valid claim. But there may be recourse against brokers and investment advisors for part or all of an investor's market losses. In fact, many investors may have a better chance of recovering some of their market losses by filing arbitration claims against their brokers than they do by investing with those brokers again, which isn't saying much.

By the time I meet a prospective client, or talk for the first time over the telephone, he or she has been thoroughly beaten up—first by a stockbroker, then by the brokerage firm that employs the broker.

I live on the Gulf Coast of Florida, and some of my prospective clients are relatively well-to-do retirees who were hoping to live comfortably on the savings they had accumulated over years of hard work. They were teachers, small business owners, doctors, dentists, and social workers. They are men and women who have worked hard to build an investment portfolio. But when I see them, they often collapse in tears, clutching each other. Many are panicked. Some seem almost to be in shock. Their brokerage account, the nest egg on which their hopes and dreams had been based, has been plundered.

They have been lied to, cheated, and stolen from. They have been told that their savings would be placed in safe, prudent investments, only to find out later that their money had been invested in the stocks of small companies and sometimes in complex and risky investment vehicles. Their accounts have been aggressively traded, selling one investment and buying another, to the point where their portfolio would have had to earn 20 or 25 percent, or maybe even more, just to break even. Even during the stock market's best years, a well-diversified portfolio is unlikely to make any profit when burdened by costs of that magnitude.

What's worse, they have been led to believe that their investment losses are their fault.

Often, they noticed steady losses in their portfolio for a period of months. They questioned their broker about what seemed to be excessive trading, or investments they had not asked to be made, and they were lied to. They were told that they just didn't remember agreeing to the trades, that the investments had been made after discussions with their broker.

They may have had meetings with the manager of the branch office where their broker works, where the manager told them in one way or another: "Tough luck." The manager told them that they received confirmation slips and monthly statements, all of which documented what had been done. They never questioned the amount of trading or the investments they had when their monthly statements were showing steady market gains, the manager told them, so they have no right to complain now that the market has gone down.

They have been told, in other words, that they are stupid and that it is their fault they lost money. Because they believe they bear some, most, or even all of the responsibility for their losses, many are reluctant to take action against their broker, even when I explain to them that the broker has engaged in improper, if not outright illegal, behavior.

Ignorant, but Not Stupid

Most investors are not stupid. My clients certainly are not. Many are quite intelligent.

However, by and large, investors are ignorant of the realities of investing, of how stock markets work, and of how brokers and brokerage firms operate. Two surveys tell this tale in stark terms.

In 1998, the AARP (formerly referred to as the American Association of Retired Persons) surveyed 827 investors aged 50 and over on the issue of how brokers are compensated. Among other findings, this survey revealed that:

■ Nearly half (48 percent) do not know that the amount of commission a client pays on the purchase or sale of an investment product can be negotiated.

■ Almost four in 10 (37 percent) do not know that the term "load" refers to a sales charge for a mutual fund.

■ About one-quarter (24 percent) do not know that brokerage firms offer incentives to brokers for selling products they have created or that they manage.

When told of various compensation practices in the brokerage industry, those surveyed expressed strong disapproval, with 90 percent saying they wanted to be told of such arrangements in advance. Yet few said they had ever asked their brokers about how the broker is compensated. Those surveyed by AARP were not stupid, just ignorant. Without a basic understanding of how the securities markets and brokerage firm practices work, it is difficult for people to know where to begin asking their "trusted advisor" or "financial professional" questions.

A second survey, conducted in the first few days of June 2001, well into the stock market downturn, is perhaps more revealing. This survey of 933 investors, conducted for the Securities Investor Protection Corporation (SIPC) and the National Association of Investors Corp. (NAIC), found that:

■ Fewer than 40 percent know what to do first if they have a dispute with their broker.

■ Fewer than 20 percent know there is no insurance for stock market losses.

■ Fewer than 20 percent understand how a margin call works. Only 14 percent know that under Federal Reserve rules, a brokerage firm must issue a margin call when the value of the assets used as collateral for the account falls below 25 percent of the amount of the margin loan.

Michael Don, president of SIPC, told Reuters News Service that "it has become increasingly evident . . . that investors have either no knowledge or, even worse, the wrong information about a number of key issues that can haunt them during tough financial times."

What investors need is education. Unfortunately, few of them get any from stockbrokers. Many, if not most, brokers don't know enough about economic and financial theory to educate their clients; after all, they are primarily salespeople. And those brokers who do know enough to educate their clients have little incentive to do so; it is time spent not selling. And, in fact, if their clients were properly educated, many would (and should) choose not to purchase investment products from brokers and would invest in other ways, such as with a fee-based registered investment advisor who believes in broad asset allocation and passively managed mutual funds or by purchasing shares of no-load index mutual funds themselves.

Misplaced Trust

Regardless of the particular circumstances these prospective clients find themselves in, the underlying reason for their being in their current predicament is always the same: They have trusted a stockbroker.

By doing so, my prospective client has become a victim. Just about every broker tells his or her clients:

- ■ "I have a buy-and-hold philosophy"
- ■ "I believe in diversification"
- ■ "I can help you devise a plan to outperform the market"

Unfortunately, the sad truth is that the third point fundamentally contradicts the first two.

One of the major benefits of buying and holding is to reduce transaction costs and, in taxable portfolios, to reduce the overall tax liability as well. The goal of asset allocation and diversification within asset classes is to create a portfolio that, to some degree, mimics the broad market while reducing volatility (risk). I'll discuss the theoretical underpinnings of stock market risk in Chapter 6. If you do these two things, you should essentially track the various markets' ups and downs fairly closely.

Once you let a broker try to "outperform" the market, you are doing two things. First, you are accepting added volatility. Second, you are accepting increased costs, which practically assures that your strategy is doomed to failure.

Every study by academics in economics and finance confirms that the only way to increase return significantly above the return generated by the market is by taking on additional risk.

And allowing the broker to try to pick stocks, time the market, and constantly trade increases the transaction-cost burden on the portfolio to such an extent that it must outperform the market by a lot just to cover those costs.

Let me review quickly the three ways investors are victimized. They are:

■ Conflicts of interest between brokers and brokerage firms on one hand and their clients on the other

■ Broker frauds and violations of securities laws, professional standards, or rules of the stock exchanges where they trade

■ A false belief that their brokers have an ability to "beat the market" because of ignorance about transaction costs, asset allocation, diversification, and the fact that, over time, all investment returns tend to gravitate toward the mean (which is what a market index is)

Each one of these will be discussed in greater detail in the next few chapters.

Conflicts of Interest

Conflicts of interest, which will be discussed in more detail in Chapter 2, are rampant in the brokerage industry.

Despite the fact that brokers should be working for their clients—in fact, brokers have a fiduciary duty to act in their clients' best interests—brokers also have a legal responsibility to their employer. For the broker to truly look after your interest while at the same time earning the best living possible is like trying to ride a horse in both directions at the same time. More often than not, brokers ride in the direction of income for themselves and profits for their firms, behaving in ways that put their interests and the interests of their employers ahead of their clients' interests.

The bottom line in all of this is that your broker is not your friend, and your broker is not necessarily looking out for your best interest.

The first conflict, of course, is that many brokers are still compensated through sales commissions. The more they sell, the more they earn. The more they recommend that you invest in products that pay a high commission, the more they earn. But their earnings are your costs. And, as I'll illustrate in some detail in later chapters, costs are one of your portfolio's worst enemies.

In most large brokerage firms that "manufacture" their own investment products, such as mutual funds and limited partnerships, brokers are provided various incentives to get their clients to invest in products the firm creates and manages, even if they perform worse than similar products managed by other organizations. These can range from a larger slice of the commission to event tickets, trips, and other prizes. In 1998, the NASD (formerly the National Association of Securities Dealers) outlawed such sales contests and incentives, but that has not stopped the practice; in September 2003, the NASD fined and censured the large, well-known brokerage firm Morgan Stanley for continuing to run such incentive contests focused on selling its in-house mutual funds from 1999 through 2002.

In addition, at some brokerage firms (not generally the better-known and well-regarded firms), brokers have other ways to squeeze out more income for themselves from a trade made for your account, including:

■ Getting a cut of the markups charged by the firm when it acts as market maker, or "principal," and not just as your agent in a transaction. (Many firms act as market maker for Nasdaq stocks, matching buyers and sellers and collecting the "spread" between the bid price and the offer price as a fee for making the market.)

■ Receiving a portion of the interest charged on margin loans. (Margin is the use of securities in your portfolio as collateral for borrowing money, used so you can buy more securities.)

■ Getting a cut of the management fees for accounts where the broker has discretion to trade, for "wrap" accounts, and for margin accounts.

Market making, margin-loan interest, and fees from managed accounts are three enormous profit makers for stock brokerage firms, and even in those firms where brokers are not given a cash portion of the profits earned, they earn "brownie points" for these efforts. Incentives often take the form of private offices, extra sales support from the branch manager—such as leads to potential clients—or being allowed to take over wealthier clients from other brokers who retire or leave the firm.

A second major conflict occurs because of the many different business lines within a modern, full-service brokerage firm. These business lines are:

- Retail sales (sales to you and individual investors like you)
- Institutional brokerage (actually conducting trades for money that is managed by financial managers on behalf of institutions like universities, hospitals, foundations, corporations, pension plans, and mutual funds)
- Investment banking (underwriting the sale of new securities for corporations)
- Trading for its own account

Not all of these various business lines are created equal. As became evident in the investigation of analyst practices by the New York Attorney General, which eventually led to the so-called "global settlement" between the New York Attorney General, the Securities and Exchange Commission (SEC), the NASD, and the New York Stock Exchange (NYSE) with 10 of the largest brokerage and investment banking firms, investment banking is clearly the tail that wags the brokerage firm dog. In order to curry favor with investment banking clients or potential clients, brokerage firms assured these companies that their stock market analysts would write positive reports about the company. Analysts actually went with bankers on sales calls to potential investment banking clients to make these promises. These analyst reports were then given to brokers to use as sales tools to get retail investors like you to invest in these companies' stocks. At many firms, brokers are not allowed to recommend that a client sell a stock that the firm's analyst rates as a buy, even if the stock is inappropriate for the client at a particular time.

The global settlement, in which the investment bank/brokerage firms paid $1.4 billion in fines, restitution, and payments to investor education funds run by the states, calls for investment banking and stock research to be completely severed, for research analyst compensation to be decoupled from investment banking fees generated, and for recommendations made by analysts in reports that brokers give retail investors to match the recommendations given by analysts to favored institutional clients. Additional guidance by the SEC, NASD, and NYSE calls for analysts to make recommendations less opaque and easier for the average investor to understand, and for firms to state clearly any time the firm has an investment banking relationship with a company that is the subject of an analyst report, or holds stock in the company in its own trading account. The underlying assumption here is that unbiased analyst reports might actually be of assistance to investors. Unfortunately, as I explain in later chapters, all of the academic evidence refutes the premise that it is possible for anyone to consistently pick undervalued stocks over a long term.

Broker Frauds and Violations

The Securities Exchange Act of 1934 is the federal law that, among other things, defines the basic relationship between someone who sells securities and those who buy securities from that person. Securities are stocks, bonds, limited partnerships, annuities, and other financial instruments. Every security that is going to be sold, with a few exemptions for small offerings made to family, close friends, and small groups of "sophisticated investors" who fit into narrow criteria, must be registered with the United States Securities and Exchange Commission (SEC) and with the securities regulators in each state in which the securities will be marketed.

The most frequently cited section of this law in securities arbitration cases is Section 10(b), which defines fraud committed by a seller upon a buyer of a security. Section 10(b) was expanded and elucidated by the SEC in its Rule 10(b)-5.

Section 10(b) and Rule 10(b)-5 have also been incorporated into the rules of the NYSE and the NASD, where most securities arbitration cases are heard.

States also have their own securities laws, which are sometimes more stringent than federal laws and sometimes less so.

When you file a claim against an individual broker, a branch-office compliance officer or manager, or the broker-dealer firm the broker works for, you typically claim a violation of:

- Federal securities law
- State securities law
- NYSE rules
- NASD rules
- Common law as established by court precedent

There are a number of out-and-out frauds that brokers commit against their clients. These practices, listed here, will all be defined in Chapter 3, and examples will be provided:

- Churning
- Unauthorized trading

- Price manipulation
- Forgery
- Misrepresentations and omissions

In addition to these frauds, there are a number of practices that, while they may not technically be fraudulent in and of themselves, are violations of either NASD rules or rules of the stock exchanges. These violations, which will also be defined in detail and discussed in Chapter 3, are often committed within the context of the commission of a fraud. The major violations are:

- Frontrunning
- Order failure
- Selling away
- Failure to supervise
- Over-leveraging in margin accounts

Possibly the most frequent claim brought against brokers, brokerage firms, and investment managers is the claim of "unsuitability." This is where I believe many investors who lost money in the last few years have the greatest chance of recovering their losses. Suitability is the subject of Chapter 5.

Briefly, under the rules of the NYSE and the NASD, a broker has a duty to understand clearly his or her clients' financial condition and investment objectives, and only to recommend investments that are suitable for each client and consistent with his or her objectives. In addition, the broker has an affirmative duty not to allow clients to put money into investments that are not consistent with the clients' investment objectives.

I and many others believe this affirmative duty extends to refusing to execute a transaction requested by a client that the broker believes is unsuitable for that client under the legal concept of not allowing a client to commit "financial suicide." Needless to say, few brokers or investment advisors are willing to turn down a commission or a fee because a client wishes to be "too aggressive," and financial suicide cases are, admittedly, very difficult to win in arbitration.

The second big issue with regard to suitability is how to determine what investments are suitable for a particular individual.

It is a fact known well to finance academics and economists, but little known to investors, brokers, or even to many securities lawyers, that you can make a determination as to whether a portfolio is suitable for a particular investor using a set of mathematical calculations that determine the historical amount of risk in the portfolio, as well as the transaction costs associated with the portfolio. Since brokers rarely perform these calculations and usually have no idea how risky a particular portfolio really is, it is not surprising that investors are ignorant of this critical aspect of their investments.

This is where the bodies are buried. Investors are leaving tens, if not hundreds, of millions of dollars on the table (money they have lost in the market but could possibly get back from their brokers) because they do not understand that the risk associated with their portfolios was unacceptably high given their risk tolerance and their investment objectives. If a mathematical calculation of three factors I'll explain in Chapters 3 and 6—beta, standard deviation, and cost-equity ratio—shows this to be true, they may have legitimate suitability (and other) claims against their brokers and the firms that employ them.

There are also some claims that frequently occur against online brokers. These will be discussed in detail in Chapters 5 and 7. The ability of individuals to trade for themselves through online brokers or the online order systems of full-service or discount brokers is a new phenomenon, and the law is evolving rapidly in this area.

Most disputes with online brokers are variations on the theme of order failures due both to system failures and to the way systems are designed. However, the issue of unsuitability is also coming into the fore as arbitrators and courts are asked to determine if online brokerages, even though they don't "make recommendations" in the traditional way, are doing so through e-mail and other communications, and whether they have an affirmative duty to make sure investors are not exceeding their financial capacity (as measured by the actual amount of cash or margin capacity in their account), are buying suitable investments, and are not committing financial suicide.

False Beliefs

As I said before, while some investors are victims of out-and-out fraud and many are victimized by the conflicts of interest inherent in the brokerage industry and in the broker/client relationship, there are also a number of investors who are victims of false beliefs.

Being a victim of false beliefs is what allows many investors to become involved in conflicts with brokers over suitability of their investments. And it is what causes them to blame themselves when their investments turn bad.

These false beliefs, in brief, are:

■ "It is possible to consistently beat the market by picking mispriced stocks, timing the market, or doing both."

Under the laws of probability, many investors, advisors, mutual funds, and money managers will "beat the market" in any one year. Fewer of them will do it two years running. And a minuscule number will be able to consistently beat the market over a five- or ten-year period. But every academic study of the subject shows that the number of people who beat the market over long periods is actually less than you would expect to do so through pure mathematical "chance."

■ "My broker does this for a living, so he or she can do it better than I can."

No, he can't. A very few money managers, who buy and sell securities for funds, consistently beat the market. And brokers, who mostly are just salespeople with no training in finance, have an even more dismal record.

■ "It's possible to have a well-balanced portfolio that is totally invested in stocks."

Not true. A well-balanced portfolio implies a portfolio that is allocated across the three basic asset classes of stocks, bonds, and cash, in order to smooth out the ups and downs of each of these asset classes, which do not move in tandem.

■ "If I invest only in bonds, my portfolio is safe."

Not true. Bonds tend to move up and down in value in opposition to stocks. A portfolio invested totally in bonds is vulnerable to swings in the bond market, while a portfolio invested in both stocks and bonds tends to smooth out such swings.

■ "There is not much I can do about transaction costs, so I don't have to pay much attention to them."

One of the largest mistakes investors make is failure to take transaction costs into consideration. Vanguard, which manages a number of passively invested index funds with low minimum investments, provides the following example:

Two investors invest $25,000 dollars each in a mutual fund. One fund has annual expenses, including transaction costs for active trading, of

1.30 percent, while the other fund, a passive index fund that does little trading, has annual expenses of 0.30 percent. Each fund earns 8 percent annually on its investments. In 20 years, the value of the "high-cost" fund will be $89,997, while the value of the "low-cost" fund will be $109,748; a 1 percent difference in annual costs accounts for an 18 percent difference in the value of the investment.

■ "Big brokerage firms, with all of their resources, must have valuable advice to convey about stock selection and market timing."

Not necessarily true. Most large brokerage firms have, since the beginning of the 1990s, purchased mutual fund companies and/or started their own in-house mutual funds. Consistently, brokerage-owned mutual funds—especially those managed and branded with the brokerage firms' names—have ranked low against independently managed mutual funds with the same investment philosophy, while often being far more costly to the investor, with high up-front sales charges and high annual fees.

■ "If a brokerage firm is a member of the NASD or the NYSE, it must have significant financial resources."

Oh, don't some of my clients wish this were so. Unfortunately, it does not take a lot of capital to start and operate a brokerage firm and become a member of the NASD. During the 1990s, many fly-by-night brokerage firms racked up numerous complaints from clients to the SEC and NASD, as well as claims for arbitration. Many turned out to be little more than shell companies, with their owners siphoning off profits as fast as they came in, leaving nothing with which to pay arbitration judgments, SEC fines, criminal fines, or to make restitution to deceived investors.

My goal in writing this book is to keep you from becoming my client, or a client of another lawyer who sues brokers and brokerage firms on behalf of investors who have become victims of broker misconduct.

Arbitration

For an investor who believes he or she has been victimized, an attempt to get redress takes place within an arbitration forum. An arbitration claim is usually filed through either the NASD or the NYSE, both of which are organizations operated and controlled by the securities industry. The mandatory agreement to arbitrate rather than litigate in federal or state court is a standard part of all brokerage firms' new account paperwork, and its validity was upheld by the U.S. Supreme Court in 1987, when it refused to overturn lower-court decisions in two securities cases that defined broker/client disputes as "arbitrable." Since then, there have been few attempts to move broker/client disputes back into the courts. Thus, for all intents and purposes, arbitration of disputes between stockbrokers and customers became the law of the land.

Since the Supreme Court's 1987 decisions regarding arbitration, there has been much debate about whether investors fare better in arbitration than they would in litigation through the courts. To be sure, there are a number of positive aspects of arbitration for investor claims. But the evidence is mounting that the arbitration forum has a pro-broker and brokerage firm bias. To this day, many investors and securities lawyers believe that investors cannot get a fair hearing in arbitration before the NASD or the NYSE.

While the arbitration system was established with good intentions—to create a faster, more streamlined, and less expensive forum for resolving conflicts between clients and brokers than civil court—unfortunately it has today become unwieldy, expensive, time-consuming, and lopsided in favor of brokerage firms against investors. The longer the mandatory arbitration system is in place, the more its flaws become apparent. Among these flaws are:

■ It is administered by industry organizations, so-called "self-regulatory organizations" (SROs), specifically the NYSE and the NASD. This gives the industry great power over the selection of tribunal members, and ultimately over the resolution of procedural issues.

■ The rules of these organizations require that one of the three members be an industry representative (in reality, many of the so-called "public arbitrators" also have close ties to the securities industry), which means that at least one-third of the panel is often biased against the investor.

■ It deprives investors of their constitutional rights of trial by a jury of their peers.

I am calling for an end to mandatory arbitration conducted by the NYSE and NASD, and in its place recommend that investors be given the option of arbitration administered by an impartial organization (e.g., the American Arbitration Association) with three neutral arbitrators or the right to sue in

The following is a list of arbitration pluses:

■ Faster, more convenient than litigation.

■ Less formal than litigation.

■ Less costly than litigation, but becoming more expensive all the time.

■ Greater confidentiality than court cases.

■ Arbitrators are supposed to seek "fairness" and "justice" in decisions.

■ Arbitrators have more expertise in industry "norms" than jurors.

■ Arbitration awards are less likely to be appealed than court judgments. (Appeals are costly, time-consuming, and have little chance of success. If the appeal is lost, interest accrues on the award.)

The following is a list of specific arbitration minuses,
in addition to the systemic problems with mandatory arbitration previously discussed:

■ Broad discovery tools are not available, and it is sometimes difficult to obtain all relevant facts.

■ Hearings are scheduled "at the convenience" of all parties. Sometimes individual hearing days are far apart, which adds to the costs and is disturbing to the "flow of proceedings."

■ Because of greater confidentiality, there is less incentive to settle in order to avoid bad publicity.

■ Arbitrators are more conservative than juries; there are fewer large awards and even fewer punitive damages awards.

court and to have their dispute resolved by a jury of their peers. I will lay out this recommendation in detail later in this book.

When Courts Are Applicable

Arbitration is still not the way investors seek redress in all cases where they have lost money in stocks, bonds, or other investments. There are a few different circumstances when investors can get some redress through forums other than arbitration.

For instance, in the case of investors in a particular company such as Enron who believe they have been victimized by fraud perpetrated by company executives, directors, and/or officers, or the company's auditors and attorneys, the courts are still open.

Also, it is still possible to bring lawsuits in federal court against investment advisors, investment managers, trust officers, and the institutions that employ them, since many of these individuals and entities do not belong to the NASD or the NYSE and their agreements with clients do not require that disputes be arbitrated.

Finally, all class actions are expressly excluded from the mandatory arbitration process. For example, in 2003 a number of investors filed suit in United States District Court in Nashville seeking class-action status, alleging that Morgan Stanley brokers had a pattern and a policy of selling investors inappropriate mutual fund classes. I'll discuss this particular case in more detail in Chapter 4, which focuses on mutual funds.

Arbitration Statistics for 2005

In 2005, the NASD Dispute Resolution office received 6,074 arbitration cases filed by customers against brokers and/or brokerage firms. This was a sharp decline from the 8,201 cases filed in 2004.

NASD Dispute Resolution closed 9,043 arbitration cases in 2005. Of those, 4,850 settled, either through direct negotiations or through mediation. Of the 1,610 cases where arbitrators ruled after a hearing, 687 rulings, or 43 percent, were in favor of the investor. This percentage of "wins" for investors is down from 53 percent in 2000 and represents a troubling trend.

The NYSE arbitration department received only 302 customer cases in 2005, less than half of the 719 cases filed in 2004. Investors prevailed in only 39 percent of these cases.

For better or worse, most investors are stuck with arbitration before the NASD or NYSE as their only recourse to try to recover money lost to broker misconduct. I, like most lawyers who practice before these forums, find the process fundamentally flawed. But at the end of the day, the problem is not only with the arbitration process itself, but with the fact that most investors simply do not know that they have a claim worth pursuing. I believe there are literally hundreds of millions of investor dollars lost through broker misconduct—during the bull market as well as since the downturn of 2000 and thereafter—waiting to be recovered by investors who are aggressive about claiming their rights to be treated fairly.

2 You and Your Broker: A Relationship Fraught with Conflicts

I have a client I'll call Kathleen. She worked her entire life as a clerk with the telephone company in a small New England town. Married, with no children, she invested her life savings of $380,000 with her neighbor and friend, who was a broker at a major national brokerage firm. Her investment objective was moderate growth.

Over a five-year period, her account lost about $275,000, almost 75 percent of its value.

An analysis of the trading in her account found a turnover ratio of 3.41 (341 percent of the value of her account was traded each year), commissions and interest on margin loans of over $250,000, and a cost-equity ratio of 16.19 percent (her costs per year were more than 16 percent of the value of her portfolio, meaning she would have had to have more than a .16 percent gain in her portfolio's value just to break even).

Kathleen's portfolio was invested almost exclusively in stocks, with over 30 percent in volatile technology stocks.

Confronted with the evidence of this clearly inappropriate portfolio, as well as the egregious behavior of the broker, the brokerage firm settled on the day before an arbitration hearing was supposed to begin by reimbursing Kathleen for 100 percent of her losses.

Brokers and the firms they work for want you to trust them. They want you to believe that they have a special expertise that is of value to you and that you cannot obtain elsewhere, much less by investing on your own. They spend millions of advertising dollars each year so you will believe this, and so you will pay them for their services.

They want you to have a personal relationship with them. They use terms like "wealth management" and "individualized investment plan" to tout their wares.

The truth is that brokers and brokerage firms are far more concerned about their money than they are about yours. There are a great number of ways brokers and the firms they represent can earn money. Don't worry if some of what I discuss in this chapter seems confusing at first; many brokers and their firms prefer that you not truly understand how they make money. They prefer that you just trust in their expertise and judgment. However, it is my desire that you somehow understand that the ways brokers make money in their dealings with you are costs—some of them hidden costs—that subtract from your portfolio's ultimate value.

In order to understand how and why you might have a claim against a broker and/or brokerage firm, it is necessary first to understand the legal relationship between a broker and his or her client, and how that relationship conflicts with the behavior of brokers and brokerage firms.

Many people have in their mind a notion of "my" broker. They believe that "their" broker is working for them and their interests. But the reality is that your broker may not always be working for you, but rather working for his or her employer, and primarily for him- or herself.

Brokers are taught first and foremost to sell; and the investment vehicles you put your savings into are called "products." The stock market analysts who work for brokerage houses are called "sell-side analysts." Every single incentive plan put in place by a brokerage firm is geared toward brokers selling.

Brokers and brokerage firms want you to trust them. But they don't want to be held accountable for that trust, and many investors blindly assume that even when things go wrong, it's not their broker's fault.

But if a broker has created a condition where the client trusts the broker's expertise and judgment, and the broker recommends an investment to a client that is not appropriate for that client's financial condition and/or investment objectives, and the investment loses money, it is the broker's fault. That is because the broker who has created a condition of trust has created a condition where he or she has "control" over the investments being made, and thus has created a fiduciary duty for him- or herself to act with the client's interest as his or her primary concern.

If a brokerage firm, one that spends millions of dollars advertising that its clients have a "relationship" with it and are not merely "customers," is successful in getting you to open an account, it has put itself in a position of becoming your fiduciary. If a broker who has pumped him- or herself up as a trusted advisor, someone who has (supposedly) been successful in making oodles of money for clients, suggests a particular investment strategy or a particular investment, that broker has put him- or herself in the position of a fiduciary.

In doing so, the broker and the firm have put themselves in a position to be held to a very high standard of conduct with respect to their activities. The standard of conduct was described by one California appeals court as follows:

> *The relationship between broker and principal is fiduciary in nature and imposes on the other the duty of acting in the highest good faith toward the principal. . . . The duties of the broker, being fiduciary in character, must be exercised with the utmost good faith and integrity.*

Some courts have viewed the relationship between a broker and a client to be fiduciary in nature, and held that this relationship exists regardless of whether the investor is "sophisticated" or "unsophisticated." Other courts disagree and apply a lower standard of care.

While brokers seem to have no quarrel with a fiduciary standard when they are soliciting your account (although they don't explicitly state that they have a fiduciary relationship, they do say they have your interests at heart), it is a standard they are quick to disclaim when you attempt to hold them accountable for their misconduct. They try to duck out by claiming that they owe this highest standard of care only when the account is discretionary—where they actually have control over the trading. This position, of course, is news to you, who routinely believe that "your" broker is always looking out for you.

Or a broker will argue that he or she only acts as an order taker, saying that you agreed to any recommendation, or that the ideas for trading in your account were generated by you and simply implemented by the broker. This, of course, makes you think that you are at least partly to blame. Brokers have a duty to recommend only investments that are suitable to the client's risk tolerance and investment objectives. If an investment is not suitable for your risk tolerance and investment objectives, the broker should never recommend it to you.

In a lengthy on-camera interview in April 2001 with Scott Cohn of CNBC, Robert Magnan, a former broker barred from the industry for life, told of how he received substantial training on how to sell over the telephone, build relationships, gather assets, and convince people to send him their money. But, he told Cohn, he never received any training in how to actually help clients make money.

The Shingle Theory

Because of these efforts by brokers to avoid responsibility for their conduct, another theory—the so-called Shingle Theory—is often used by investors' attorneys to establish the nature of the relationship between broker and client. The Shingle Theory was first outlined by the Securities and Exchange Commission (SEC) in administrative actions against brokers and has since been accepted by courts.

The Shingle Theory basically holds that a broker-dealer (the brokerage firm) and each individual broker "hangs out a shingle" as would a doctor or lawyer. The broker and firm are both licensed and can have that license revoked.

To the client, that license—that "shingle"—confers on the broker and the firm an implied level of professionalism; part of that professionalism is an implied fiduciary duty to professionally conduct the business of helping the client invest his or her money consistent with the client's investment objectives and risk tolerance.

Viewed in this context, the Shingle Theory is simply another way to impose a fiduciary duty on brokers. Regardless of whether you call this obligation a "fiduciary" one, or one premised upon the Shingle Theory, you would think that brokers would willingly acknowledge that, in dealing with their clients' life savings, they should adhere to the highest professional standards imposed by the law. Unfortunately, this is not the case.

If you give the broker your permission to make investment decisions and act on them—known as a discretionary account—there is no doubt that the broker has a fiduciary duty to you. Fortunately, some courts have held that even if you do not give the broker discretion to trade, he or she also has a fiduciary duty toward you. This is especially true when you can establish that the broker has de facto control over your account, because you basically follow the broker's advice and agree to any trade he or she recommends. And why wouldn't you, since if you knew as much as the broker supposedly does, you'd handle the transactions yourself through a discount brokerage and wouldn't need the broker to provide any advice?

The truth is that investors want their stockbrokers to be confident of their position (even though, in reality, the broker may be totally uninformed about what he or she is confident of).

As one former broker said to me of the training process:

A Case of Misplaced Trust

In 1994, Robert Ravenscroft bought 10 shares of Mesa Airlines. It was the first stock investment he had ever made. The 28-year-old Ravenscroft made his stock purchase through Dennis Dixon, president of Simmons & Bishop, a small Phoenix-area brokerage firm.

Over the next couple of years, Ravenscroft came to trust Dixon. So when Ravenscroft inherited $10 million a few years later, he went to Dixon with $7 million and asked the broker to set up two investment accounts, one for speculative trading and the other to house safe investments that would be used as a nest egg. Ravenscroft and his wife used the other $3 million to start a business.

Between 1996, when the Ravenscrofts opened the accounts, and April 2000, the $7 million had turned to dust. During one of the most ferocious bull markets in history, Dixon had lost the Ravenscrofts' entire investment while generating more than $1 million in commissions.

While Ravenscroft initially gave Dixon discretion to trade the accounts and approved of risky trading strategies, including taking large positions in stock options and short-selling stock, he withdrew discretion and approval for the risky strategy after suffering losses in 1998. Despite written instructions to stop selling short and telephone calls asking Dixon not to trade from the second account, the practices continued.

The Ravenscrofts filed an arbitration claim against Dixon, the firm, and the firm's trading supervisor and compliance manager. In October 2001, an NASD arbitration panel awarded the couple $1.16 million, finding for them on their charges of breach of fiduciary duty, unsuitable investment strategy, churning, unauthorized trading, and failure to supervise.

We spend three months or so taking tests, three weeks in initial train-
ing, and when we come back, [each broker] gets a desk and a phone.
No one shows you how to put a portfolio together. If the Nasdaq is
exploding, that is where you put your clients. You do this because they
think you are an idiot if you don't, and you succumb to client pressure
because you have never lived through a bear market and can't imagine
what one could feel like.

If brokers really told investors of all the risks involved in the investments
the brokers recommend, many people would choose not to deal with them.
As I will show in coming chapters, staying away from brokers is a very prudent path to follow.

Confidence Trumps Knowledge

An article in the broker's trade magazine *Registered Representative* tells it
all. In an experiment performed by a Wake Forest University psychology
professor, 600 students were given the choice of investing with two different
stockbrokers who each recommended the same stocks.

One stockbroker took a cautious approach, explaining all of the risks
involved as well as the potential rewards. The other broker didn't mention the
risks and gave a more confident recommendation. Students overwhelmingly
said they would invest with the broker who told them nothing of the risks.

"People are overly impressed with confidence," Professor Eric Stone told
Registered Representative. "In situations where the average person feels out
of their league, they prefer to rely on an expert who's confident."

When I recounted this study to a former client of mine who used to be a
stockbroker (I also represent brokers in arbitration against firms that formerly
employed them), her response was "Yes, so is this a broker problem or a problem with the consumer?"

That's a valid, and important, question.

Clearly, as I discussed in Chapter 1, many investors today are ignorant
both of investing and of the ways of Wall Street. As Amy Feldman wrote of
investors' arbitration claims against their brokers in the October 2001 issue
of *Money* magazine:

A large number of the claims appear to be something new: fallout
from the explosive mix of inexperienced investors and overly confident

brokers in a stock market where everyone, it seemed, was making easy money. . . .

While some of the complaints are compelling, what's really astounding is the extent to which some investors abdicated responsibility for their accounts—signing documents without filling them out, not opening monthly or quarterly account statements, remaining ignorant of basic margin rules even as their own margin debt ballooned. Equally astounding, on the other side, is how little many of these brokers—even those at the top-name firms—seemed to focus on their clients' financial goals and long-term well-being. . . .

So I say to my former-broker friend, yes, many investors were ignorant, naive, and some may even have been lax in their oversight of what their brokers were doing. But brokers clearly have an advantage in the broker/client relationship. They have used their salesmanship and powers of persuasion to get clients to believe in their professionalism, and in their ability to "beat the market."

They have professional accreditation. They work for a firm that advertises its qualifications and professional abilities, as well as its "customer service." And, the ones who make a living year in and year out in the brokerage industry are blessed with sales abilities. It simply is no match.

Of course, if the investments you've had touted to you by your confident broker turn sour and you file a claim of arbitration against your broker and/or the firm for your losses, both will argue that they had absolutely no fiduciary duty toward you. This position drips with irony.

After working to obtain your business by convincing you of how trustworthy they are, when they break that trust they seek to avoid responsibility for that conduct by asserting that they owe you no fiduciary duty. Unfortunately, the mandatory arbitration system permits many to get away with it.

Can't Avoid the Conflicts

Many stockbrokers are perfectly ethical and law abiding, and they consciously try to place their clients' best interests above their own. But even the most ethical brokers can't escape the conflicts that exist: primarily the way they are compensated and the fact that retail brokerage—sales by brokers to investors like you—is increasingly the least important profit center for many large brokerage firms.

Brokers and brokerage firms do, of course, have many incentives to treat their clients appropriately:

■ Economic principles tell you that if brokers for a particular brokerage firm continue to treat their clients badly, the firm will lose clients, lose money, and possibly go out of business.

■ Self-regulating organizations (SROs) such as the New York Stock Exchange (NYSE), the NASD, the Chicago Board of Options Exchange (CBOE), and other securities exchanges all have rules regarding fair dealing with clients and can impose penalties on brokerage firms ranging from fines to expulsion in addition to any money recovered by individuals through arbitration. Unfortunately, these organizations are fraught with conflicts themselves and are frequently only paper tigers.

■ The Securities and Exchange Commission (SEC) looks over brokers' and firms' shoulders, and can impose penalties on either a firm or an individual broker for violations of SEC rules and federal securities laws, including barring a broker from ever working in the securities industry again.

■ State securities regulators, who might be the secretary of state or the attorney general, can initiate actions against a broker or firm. Sometimes, as was made clear in the 2002 investigation of analyst behavior and the 2003 investigation of timing and "late trading" of mutual funds—both cases brought by New York Attorney General Eliot Spitzer—a state securities regulator's actions can be profound.

■ Entire groups of individuals who have been treated unfairly in the same way by the same firm have, on occasion, been successful in class-action lawsuits brought in court.

■ Every brokerage firm has a compliance department and a compliance manager. They do help keep brokers out of trouble, although during the bull market in the 1990s the business was expanding so rapidly that some industry insiders, including some of my former-broker friends, say compliance staffs simply couldn't keep up with the number of new brokers coming into the industry.

■ Finally, of course, individuals can file an arbitration claim against a broker or a firm before an arbitration panel.

Despite the incentives to do the right thing, conflicts are still overwhelming. For instance, brokerage firm compliance departments have a number of problems. On May 23, 2002, a House subcommittee held a hearing on the matter, prompted by the case of the Cleveland broker Frank Gruttadauria, then under arrest and later convicted of bilking wealthy clients out of up to $125 million over 15 years. Gruttadauria was a so-called producing branch manager, who both supervised other brokers and managed his own book of client business. Gruttadauria brought in over $1 million in commissions most years, and the branch's compliance officer reported to him. Despite a number of obvious problems in Gruttadauria's handling of clients, the branch compliance officer was fearful of reporting his boss to higher-ups. Compliance officers have always been considered by brokers to be essentially unarmed security guards.

Remember, few brokers want to do the wrong thing for any client. Many truly believe (despite the overwhelming academic evidence to the contrary) that they can add value over and above the costs you incur. However, as you'll see in detail later, they rarely actually do add significant value, and many times they destroy value, whether meaning to or not.

Broker Compensation: The Biggest Conflict

The financial services industry is big business. It employs nearly 800,000 individuals and manages the accounts of of almost 93 million investors, either directly or indirectly through corporate retirement plans. In 2005, the industry generated an estimated $322.4 billion in domestic revenue and an estimated $474 billion in global revenue.

Brokers are some of the highest-paid salespeople on the planet. There are over 600,000 registered representatives (the technical name for a stockbroker) in this country, employed by more than 4,000 brokerage firms. Nearly all of them are compensated through sales commissions, generally keeping about 40 percent of the gross commissions they earn, while the firm keeps the other 60 percent. Some investment products do provide a lower-percentage payout to the broker, and some firms give a smaller payout to brokers who have lower gross commissions, but brokers generally make at least 28 percent of the gross commission on any investment product they sell.

In 2004, according to the Securities Industry Association (SIA)—the stock brokerage industry's trade association—the average broker generated

$418,003 in gross fees and commissions, keeping an average of $174,105 for him- or herself in W-2 earnings (a payout of about 42 percent of gross fees and commissions). This general income level puts the average stockbroker comfortably in the top 5 percent of American families in terms of annual income, even if his or her spouse does not earn a penny.

While the split is generally 40 percent for the broker and 60 percent for the firm, the broker can get a better split by—you guessed it—generating larger commissions. Because the "cost" of a broker to the firm is essentially fixed (office space and utilities, furniture, telephone, etc.), if a broker generates higher commissions, the firm can let the broker have a larger share and still make more money.

At some firms, brokers who bring in more than $1 million in gross commissions get to keep upward of 50 percent of the gross—as well as being assigned a full-time sales assistant or two who is paid by the firm—while lower-producing brokers earn less than 40 percent, and the lowest producers are regularly asked to find another line of work.

And how do you think firms move riskier, more difficult investment vehicles? Right again—they increase the commission. While the typical commission on a trade of common stock, municipal bonds, corporate bonds, or mortgage-backed securities is 1 to 2 percent, the commission on an initial public offering (IPO) of stock, annuities, or thinly traded stocks can be as high as 7 percent, and limited partnerships or private placements of stock in nonpublic companies can carry commissions as high as 9 percent. It should be said that many of the industry's more reputable brokerage firms have stopped selling limited partnerships and private placements because of their riskiness.

Risk does not always equate with high commissions. Sometimes the higher commissions are paid for more popular investment products or products that investors feel they can't be without. For instance, mutual funds, which are not necessarily more or less risky than individual stocks, often carry a front-end load (commission) of 3 to 6 percent, which is reduced as the amount invested in the fund or fund family increases (mutual funds are the subject of Chapter 4). And whole life, variable life, and universal life insurance products often carry commissions that eat up much of the first year's premium.

While firms pour resources into "training" brokers to sell, they spend relatively little time working with brokers on how to deal ethically with their clients.

The NASD and NYSE have rules requiring brokers to recommend only suitable investments to their clients. In order to do this, the broker needs to have a full understanding of the client's financial situation, objectives, and risk tolerance. However, the time it takes to learn these essential facts about customers is time not spent selling. Therefore, it is not uncommon for brokers to make recommendations of totally inappropriate investments, saying that some clients prefer to be more aggressive, and therefore it is difficult to say that any investment is "unsuitable."

In some cases, brokers get clients to sign blank new-account forms, then fill in the investment objectives and risk tolerance boxes themselves, a violation of exchange and NASD rules. As the barred-for-life broker Robert Magnan told CNBC's Scott Cohn in 2001, if the boxes are filled out by the broker showing the investor wanted an aggressive account, any future dispute becomes the client's word against that of the broker.

It is not uncommon for brokers who produce large commissions to win prizes, including trips for themselves and their spouses to exotic locations. On some of these incentive trips, mutual fund and other promoters spend a few minutes each day presenting the virtues of their "products" to the brokers; but most of the time is spent on golf, tennis, or skiing. Suffice it to say, there are no trips given to those whose only virtue is professional behavior toward clients.

A few years ago I engaged in the following cross-examination during an arbitration hearing with the branch manager of a well-known and well-respected brokerage firm:

Q: [Your firm] has many programs in place to incentivize its brokers to produce commissionable income to the firm. Is that a fair statement?
A: In general, I suppose so.
Q: Okay. And it has a number of kinds of clubs or awards which it uses to incentivize its brokers to generate commissions, correct?
A: To award them at certain levels, yes.
Q: Thank you. Okay. So, for example, there's something called the Executive Club, right?
A: That's correct.
Q: The President's Club?
A: Correct.
Q: The Chairman's Club?
A: Yes.

Q: The Circle of Excellence?

A: Yes.

Q: And last, but obviously not least, the Circle of Champions?

A: That's correct.

Q: And the way you get into these various clubs or circles is a function of your commissionable production, correct?

A: Revenues, yes, sir.

Q: [Are there] also clubs and awards that [your company] gives brokers regardless of commissions they generate for being excellent with compliance [with the rules and regulations of the self-regulatory organizations]?

A: Not that I am aware of.

This discussion clearly shows how brokerage firms would rather provide incentives to their brokers to sell products than to be worried about whether they are doing the right thing for their clients.

Titles are also given to brokers on the basis of commissions earned. Clients are very impressed by the fact that they do business with a "Vice President" or, even better, a "Senior Vice President: Investments." They ought to be—it's their commissions that are paying for those titles.

In addition to commissions that are often transparent as part of the purchase price for all kinds of products (and not so transparent in other cases), brokerage firms also earn income in a number of other ways, mostly from stock transactions. In some instances, individual brokers are cut in on these income sources as well. They are:

- Hidden commissions
- The bid-ask spread
- Markups
- Margin interest
- Management fees (wrap accounts)
- Mutual fund shelf-space fees

HIDDEN COMMISSIONS

When a company makes its first offering of stock to the public through an IPO, the brokerage/investment banking firms underwriting the stock spread the millions of shares being issued out among many brokerage firms. This way, the stock can find its way into the hands of many different investors. (In a market manipulation of an IPO, discussed in Chapter 3, the underwriter keeps the stock within a very small group of firms.)

If you buy shares in an IPO, there is no commission price attached to the purchase on your confirmation slip. However, brokerage firms take the stock at a discount to the actual offering price, and the difference between the discounted price and the offering price you buy at is a hidden commission. In fact, IPOs carry some of the highest commissions, up to 8 percent of the purchase price (e.g., for a stock issued at $15 a share, the firm probably paid around $13.75 to $14).

Another source of hidden commissions is in the so-called "trailing commissions" in shares of mutual funds paid to brokers each year the mutual fund investment is held. The myriad of conflicts involved in mutual funds is the subject of Chapter 4.

THE BID-ASK SPREAD

Your broker does not necessarily make any more money through the bid-ask spread, but the firm does, and the broker may be given incentives to sell shares in companies with a wide bid-ask spread.

Within any stock market, there are traders who have an obligation to keep the market working efficiently by being the "counterparty" to any trade an individual or institution wishes to make.

In an open-auction exchange, such as the NYSE, these traders, and the firms they work for, are known as "specialists," who maintain a stationary "post" on the floor of the exchange where floor traders come to buy or sell each particular stock.

The Nasdaq (formerly the National Association of Securities Dealers Automated Quote system) is a totally electronic exchange where firms known as market makers (sometimes many for each stock) match buyers and sellers.

These firms need to be paid for the risk they agree to carry in being willing to take the opposite side of any trade. This payment comes in the form of the spread between the bid and ask price.

If you wish to buy stock for $25 a share, you make a "bid" at that price, and the specialist or market maker is obliged to find a counterparty who is willing to "offer" the stock at $25, or very close to it. Of course, this is all happening almost instantaneously, with the stocks of hundreds of companies.

So the bid and ask prices that market makers or specialists are willing or able to transact business at are always changing.

In theory, the market maker should find a bid slightly higher than the offer price, keeping the difference (the spread) as the commission for engineering the trade. Until 2000, the bid-ask spread was always quoted in increments of at least $1/16$ of a point (a point being one dollar), or about six cents. Since all U.S. stock markets went to decimalization, spreads can now be as little as one cent.

For stocks with heavy daily volume, bid-ask spreads will be a few pennies. But for stocks that trade infrequently, the spread can still be 50 cents or more.

NYSE specialists are members of independent firms (some are subsidiaries of larger firms) that do nothing but work in this capacity. They make their living by holding in inventory the minimum amount of shares in the stocks they make a market in necessary to maintain orderly flow. They make the market in most trades by matching up buyers and sellers; where willing buyers or sellers cannot be found, they trade by taking stock into or selling stock from their own inventory. In 2003, the NYSE opened an investigation of its specialist firms to see if they had been "getting in front of" trades (deliberately buying or selling just ahead of an order to buy or sell in order to remove stock from the market so buyers and sellers could not be matched and they could conduct the trade themselves, pocketing the few pennies, penny, or even fraction of a penny of spread in each share traded).

Nasdaq market makers, however, are usually brokerage firms that also sell investments to you and other retail customers. The profit they make on the spread is added to any commission they charge you.

If the brokerage firm you deal with is a market maker in the stock you are buying or selling, it is said to be acting as a principal in the transaction rather than as an agent. In this case, the firm is taking the spread as income over and above the commission it takes as an agent in the trade.

But even if the firm you deal with is not the market maker, it still might be profiting from the spread. The firm can be receiving payment from the market maker through a system known as "payment for order flow," which is essentially a legal kickback.

Under NASD rules, when making a transaction in a Nasdaq stock, the brokerage firm's trader is supposed to check with three market makers to determine the best bid or ask for you (depending on whether you are buying or selling). But in the world of payment for order flow, some market makers may share part of their spread profits with other firms that send business their way, and many brokerage firms cut this corner in order to collect the payment for order flow.

MARKUPS

Say the firm you do business with makes a market in a particular stock. When that stock moves from the firm's trading desk to the brokers (including yours) and then on to you, the firm and the broker sometimes split the profit generated from what is known as a markup (or a markdown if you are selling).

Here's how it works: The firm's trader may have been buying the stock for a while for prices below the current spread and building up an inventory. At some point, the trader will then turn the stock over to the firm's brokers to begin pushing out to their clients.

Traders are not supposed to know what brokers are doing, and vice versa. However, at less scrupulous firms brokers can get a good idea of how the trader has been "working" the stock over time by what their internal trading price is (this is a bookkeeping entry so the trader gets proper credit for generating profits to the trading desk, which in turn enhances his or her bonus).

For instance, on a stock that has a market "ask" price of $8 a share (what the firm wants you to pay), the firm's trader may have been building a position over time by buying the stock for less than the current $7.50. He charges the brokers $7 a share to get rid of the inventory.

(Robert Magnan, the barred-for-life former broker, told Scott Cohn of CNBC of how he would arrive at the office and talk to the trading desk, which would tell him which stocks the firm was trying to "move" that day and what portion of the markup he would get to keep.)

Your broker offers the stock to you at $8, with a 3 percent commission included in the $8 price. The profit is really $12\frac{1}{2}$ percent on the trade (the difference between $7 and $8); 3 percent (24 cents) is credited as commission, to be split with the firm (about eight cents goes to the broker) and shown on your trade confirmation as the commission. The difference between $7.50 and $8.00 minus the 3 percent commission (26 cents) is the spread, which belongs entirely to the firm. And the difference between $7.00 and $7.50 is the markup "paid out" to the broker as a "trading credit" or "sales credit." The total "cost" of the trade to you is $1 per $8 share, or $12\frac{1}{2}$ percent; the broker's total take is about 58 cents per $8 share, or about 7 percent.

Not disclosing such an arrangement to a client can be argued to be a violation of Section 10(b) and Rule 10(b)-5 by failing to state a material fact that, had it been stated, might have caused the investor to behave differently (i.e., not buy the stock).

MARGIN INTEREST

A margin account allows you to use the securities held in the account as collateral to borrow money in order to purchase more securities.

In some firms, margin interest income is one of the largest profit centers from the retail brokerage division. Brokerage firms borrow money at their cost of capital and lend it to you at a higher interest rate. It's that simple.

Margin interest is something that can be negotiated by a client, but you have to ask, and be forceful about it. And, if you are a small client, you can't drive down the margin interest rate as far as a large client can.

Even though the broker is not earning a piece of the margin interest, by convincing you to use margin (which substantially raises your portfolio's costs and increases your portfolio's risks), the broker can make bigger trades and generate more commissions.

MANAGEMENT FEES (WRAP ACCOUNTS)

Brokerage firms are increasingly trying to move their clients into managed accounts, often called wrap accounts, where for a single annual fee the client can perform as few or as many transactions as desired. A survey of 4,106 registered representatives (stockbrokers) conducted in 2001 for *Institutional Investor Newsletters* found that, despite the extensive effort by brokerage firms to get their clients into wrap accounts and other managed accounts, only 5 percent of brokers actually focused their efforts there. These brokers overwhelmingly cater to wealthy investors.

In theory, fee-based accounts take away many of the broker's incentives to constantly trade the account to generate commissions or otherwise mismanage the client's funds. They also align the broker's incentive (a larger fee) with the client's goal (to see the account grow).

Unfortunately, fee-based accounts are not equal. While a fee-only money manager will often charge 1 percent of the first $1 million invested, and lesser amounts for larger accounts, brokerage firm wrap accounts (which you can open at many firms with as little as $100,000) usually charge at least 1 percent and can go as high as 3 percent, with no reduction in fee as the account gets larger.

The fee-based account is an alternative to individual commissions on individual transactions. For people who trade a lot this might be an advantage, but for folks who don't move their money around, the fee can add up to a lot more than the annual transaction costs. The reason brokerage houses charge so much is that they use outside advisors to manage the money—and if they have to pay 1 percent to have an account managed, they need to charge 2 percent to make money. If a broker has a client with a $500,000 account, the 2 percent fee is $10,000, of which the broker/firm keeps $5,000 for doing nothing more than matching the client up with a money manager or managers. The manager(s) earn $5,000 for managing the money. For brokers, getting money under management means a flat fee for little work; they don't need to charge more fees for more stuff.

MUTUAL FUND SHELF-SPACE FEES

Why do you think your broker recommends a particular mutual fund over all the other funds with similar investing styles? While many brokers focus on funds' performance, for others the size of the load (the commission) is the most important factor.

But fund companies also pay hundreds of thousands of dollars to brokerage firms to get "shelf space" for their funds, just as consumer-products companies pay for shelf space in grocery or drug stores, and just as publishers pay for preferred space in bookstores. Just as no grocery store can carry every brand of toothpaste and no bookstore can house the more than 100,000 titles published each year in the United States, no brokerage firm's brokers can be asked to know even the slightest amount about the more than 8,000 mutual funds that compete for the investment dollars of the American public. Again, I'll discuss the various forms of payment from fund companies to brokerage firms and brokers in Chapter 4.

Retail Brokerage Is Lowest in the Firm's Hierarchy

Before the mid-1970s, when brokerage fees were set, most brokerage firms earned the bulk of their annual revenue and profits from the sale of stocks and bonds to institutions and individual investors. Since the "big bang," when commissions were deregulated, commissions from both retail investors (you) and institutional investors have fallen as a percentage of every major firm's revenues.

At the same time, the entire financial services industry has consolidated, and regulations have allowed for a combining of commercial banking and investment banking (the Depression-era Glass-Steagle Act was overturned in the late 1990s). This has allowed companies to consolidate to a huge degree.

As an example, take the world's largest financial services company, Citigroup, a 1998 combination of the huge Citibank and the equally huge Travelers' Insurance, which owned the Salomon Brothers investment banking firm and the Smith Barney brokerage firm, along with a host of other subsidiaries. Through combining subsidiaries and divisions, Salomon Smith Barney came into existence, with one of the largest broker networks as well as one of the largest investment banking businesses.

Most giant brokerage and investment banking firms today earn the bulk of their revenue from underwriting issues of stocks and bonds for corporations. This has major implications for you. They may have split the operating units for these activities on paper, especially after the global settlement on securities analyst behavior in 2002, but profits from all of these divisions still drop to the same bottom line.

When a firm underwrites a stock offering for a company (either an IPO or a secondary underwriting of an already public company), it usually directs one of its stock analysts to begin coverage in research reports of the company (if the firm does not already cover the company). If the stock issue is an IPO, SEC regulations require analysts from the firm performing the underwriting to wait for a period of time before they can begin writing reports about the company.

These reports, which are often glowing and rate the company a "buy" or a "strong buy," are then used as fodder for brokers to tout the company's stock (hence the term "sell-side analysis"). Analysts rarely issue negative reports, especially if they want the company to give them more underwriting work. This was shown starkly in the affidavit filed by the New York Attorney General to a court in an effort to get an order for Merrill Lynch to change its policies in this regard. A number of times stock analysts e-mailed each other saying there was nothing interesting about a company except investment banking work. (The spring 2002 investigation into Merrill's behavior ultimately led to a more comprehensive study of analyst behavior at many large investment banking/brokerage firms, and to the global settlement, in which 10 firms agreed to pay fines, restitution, and contributions to investor education of a total of $1.4 billion, as well as to restructure the way their analyst organizations operate.)

One academic study of analyst recommendations found that analysts did fairly well making recommendations about stocks their firm had no underwriting relationship with, but poorly when there was an underwriting relationship.

So, if your broker is with one of the large firms that have investment banking operations, in the late 1990s, during the height of the stock market bubble, he or she was basically pushing stock at you in order for the brokerage/banking firm to show the company it was performing the underwriting for that the brokerage firm was worthy of future business. The broker was basically doing the bidding of the underwriting department.

An even bigger scandal here is that once a retail investor is in the IPO, the retail broker cannot sell that client's IPO stock for 15 to 45 days (depending on the brokerage firm) or until the stock price has moved a particular percentage up or down. Some firms penalize the broker by taking back the commission on the initial sale. Yet institutional clients can sell any time they want.

Secondly, since the firm is a principal in the trade, the commission it earns on these sales is hidden as part of the internal accounting done as part of the underwriting fee. But you can bet that the broker is earning more by selling this "house" stock than he or she would by selling other stocks. Usually, the allocation of IPO stock given to individual retail brokers is not large (most has been allocated to the institutional brokers for their institutional clients), and most retail brokers are not cleaning up selling IPOs to their clients.

Of course, most retail investors never got near an IPO, since most of the IPO stock was doled out to preferred customers, which created a scandal in itself, for two reasons. This should make you happy, because you weren't the only folks being victimized. Some of the largest investment banks have agreed to censures and fines (although never admitting guilt) for engaging in practices known as "spinning" and "laddering."

When "spinning" an IPO, the underwriter, in effect, bribed leading officials (chief executive officers and chief financial officers mostly) in large companies with which they hoped to do investment banking business by putting large dollops of IPOs in their personal brokerage accounts, sometimes without the executives even knowing about the actual amount and timing of the stock being placed in the account.

When "laddering," they assigned shares in IPOs before the stock went public to clients who agreed to buy additional shares after the issue was released, at increasingly higher prices. This, of course, drove the market higher (a subtle form of market manipulation, although not an actual "pump-and-dump" fraud like the boiler room firms were running).

No Good Deed Goes Unpunished

In the battle between retail brokers and investment bankers, the brokers always lose—even when they try to do right by their clients. Take the example of Chung Wu, a broker in the Houston office of PaineWebber, a division of UBS PaineWebber.

On August 21, 2001, Wu sent an e-mail to all of his clients who held Enron stock, among them a number of Enron employees who held the company's stock after exercising options given them as part of their compensation package. PaineWebber was paid by Enron to handle the company's stock-option plan, and by doing so had first crack at managing brokerage accounts for Enron employees who exercised those options to purchase stock. (Chapter 3 discusses in detail how such systems work.) PaineWebber's investment banking group was also a major underwriter of Enron securities.

Wu, like many brokers, had used e-mail regularly to communicate with his clients. E-mail with market news and recommendations is one "value-added service" brokerage firms tout to their clients. But this e-mail cost Wu his job. It read, in part, "Financial situation is deteriorating at Enron. . . . I would advise you to take some money off the table even at this point." Within hours of the e-mail, the Enron executive who ran the company's stock-option plan had e-mailed PaineWebber officials in Houston and New York to "Please handle this situation. . . . This is extremely disturbing to me."

By the end of the day, Wu had been fired. PaineWebber said Wu had violated company policy by not having a supervisor look over any communication to clients and for contradicting the firm's research guidance. PaineWebber's last research report before August 21 rated the company a "strong buy" and said "we would be aggressive buyers of Enron at current levels."

On the day Wu was fired, Enron's chairman, Kenneth Lay, sent an e-mail message to employees saying the company placed a high priority on restoring investor confidence and lifting the stock price, and asking them to hang on to their stock. On that same day, Lay sold $4 million of Enron stock and brokers at PaineWebber's Houston office were busy selling large blocks of Enron stock for other Enron executives.

A group of PaineWebber retail clients, including many of Wu's clients, have sued the firm in a class-action complaint in United

States District Court in Houston, alleging among other things that PaineWebber "directly lied to its clients for its own pecuniary gain by failing to reveal adverse information which it knew about Enron." PaineWebber has denied all allegations, which remain to be proven. Wu, who immediately went to work for one of Paine-Webber's competitors, A.G. Edwards, in its Houston office, has also sued PaineWebber, for wrongful termination, seeking $2.7 million in damages.

The Wu firing, and the close relationship between PaineWebber's Houston office and top Enron officials, has also been the subject of an investigation by U.S. Representative Henry Waxman (D-CA), the ranking minority member of the House Committee on Government Reform. Waxman, in a letter to the PaineWebber Houston branch office manager Patrick Mendenhall, who had fired Wu, cited another (unidentified) broker who told committee staff that "advisors in the Houston office were instructed by supervisors not to encourage Enron employees to exercise their stock options and diversify their holdings, even if the employees were overly concentrated in Enron stock."

Finally, they even victimized the entrepreneurs whose companies they were taking public. In order to guarantee that stocks would have a "pop" (a huge run-up in price in the first few days, often in the first day), the investment bankers deliberately underpriced the IPO. When an IPO prospectus is issued, a price range for the offering is given (e.g., $12 to $17 per share). When the underwriters have a sense of how much demand there actually is for the new company in the marketplace, just before the issue launches, they set a firm price. You would think that a stock with a lot of demand would be priced at the top of its range, but often it wasn't.

If an IPO with a lot of demand was priced at $17, and it rose the first day to $20, this would be about a 17 percent increase (not bad for a day). But if the price were set at $12, and the stock went to $20, the first-day increase would be about 65 percent, often worthy of a business-section headline. By the 1998 to early 2000 time frame, just before the stock market bubble burst, some IPOs were oversubscribed by 500 percent or more (meaning there was desire for five times the number of shares being offered). Since entrepreneurs, investments bankers, and others whose stock was not included in the IPO could not sell for up to 180 days, this created an artificial imbalance of supply and demand in the stock, driving some prices up by 300 to as much as 1,000 percent in the first day or two of trading (i.e., an IPO priced at $15 would go as high as $150).

Of course, the entrepreneurs and venture capitalists who were selling their stock to the public in the IPO received less for their shares (known as "leaving money on the table"), but the brokerage firm got great publicity from the IPO, and more entrepreneurs came knocking on its door to underwrite more IPOs. The psychology of having a "hot IPO" and a huge "market cap" (how much the stock was valued at in the marketplace) began to outweigh how much capital actually came into the company to grow its business from the IPO, which, after all, is the purpose of floating stock to the public.

Ramifications of These Conflicts

There are three ramifications of these conflicts that inhabit the relationship between you and your broker.

First, simply knowing about the conflicts should serve you well in your future dealings with stockbrokers, assuming you ignore my advice and insist on dealing with them at all. You should not be so easily convinced in the future that your stockbroker is your trusted friend and advisor, looking out solely for your best interests. It is just not so.

Second, consider very carefully whether your broker can effectively serve two masters: him- or herself (and the brokerage firm) and you. It may well be that these conflicts are so pervasive and so overwhelming that you should not be placing your trust in (or money with) someone who is burdened by them.

Third, assuming that you believe your broker's value outweighs the conflicts inherent in the relationship, take a hard look at that "value." If you knew there was no evidence that your broker could outperform the market by picking "winners" and timing the market, would you still deal with that person—especially now that you understand the "real" relationship between you and "your" broker?

Understanding these conflicts and asking your broker questions about them makes you a far more informed investor than most people and reduces the likelihood that you will fall prey to one of the frauds and abuses discussed in the next chapter.

For example, here are seven questions to ask of any broker recommendation:

1. "Why do you think this (stock, bond, fund) is right for me? How does it fit with my investment goals and my risk tolerance?"

2. "Does your firm make a market in this stock?" If a fund: "Does your firm or any subsidiary of your firm or another subsidiary of your parent firm manage this fund?"

3. If a stock: "Are you buying the stock out of your firm's inventory?" If the firm is rating the stock a "buy," ask: "Why is the firm selling the stock from your inventory if it's rated a buy?"

4. "What is your commission on this (stock, bond, fund) and are you being given any special incentives to sell this (stock, bond, fund)?"

5. "Why are you recommending this purchase now as opposed to some other time?"

6. "Did your company underwrite the stock?"

7. "Since all information about a public company is instantly incorporated into its marketplace price, why do you believe this stock is underpriced?"

Asking these types of questions will keep you from becoming another victim of the types of practices that plague the relationship between investors and brokers.

How to Investigate and Interview a Potential Broker

If you insist on working with a stockbroker, or if you decide to work with any other financial advisor, you must believe that the relationship you will create with that individual will be one based on mutual trust.

It is often said that people do more planning about a two-week family vacation than they do about their investment portfolio. A good broker can and should help you think through your short- and long-term investment goals and help you create a plan to reach those goals.

A good broker or other financial advisor should work with you to buy the investment vehicles that help you reach your goals, regardless of whether they are the most profitable products for the broker. Possibly most important, a good broker should temper your enthusiasm for fad investments you read about in the financial press and help you stay on course with your investments.

You should never agree to open an account with a broker who cold-calls you on the telephone. You should undertake a search for a broker or investment advisor the same way you would hire any other professional to work for you, using referrals from friends and relatives you trust, as well as having discussions with any brokers you happen to meet through your social circle.

Most important, you should take your time and talk to a number of potential brokers to determine who makes you feel most comfortable. Before you agree to open a new account with any broker, even one who comes to you highly recommended, you should investigate that person's professional record and interview that person about how he or she would work with you.

Prior to interviewing the broker, go to the NASD website, www.nasd.com. Click on "Securities Industry Regulation" and follow the cues to "Perform an Online Search." Check out the disciplinary record for the broker you are interviewing. The record, called the Central Registration Depository (CRD), shows how many times the broker has been named as a respondent in an arbitration proceeding and the results of any such proceedings, as well as any sanctions placed on the broker by the Securities and Exchange Commission, any civil actions against the broker by state regulatory agencies, and even any criminal record the broker may have (even charges not related to selling securities). Also prior to interviewing the broker, ask him or her to send you the financial statements of his or her firm. You may be surprised to learn that you are worth more than the firm. As a general rule, do not do business with any firm that is not large, reputable, and well established. Although brokers at reputable firms have disputes with clients, these firms generally have stronger compliance departments than smaller, less-established firms. More important, if you do have to file a claim and you prevail, the odds are better you will be paid by a large, well-known firm. Many judgments against small firms turn out to be uncollectible.

At the interview, ask the following four questions:

1. **"What is the broker's investment philosophy?" A broker should be prepared to discuss the following issues with you:**
- Asset allocation
- Diversification within asset classes
- The relationship between risk and return
- Market risk
- Inflation risk
- Long-term holding of stocks
- Portfolio rebalancing

(I will discuss all of these concepts in detail in Chapter 6.)

2. **"How many times does he or she anticipate turning over your portfolio on an annualized basis and what cost-equity ratio does he or she believe acceptable for a client portfolio?"**
For turnover, anything more than one complete turnover is suspect, and many buy-and-hold portfolios turn over less than one time every three years. For cost-equity ratios, anything over 5 percent is clearly unacceptable, and it should be much less.

3. **"How does he or she calculate the risk of your portfolio?"**
If the answer isn't "by calculating its standard deviation," look elsewhere. If it is, ask what he or she believes an acceptable standard deviation would be. Remember, the S&P 500's historic annual standard deviation is around 15.

If the broker claims he or she can time the market and pick "winners," ask to see objective academic studies that show that anyone has been consistently successful in these endeavors over 15 years or longer.

4. **"What kind of return does he or she expect your portfolio to generate over the risk-free rate of return (the return on short-term U.S. Treasury instruments)?"**
Anything over 7 percent is suspect and would expose you to very significant risk.

Finally, don't be swayed by a broker's title. In the brokerage industry, titles are handed out like jelly beans, and the best titles go to the best producers. The fact that a broker is a senior vice president may not mean anything more than that the broker brings in a lot of commissions.

And big producers are not necessarily the safest bet for your portfolio. Brokers who generate a lot of commissions often don't help their clients produce better results than brokers who bring in less commissions; they are just better salesmen.

In fact, brokers who generate a lot in commissions for the firm are often allowed to run roughshod over the branch manager and branch compliance officer, who fear that the brokers may take their book of clients (and a hefty chunk of the branch manager's bonus) to another firm if they are questioned too closely about their sales techniques.

TERMINOLOGY

COMMISSION: A payment received by the sales agent for selling an investment product. Commissions are split between the broker and the brokerage firm.

FIDUCIARY: An individual (or organization) that has a special relationship with and duty toward another individual or organization to act "in the highest good faith" and "with integrity."

MARGIN ACCOUNT: A margin account allows an investor to use the value of the securities held in the account as collateral against a cash loan that can be used to purchase additional securities.

SELF-REGULATING ORGANIZATIONS (SROS): Organizations that regulate their members' actions outside of the legal system. An SRO can establish policies and procedures that sanction members or adjudicate disputes without using the courts.

SHINGLE THEORY: A legal theory that holds that the brokerage firm and individual broker, by "hanging out a shingle" as a licensed professional, imply a level of professionalism and ethical dealing with clients.

SPREAD: The difference between the bid and ask price on a security being offered for sale in the marketplace. The bid-ask spread provides an automatic profit for the firm making a market in the security, which compensates for the market maker's being required to maintain an orderly market by buying from any seller or selling to any buyer.

WRAP ACCOUNT: A managed account held by a brokerage firm. Instead of commissions being charged on each transaction, an annual fee is charged (usually 1 to 2 percent of the account's value).

3 Ripped Off by Broker Fraud

I have a client I'll call Fred. Fred, like you, is not stupid. In fact, Fred is quite intelligent. He is a professional in a major American city. One day in June of 1995, Fred answered a cold call from a stockbroker who worked for a small brokerage firm he had never heard of. Many of us get calls like this, and in the 1990s, during the great bull run in the stock markets, we all got a lot more calls than we get now.

Most of the time, we simply tell these people we're not interested and hang up quickly. But sometimes we get caught up in the story these cold callers have about their ability to make us rich. Fred moved money from his individual retirement account (IRA) into a new IRA account with the small firm. A year later, in June 1996, Fred allowed himself to be talked into investing $58,750 of that IRA (more than 60 percent of the account's value) in 5,000 shares of the initial public offering (IPO) of a company he had never heard of, which I'll call Widget Inc.

Unfortunately for Fred, Widget was one of a number of stocks involved in a "pump-and-dump" stock manipulation scheme. It crashed, and today is worthless. The small brokerage firm is no longer in business. A managing director of the firm was indicted and pled guilty to fraudulently manipulating a number of thinly traded stocks, including Widget. The criminal scheme involved the creation of an artificial demand for these stocks through payment of undisclosed commissions to induce brokers to recommend and sell them to their clients. Fred was a victim of this scheme.

I filed a claim for Fred with the NASD, charging the small brokerage firm and its president and majority shareholder with failure to supervise its brokers; breach of fiduciary duty to Fred; securities fraud for the role one of its managing directors played in the manipulation and fraudulent sales of Widget stock; misrepresentation of material facts in the sale of Widget stock; and violation of the NASD's rules of fair practice, which state in Rule 2110 that "[a] member, in the conduct of his business, shall observe high standards of commercial honor and just and equitable principles of trade."

I also filed an arbitration claim, this one with the NYSE, seeking to recover damages from the clearing broker for the small brokerage firm which during the 1990s acted as clearing broker for a number of small brokerage houses that turned out to be boiler rooms.

In May 2002, an NASD arbitration tribunal ruled in Fred's favor, finding against the small brokerage firm and awarding him over $54,000. However, the NASD tribunal did not find any liability on the firm owner's part, and since the firm has gone out of business, Fred will never collect this award. The clearing broker denied any wrongdoing in Fred's case, and in a decision dated August 26, 2002, an NYSE arbitration tribunal sided with the clearing broker.

Fred is out the $58,750 he gave to the boiler-room broker, plus his arbitration fees to the NASD and the NYSE.

The kind of egregious market manipulation by the small firm that Fred fell victim to is just one of many criminal frauds and violations of NASD or NYSE rules that should entitle investors to get their money back from their broker.

The late economist Charles Kindleberger wrote a book in 1978 called *Manias, Panics, and Crashes*. In that book, Kindleberger wrote that the tendency to "swindle and be swindled run in parallel" to the tendency to speculate in boom times, and that after the boom crashes there follows a time when frauds are revealed and "the curtain rises on revulsion."

Kindleberger's insight is important. Between 2000, when the booming stock market began to deflate, and 2003, when the economy and stock market again picked up steam, arbitration claims increased both at NASD and the New York Stock Exchange (NYSE), where almost all client/broker dispute arbitrations are conducted. They have since declined as the market has recovered. Many brokers and brokerage houses defend claims made against them by saying their clients are falling prey to "sour grapes" now that their stock portfolios are declining, and that nothing is happening other than the movements of markets.

The fact is that some brokers and brokerage houses were engaging in fraudulent practices during the boom times; but, human nature being what it is, clients were not complaining because the rising tide of the boom market was indeed lifting their boats. The point is, however, that had the frauds not taken place, their boats would have risen even further.

Securities fraud is defined in the federal securities laws, as well as in state securities statutes. Fraud is also a theory in common law.

The basic federal statute governing fraudulent practices committed by brokers is Section 10(b) of the Securities Exchange Act of 1934. Section 10(b) prohibits brokers from using any "manipulative or deceptive device or contrivance" that contravenes any rule or regulation established by the Securities and Exchange Commission (SEC).

Rule 10(b)-5 of the SEC prohibits brokers from misleading investors by making any false statements about a security, by failure to disclose material information about the security, or by engaging in any other acts or practices that "would operate as a fraud or deceit on any person." The reach of Rule 10(b)-5 is broad, giving investors the possibility of recovering their losses from brokers for a range of conduct that is far more common than you might believe.

State securities laws and the common law also provide similar redress for fraudulent conduct.

As you'll see in the discussion of common broker frauds that follows, sometimes it's pretty simple to figure out that one of these frauds has been committed, since the conduct of some brokers is so egregious.

But many brokers are getting away with failure to disclose a very basic material truth to all of their clients—that stock picking and market timing is a losing game. This failure to disclose is what leads to the vast number of unsuitable investments in my clients' portfolios, and possibly in yours.

While the discussion in this chapter is limited to practices that are blatantly fraudulent, I will discuss in Chapter 7 why the failure to disclose the fact that there is no basis for brokers' claims that they add value by picking stocks and timing the market should give rise to recovery of millions of dollars of losses suffered by investors in recent years.

The five big broker frauds are:

- Churning
- Unauthorized trading
- Price manipulation
- Forgery
- Misrepresentations and omissions

Churning

Churning is what happens when a broker makes trades in an account more frequently than necessary, with the sole intent of generating commissions. That's the rub: Commissions.

In its booklet for all registered representatives "Understanding Your Role and Responsibilities as a Registered Representative," the NASD writes:

> *Churning: You must not abuse your control over the customer's account by initiating transactions that are overly frequent and disproportionate in view of the financial resources and character of the account.*

This is a very artfully written little message. While the intent is clear—don't abuse your client's trust—the language is vague enough so that there is no clear delineation of when an account is churned. "Overly frequently" is subjective.

Even though broker/client disputes have only been dealt with in arbitration since the late 1980s, there is an ample body of case law precedent from earlier court cases to provide guidance on how to prove churning, or any other fraud or violation for that matter.

In the case of churning, courts have laid out three tests that must be met:

1. The broker had "control" over the trading activity. This control can be written trading authorization giving the broker discretion over the account, or it can be de facto control, which happens when the investor agrees willingly to trades the broker suggests because of the trust the investor puts in the broker.
2. The broker engaged in trading that is excessive and contrary to the customer's risk tolerance and/or investment objectives.
3. The broker acted either with reckless disregard for the investor's interest or with scienter. Scienter is a legal term that means intent. Scienter is a very important concept when making a claim of securities fraud.

CONTROL

Control is not always easy to prove. If the new-account forms show that the investor signed the page giving the broker discretion over the account, it's a slam dunk. But that is not usually the case.

Usually you have to demonstrate that you trusted the broker and relied on the broker's judgment, thereby giving him or her "control" over your account. I find it ironic that brokerage firms spend millions of dollars in advertising to convince investors of their special expertise but are quick to assert in a churning case that the customer did not really rely on the broker for advice.

Obviously, an inexperienced or unsophisticated investor is better able to argue that the broker "controlled" his or her account than is a longtime investor or someone who is familiar with the markets. However, the plain fact is that most investors do rely on their brokers; otherwise, they would not use them for financial advice and counseling.

Brokerage firms also seek to avoid liability for their conduct by asserting that the investor "ratified" the broker's conduct by reviewing and approving monthly statements and confirmation slips that set forth each trade. While this defense makes little common sense, it can be persuasive to an arbitration tribunal. Essentially, what the brokerage firm is shamelessly asserting is that "we may have cheated you, but you should have been smart enough to catch us."

At the end of the day, an investor should be able to convince a tribunal that the broker had control of his or her account simply by demonstrating that he or she relied on the broker and routinely followed the broker's advice. Nothing more should be required.

Unfortunately, this is not always so. Take the case of my client Phil as an example. Phil was 50 years old when he came to me. A part-time maintenance worker at a factory in Alabama who made $200 a week, he was married with two children. Phil had inherited land that had been in the family for many years. He sold the land, realizing $625,000 on the sale after paying all of his costs.

Phil was an extremely unsophisticated investor, with little prior experience in financial markets. He called a discount brokerage firm and spoke with a broker there. The broker suggested that he invest 100 percent of his money in the Rydex Dynamic Velocity 100 Fund, and that he margin the investment 100 percent, permitting him to make a total investment of $1.2 million.

The Rydex Dynamic Funds were extremely speculative funds, designed with a target of 200 percent exposure to the Nasdaq 100 index, meaning the funds themselves were borrowing—using the stock in the fund as collateral—to double its exposure. After losing $100,000 of his investment in just two days, Phil sold the fund.

I brought a claim on his behalf against the discount brokerage firm with the NYSE. It seemed so obvious that Rydex Funds were a totally inappropriate investment for the entire portfolio of a man trying to raise two children on earnings of $10,000 a year.

In a 2-1 decision, with the tribunal panel chairman dissenting, the panel denied Phil's claim and awarded him nothing. The brokerage firm had made the argument that the broker had not actually made a recommendation to Phil, but had only discussed the matter with him, and that Phil had made the investment decision himself. The absurdity of this result is yet another example of the unfairness of the mandatory arbitration system. I have no doubt that a jury of Phil's peers would have sided with him.

EXCESSIVE TRADING

The courts have ruled that it is not necessary for an investor to prove that each and every trade carried out in the account was, in and of itself, excessive; only that the totality of trading was excessive. A churning claim is not made based on the outcome of a particular trade or group of trades, but rather on the effect on the portfolio of all the cumulative trading. In fact, courts have ruled that it is possible to assert a claim of churning, and recover excessive commissions, even if the excessive trading leads to market gains.

Excessive trading is determined by using mathematical formulas and then measuring the outcomes of those calculations against standards for portfolio performance and portfolio management.

Before I decide whether to take a case, I have an independent expert do an analysis of the potential client's portfolio. Two pieces of his report give me an idea of whether there is a potential claim of churning. The first is the turnover ratio; the second is the total cost-equity ratio.

Turnover is a measure of a portfolio's trading activity. It is computed by taking the lesser of total purchases or total sales, and dividing that by the average monthly net assets for the time frame being analyzed. If the time frame is more than 12 months, the turnover can be "annualized" by taking the turnover result, dividing by the total number of months being analyzed, then multiplying by 12.

Annualized turnover tells you what percentage of your portfolio has changed over a year. A turnover of 1.0 (meaning 100 percent of the portfolio value) does not necessarily mean that all securities within the portfolio have been changed, only that the total value of the securities bought or sold over the year has been equal to the average monthly net assets in the account.

Of course, to get a true turnover ratio, you have to correct for any sales of securities made in order to take cash out of the account.

Turnover is an important ratio for a lot of reasons. First, a low turnover (say, below 0.25) indicates a buy-and-hold strategy. Any ratio higher than 3.0 indicates a buy-and-sell strategy.

There is considerable debate about the degree of portfolio turnover that should be considered "excessive." Here is how I come out on this issue:

In a study by Winslow and Anderson, reported in the *North Carolina Law Review,* the authors found that average turnover rates for stock mutual funds range from 0.5 for very conservative funds (meaning low risk and low turnover, including index funds), which means that 50 percent of the fund's value turns over in a year, to 1.18 for aggressive growth funds, which means that 118 percent of the fund's value turns over annually. They found the average turnover rate for all mutual funds to be about 0.8 (80 percent of the fund's value turns over annually).

If professional mutual fund portfolio managers believe these turnover rates permit them to optimize returns for the billions of dollars of assets they manage, it should be difficult for your broker to justify any higher turnover rates for your portfolio. In any event, the burden should be on the broker to explain why such a high turnover rate was necessary or appropriate. This is a difficult burden for the broker to meet, since usually the only reason for this kind of excessive trading is to generate commission income.

The other important measure in trying to make a case for excessive trading is the total cost-equity ratio, sometimes called the "break-even" ratio. This is an indicator of the amount of return a portfolio would have to generate to cover the transaction costs (commissions and spreads) and any margin interest incurred in the account.

The ratio is calculated by taking the total costs and dividing this by the portfolio's net equity. For example, if you had $200,000 net equity in a portfolio that incurred transaction costs of $4,000 and margin interest of $2,000 during the year, the total cost of $6,000 divided by the net equity (make sure to subtract any margin debt from the portfolio's total equity) is a cost-equity ratio of 3 percent. This means that the portfolio needed to generate a 3 percent gain just to cover costs.

Let's put these numbers into some context.

Of the 6,806 domestic stock mutual fund share classes with a five-year history in the Morningstar database as of April 30, 2006, only 326 (4.8 percent) generated a five-year annualized return of greater than 15 percent (net of cost). For comparison, the Standard & Poor's 500 index, often used as a proxy for "the stock market," had an average annual return—since its inception before World War II—of 10.4 percent, net of any costs.

Ask yourself this question: If about 95 percent of the professionally managed domestic stock mutual funds cannot achieve a return of 15 percent or more while keeping their cost-equity ratio below 3 percent, what are the chances of your broker doing better for you, despite a cost-equity ratio of 5 percent or more?

When this data is presented in this way to an arbitration tribunal, it should go a long way toward supporting a claim that a broker with such a high cost-equity ratio (say, 5 percent or more) is trading to generate commissions and profits for the firm, and not for your portfolio's benefit. Indeed, as the cost-equity ratio rises, it becomes more likely that you will suffer real, and possibly significant, losses. The broker and his or her firm should be liable for these losses.

I have a number of clients whose portfolios need to generate returns in excess of 25 percent just to break even. One was a client I'll call Sam.

Sam was 55 when he came to me. He was a commercial real estate broker in a metropolitan area. One day he attended a free seminar given by a major brokerage firm. After a series of aggressive follow-up calls, he agreed to transfer his account from his old firm to the new one.

Sam deposited over $400,000 of funds intended for his retirement in the new account. Over the following three years, the account lost $365,000, about 89 percent of its value.

My financial expert calculated that Sam's turnover ratio was 22, meaning the entire value of his portfolio was turned over 22 times in one year, and that his cost-equity ratio was 24 percent, meaning that he would have had to earn a 24 percent return on his portfolio simply to break even.

The brokerage firm argued that Sam was a sophisticated investor who understood stock trading, and that he saw confirmation slips and knew that the account was being actively traded. The NYSE arbitration tribunal accepted the brokerage firm's "blame the victim" defense and awarded Sam the princely sum of $30,000.

Again, my position is that if a broker is not telling you all the ramifications of the trades, including the costs of commissions and the tax implications of the trading strategy, he or she is omitting a material fact. If you knew these facts, you might have decided you didn't wish to trade at all, except for purchases using any new cash put in the account, sales to meet any cash needs, or any purchases or sales necessary for portfolio rebalancing and tax planning at the end of the year.

SCIENTER

It seems obvious that when a broker churns an account there is intent. Aside from generating commissions, there is no reason to turn a portfolio over three or four times, or more, in a year. In 1983, the U.S. Court of Appeals for the Second Circuit ruled that churning, in and of itself, can be seen as manipulative under the fraud statute because "the scienter required by 10(b) [is] implicit in the nature of the conduct."

A CASE OF CHURNING

I have a case where a number of investors immigrated to this country from Ireland. They had the misfortune to meet a fellow immigrant who was work-ing as a broker with a well-known firm. They did not know that the broker had been disbarred from the practice of law in Ireland and reinstated only upon the express condition that he "is not to handle clients' money."

The broker solicited my clients to join an "investment club" that would engage in short-term trading at discount rates. He convinced them that the risk would be minimal because he would be monitoring their trades on a "minute-by-minute" basis. The trading strategy, such as it was, involved buying the stocks on the publication of good news and selling them shortly thereafter.

During the 13 months the club was in existence, before my clients realized what was really going on, the account experienced an annualized turnover rate in excess of 173. Keep in mind that the average turnover of a mutual fund is 0.8.

The cost-equity ratio of this account was over 31 percent. This means that my clients would have had to earn a 31 percent return on the portfolio each year simply to break even. Of the 3,227 domestic stock mutual funds tracked by Morningstar, as of March 31, 2002, exactly 16 funds had returned in excess of 25 percent annually for 5 years. One such fund is the Kinetics Internet Fund, with an annualized return of 41.15 percent. If Kinetics had an annual cost-equity ratio of 31 percent, instead of the 2 percent it actually had, its return would have been 12.15 percent.

It is obvious that the only purpose of this trading activity was to enrich the broker and the brokerage firm at the expense of the investors.

The upshot of this story was a very ugly arbitration hearing, of which I will have more to say in Chapter 8.

SUSPECT CHURNING? WHAT YOU SHOULD DO

If you believe your account is being churned, there are two numbers you need to know: turnover rate and cost-equity ratio.

Unfortunately, it is difficult to glean this information from your account statements, and your broker is unlikely to provide you with it. But it does not hurt to ask.

Assuming your broker does not provide you with this information, gather your monthly account statements (if you don't have them, you can request them from your broker and he should provide them to you promptly) and bring them to your accountant. Ask your accountant to compute the turnover rate and the cost-equity ratio.

Most accountants should be able to perform these calculations. If your accountant does not have this expertise, ask him or her to refer you to a forensic accounting firm to do this work.

If your turnover rate is 3.0 or more and/or your cost-equity ratio is 5 percent or more, you may have a claim worth pursuing. At this point, it is worth discussing your claim with an attorney who specializes in securities arbitration matters.

Unauthorized Trading

Unauthorized trading means exactly what the term implies: The broker makes trades in your account without permission to do so. Brokers and brokerage houses usually challenge any claim of unauthorized trading by saying, "You agreed to it, and you got a confirmation, so you authorized it."

This is not as cut-and-dried as it seems. It is possible to argue that you did not formally ratify the trade if you were not informed of all of the particulars of the trade (the security name, buy or sell, the quantity in the transaction, the price at which you are bidding or offering, and any special instructions). Also, some courts have found that if the broker does not inform you of your right to refuse a trade you believe is unauthorized, that is a breach of the broker's duty to you.

According to guidelines published by the NYSE, when you agree to make a trade, the broker is supposed to note all of the particulars of the trade on the order ticket and read the order ticket back to you. Then, after the order has been executed, the broker is supposed to call you again and reiterate the information, including the actual price at which the security was bought or sold (which may be different from your bid or offer). Finally, the next day the broker is supposed to match up his or her paperwork with the trade confirmation from the firm's trading desk to make sure the confirmation slip you receive is accurate.

If your broker follows these guidelines strictly with every transaction, you are in the minority. Whenever you make a trade, you should note on your phone log the specifics of the transaction, and you should also note the return phone call to confirm the trade. If you don't get one, call the broker, and note that you had to make the confirmatory call.

Sometimes, even if you have not been keeping a telephone log of your conversations with your broker, you can prove unauthorized trading by closely examining the brokerage firm's telephone logs and matching them with the firm's computer logs of your account activity. I'll discuss this more in the section of Chapter 11 on pre-arbitration discovery.

Unauthorized trading frequently occurs when brokers are under pressure to generate commissions. It is far more prevalent in boiler-room operations than in reputable brokerage firms, which is another reason for not doing business with firms you have never heard of when you receive cold calls.

A CASE OF UNAUTHORIZED TRADING

I am always surprised by the number of unauthorized trading cases there are, given that it is blatant fraud. Here is one example, as set forth in a decision by the NYSE dated December 13, 2001 (Andrew J. Parish, Exchange Hearing Panel Decision 01-223).

Andrew J. Parish was employed as a registered representative with Edward D. Jones from January 1998 until he was terminated on August 31, 1998. He stipulated to the conduct described below "without admitting or denying guilt."

Parish admitted making 10 unauthorized trades in the account of a 66-year-old retiree and his son. When the son complained, the firm reversed the transactions.

He also admitted making 10 unauthorized transactions in the account of an 82-year-old retiree with an annual income of $20,000. The firm also reversed these transactions when it became aware of them.

For these and other problems, the NYSE censured Parish and barred him from the securities business for a three-month period.

In his 1999 book *License to Steal: The Secret World of Wall Street Brokers and the Systematic Plundering of the American Investor,* an anonymous former boiler-room broker told of how brokers at the firm he worked for routinely made unauthorized trades in order to increase their commissions, or to "park" stock that another investor was insisting be sold while the firm was actively manipulating the stock and driving the price higher (see the following discussion of price-manipulation frauds). They would cover these indiscretions by:

■ Telling a client who complained that the trade was a mistake and that the commission on the next trade would be waived.

■ Buying shares of the stock for their own account on the last day of the account statement period to drive it higher, so if the client complained the broker could say, "I knew it was a winner and couldn't get ahold of you."

■ Calling the client just before the account statements came out and warning of a "clerical error" in the forthcoming statement. Of course, it was not an error, but this gave the broker another month to find another home for the stock, or for the price manipulation to hit its peak.

■ Paying off the kid in the mailroom not to send out the confirmation slip.

I should emphasize once again that these practices are very much the exception, not the norm, but that they happen with enough frequency that American investors lose millions of dollars a year to such behavior.

SUSPECT UNAUTHORIZED TRADES?
WHAT YOU SHOULD DO

In addition to sending a complaint letter, gathering your records, and beginning a phone log, you should—both orally and by letter or fax—disavow within 10 days the trade you believe has been made without your consent.

You should receive a confirmation of the trade before the fifth day, when the trade settles, so you should have ample time to reject it. If you receive a confirmation slip for a trade you do not believe you authorized more than 10 days after the trade, include this information in any complaint letter you send.

If you have to disavow two trades, write to the firm's compliance department and to the securities regulators in your state. Also, stop doing business with the brokerage firm. Finally, consider pursuing a claim against the broker and the brokerage firm for any losses you have incurred on account of the unauthorized trading.

Price Manipulation/Market Manipulation

Manipulating the price of stocks is not as difficult as it may sound. Boiler rooms and chop shops do it all the time. This is what happened to my client Fred, whose story I'll continue a little later.

Some people make the distinction between price manipulation and market manipulation, but they are almost always the same thing. There are very few cases where brokers at major legitimate brokerage houses actually manipulate price through fake trades—a practice known as "painting the tape"—lie about how much volume is being traded, or refuse to execute a client's sell order.

But boiler rooms and chop shops do all of these things, and more.

In the spring and summer of 2000, 120 people were charged in federal district courts in Manhattan and Brooklyn with stock fraud. A number of others were charged in state criminal court in Manhattan. They were principals and brokers in some of the most notorious boiler rooms of the 1990s, as well as a number of known members of New York's five Mafia families. The "Mob Stock Scam" was coast-to-coast front-page news.

In the 16 federal indictments and other "criminal informations," the defendants were charged with defrauding thousands of investors out of over $50 million from 1993 to 1996 by manipulating the prices of stock in 19 small companies.

Many of those charged had criminal histories of taking part in other stock frauds and had been barred by the SEC from the securities business. Some had worked for three, four, or even more boiler-room brokerages since the late 1980s, when frauds in the so-called microcap market began in earnest.

In September 2000, Richard J. Walker, then-director of the SEC's enforcement division, testified on organized crime's involvement in microcap fraud before the House Subcommittee on Finance and Hazardous Materials of the Committee on Commerce. He told the representatives:

> *Existing evidence indicates that organized crime activity on Wall Street has been limited to the microcap market. The reasons for this are several. Effective market manipulations require control of the sell side of the market and keeping the truth about the company from prospective*

investors. The float and trading volume for securities of large-cap companies makes it almost impossible to control the sell side of the market, even with strong-arm tactics. In addition, such companies tend to be more seasoned in terms of public reporting and, as a result, it is more difficult to create sudden, exciting hype about a company that would generate real buying volume from innocent investors. . . .

The most prevalent fraud in the microcap market is the "pump and dump" manipulation. The scheme centers on the spreading of false information—principally through either a "boiler room" or via the Internet—designed to artificially inflate a stock's price. Investors often receive information that is either exaggerated or completely fabricated. Those spreading the false information typically hold large amounts of stock and make substantial profits by selling after the price peaks. Upon selling their shares, the promoters cease their manipulative efforts, the stock price plummets, and innocent investors incur substantial losses.

Boiler-room brokers often "hook" a new investor by getting the individual to make an initial investment in the stock of a blue-chip company or to transfer securities in blue chips they currently hold with another broker to a new account, with the promise that they will make the account grow over time.

Once the money is in the account with the boiler-room brokerage, it is often as good as gone. Brokers:

- Call frequently with hot tips.
- Continue to talk until you either buy a stock or hang up the phone. "He buys or he dies" (from lack of food or sleep while he is on the call) is what one broker tells his unregistered cold caller in the movie *Boiler Room* to get him to continue talking until he can wear down a potential investor into talking to the broker so he can close the deal.
- Make unauthorized trades in your account if you refuse to buy frequently enough.
- Berate, harass, insult you and worse if you refuse to make a purchase, or a big enough purchase.
- Sell your blue chips to pay for stock you have purchased if you refuse to send more money after rethinking the wisdom of the trade.

■ Refuse to allow you to sell out of a stock that is in the "dump" phase of the scam by not taking phone calls, not returning phone calls, hectoring you not to sell, or simply refusing to execute the sale.

A stock manipulation is accomplished by a small group of people who control all of the stock in a thinly traded small-capitalization stock placing blocks of the stock in various boiler-room brokerage accounts. The large blocks are then chopped up (hence the term "chop shop") into small blocks to sell to investors.

As is so often the case, the law of unintended consequences was at work in the explosion of microcap stock manipulation that began in the 1980s. Changes in SEC regulations that were designed to help legitimate companies raise capital played right into the hands of scam artists.

The SEC regulation used to set a stock fraud in motion is Regulation S, which allows certain kinds of stock to be sold outside the United States without registering the stock with the SEC, as is necessary when stock is sold publicly in this country.

In a manipulation fraud, a few million shares of stock are issued under Regulation S and sold to dummy corporations outside the United States for a few pennies a share. The stock is then transferred to the accounts in this country of the fraud conspirators, usually at one brokerage firm.

Some of the stock is then chopped up and distributed among the boiler rooms, which release it to their sales floors, where cold callers begin marketing it aggressively for a few dollars a share as an IPO of stock in a hot new company.

As the stock begins to move up in price, it actually becomes easier for the boiler-room brokers to pass it off on successive generations of investors. Some early investors actually make money on the deal as they sell their stock to the next generation (with the broker pocketing a commission on both sides of the trade, a practice known as "crossing trades," which is against stock exchange rules).

The conspirators try to run up the stock's price by issuing false and misleading press releases about the company to the financial press, and by clogging Internet investment chat rooms with hype from "investors" about the stock's movement and the company's achievements.

When the stock seems to be getting stale, the conspirators begin to sell any stock they have held on to (the dump phase). The boiler rooms make money on all of the commissions generated, by the "spread" between the bid price and the ask price (because they are acting as market makers in these stocks, many of which trade off stock exchanges on what is known as the Nasdaq "bulletin board" system), and often through kickbacks from the conspirators.

Later-generation investors are left holding worthless stock. After running a few scams, many boiler-room brokerages close up shop and open under a new name, in the same offices, with the same brokers and the same owners. It is very difficult for individual investors to successfully recoup any losses from manipulation schemes; even if they win an award at arbitration, many of these small brokerage firms have gone out of business or have no assets that can be used to pay an award.

The heyday of microcap stock manipulation seems to have run its course. It was actually on the decline before the market began to sag in 2000. While it took the Justice Department years to put together the cases that resulted in the 2000 indictments, the SEC and the NASD had begun earlier to rewrite rules and regulations to make pump-and-dump frauds more difficult to carry out.

The last of the legal cases have finished winding their way through the criminal justice system. In May 2002, Victor Wang, the former chairman of the chop-shop brokerage Duke and Company, was sentenced by New York State Judge William Wetzel to serve $7\frac{1}{2}$ to $22\frac{1}{2}$ years in state prison. Wang pled guilty in 1999 to charges of enterprise corruption brought by the office of the Manhattan district attorney. According to prosecutors, in the three-year period before the firm was shut down in 1998, the two-office company sold investors more than $600 million worth of manipulated stocks. Twenty-four others have been convicted in connection with the Duke and Company fraud.

A CASE OF MANIPULATION
My client Fred, whose story I told at the beginning of this chapter, was the victim of a classic case of manipulation.

SUSPECT MANIPULATION? WHAT YOU SHOULD DO
Victims of this kind of scheme clearly have redress against the broker and the brokerage firm, as well as against the principals of the brokerage firm, under a legal theory known as "controlling persons," which I'll discuss in detail in Chapter 10. Unfortunately, despite this fact, manipulation cases are often situations where there are plenty of legal rights for the victim but no one from whom to collect, as happened to Fred.

If you have been a victim of a pump-and-dump manipulation, you should contact an attorney and explore the possibility of filing and pursuing a claim. The attorney may decide to include the clearing broker firm as a respondent to the suit, if the facts warrant. Clearing brokers often have the financial resources to pay a judgment, but establishing liability against them can be difficult and uncertain.

Forgery

Forgery is committed by brokers in order to enable them to commit fraud. Cases of "pure" forgery are relatively rare.

Brokers most often forge a customer's signature on a new-account form, including the section that gives the broker trading discretion over the account and the section that declares the account to be a margin account, or on a form that allows the investor to trade options (a very high-risk proposition).

Tribunals generally do not consider this practice a problem if the broker is simply carrying out the directions given to him or her by the investor. However, if this is not the case, then the broker is simply engaging in blatant fraud, and he and his firm will be held responsible for the damages caused by this misconduct.

A CASE OF FORGERY

As I previously indicated, cases of outright forgery are not common, but they are not as unusual as you might expect. The case of Marco Carnevale is a particularly egregious example of forgery engaged in by a broker employed by a reputable firm.

In the winter of 2000, Marco Carnevale, a broker in the Boston office of Prudential Securities, attended a client's funeral, acting as a pallbearer. Not wanting to lose the client, even in death, Carnevale then forged documents so he could keep trading the client's retirement portfolio.

Massachusetts Secretary of the Commonwealth William Galvin, in whose office the state's securities regulators work, uncovered the ruse in an investigation into Prudential's lack of supervision in its Boston office. In an agreement with Galvin's office, in which Prudential did not admit to any wrongdoing, the firm agreed to pay a $250,000 fine and increase supervision of its brokers.

Carnevale, who left Prudential in July 2000, was one of three brokers in the office accused by the state of unauthorized trading in client accounts.

Carnevale's con was small potatoes when seen in the light of the forgeries that helped Enrique Ernesto Perusquia bilk clients out of more than $200 million. Perusquia, who worked for a time in PaineWebber's Manhattan and San Francisco offices and in Lehman Brothers' Manhattan office, allegedly forged the signatures of at least some of more than a dozen clients who, among them, lost over $150 million.

In December 2001, an NYSE arbitration panel awarded 10 plaintiffs $429 million, including $208.7 million in punitive damages, in their claims against Perusquia, who was alleged to have invested millions of dollars from his clients' accounts in companies about to declare bankruptcy, in exchange for kickbacks, and to have sent falsified account statements to clients.

PaineWebber, a division of UBS PaineWebber Group, Lehman Brothers (where Perusquia worked when he began the con), and J.P. Morgan Chase Bank, which cleared trades for both brokerage firms, all settled with clients in 2001. In January 2002, the United States Attorney's office in San Francisco charged Perusquia with criminal and civil fraud in connection with the forged account documents and legal memoranda, as well as sending falsified account statements. In February, Perusquia signed a plea agreement and waived a formal indictment. In May, he was sentenced to $6\frac{1}{2}$ years in federal prison. He also agreed to make $68 million in restitution. In addition, the Securities and Exchange Commission (SEC) imposed civil penalties of $8.8 million against him and barred him from associating with a broker-dealer for life.

Finally, in August 2003, the SEC censured UBS PaineWebber and fined the firm $500,000 for failure to supervise Perusquia. UBS PaineWebber consented to the judgment without admitting or denying guilt. The SEC's administrative order, document number 34-48371, dated August 20, 2003, and available at the SEC's website (www.sec.gov), is a fascinating rendition of a complex securities fraud.

Brokers don't just forge their clients' signatures; sometimes they forge the signatures of their branch manager. On May 29, 2002, the *Wall Street Journal* published a set of disciplinary actions taken against brokers by the NASD after investigation by NASD Regulation (the organization's investigating and adjudicating body). In one decision, the NASD fined Alfred Vincent Ferarro Jr. (a Wayne, New Jersey, broker) $9,670, including disgorgement of $2,172 in commissions, for "sign[ing] the name of his branch manager on customers' new-account applications for investments in variable contracts and mutual funds without the manager's knowledge or consent." Ferarro was also suspended from association with any NASD member for one year.

SUSPECT FORGERY? WHAT YOU SHOULD DO

As an investor, it is very difficult to detect a forgery. You will usually encounter forgery in tandem with unauthorized trading, and what will attract your attention will be the unauthorized trading. If you suspect unauthorized trading, you should inquire about the possibility that forms have been forged to give your broker discretion over your account.

Misrepresentation and Omission

Misrepresentations and omissions are, by definition, violations of the antifraud regulations. They are willful. They occur when a broker does not disclose the risk inherent in an investment suggestion he or she makes or a trading strategy he or she suggests undertaking.

In order to win at arbitration, you must show that the misrepresentation was "material" to the investment decision. When an arbitration panel hears a misrepresentation or omission case, the question the arbitrators ask of the evidence is: "Would the investor have made the same investment decision if the facts were not misrepresented or omitted?"

Misrepresentation always involves intent. A broker misrepresents risk, or fails to discuss risk, when he or she believes that the client will balk at the advice because of the risk involved. Except in cases of a stock-manipulation fraud like Fred's, misrepresentation occurs more frequently in cases of "unsophisticated" investors, and is a frequent complaint made by my retired and widowed clients.

However, I also see cases involving misrepresentation even with investors who are supposed to be relatively sophisticated. The ability of brokers to commit these offenses rests again with the amount of trust investors put in their brokers as supposed "experts" in investing.

As David Robbins writes in his *Securities Arbitration Procedure Manual*, "brokers will be held responsible for misrepresenting material facts or failing to disclose them because customers, by and large, must rely on the representations of their brokers; customers do not often have the ability or resources to verify those representations or have the accessibility to information available to the broker."

A CASE OF MISREPRESENTATION/OMISSION

I represented an 86-year-old retired man I'll call Ralph and his 71-year-old wife, whom I'll call Edith. They are very risk-averse, and only invest in bonds. They went to a broker who specialized in bonds, and he invested their entire $1 million combined portfolios in bonds. However, this is what the broker did not tell them:

Approximately 80 percent of their portfolios were invested in nonrated "junk" bonds. A 2001 study by the bond-rating agency Fitch IBCA found that municipal securities not rated are estimated to have default rates between nine and 13 times higher than investment-grade municipal bonds.

Approximately 73 percent of bonds purchased in my clients' portfolios were in the following sectors: multi-family housing, health care, industrial development, and electric power. These sectors have a significantly higher risk of default than other sectors.

My clients suffered substantial losses when a large percentage of the bonds in their accounts defaulted.

I filed an arbitration claim on their behalf, asking for $397,443.92 in compensatory damages for Ralph and $73,132.37 for Edith. In addition, we asked for punitive damages against the firm, its principals, and the broker; attorney's fees; and all costs and expenses. In May 2002, an NASD arbitration panel awarded Ralph $100,000 and Edith $25,000 in compensatory damages, no punitive damages, and none of the fees and expenses we had asked for.

This is a classic case of misrepresentation and omission. It is also another case demonstrating how difficult it is to obtain full compensation by the tribunals appointed by the industry self-regulating organizations.

SUSPECT MISREPRESENTATION/OMISSION? WHAT YOU SHOULD DO

Again, for an investor, it is very difficult to discern that you are being a victim of a misrepresentation or omission. Your natural tendency is to believe what your broker is telling you. If your investment begins to lose money and you talk to your broker, you may be uncomfortable with the answers the broker is providing about why the investment is losing value. As you get further along, you unravel that the broker has misrepresented the safety or suitability of the investment.

Additional Frauds and Improper Practices

There are other, less common, practices engaged in by brokerage firms that are also fraudulent. Because they are less common, I will discuss them briefly. Just because they occur less frequently than the five big frauds does not mean that if you suspect your broker has committed one of these acts you should not file a claim and try to recover your losses.

FRONTRUNNING

Frontrunning occurs when a brokerage firm or individual broker—or sometimes an investment advisor—buys or sells for his, her, or its own account(s) before doing the same for client accounts.

The typical frontrunning scheme operates as follows:

A broker places an order in a thinly traded stock for his own account shortly before placing a large order for a number of clients. The broker knows the client orders he intends to place will move the stock price up. He usually sells his own position shortly after placing the orders for the clients.

A variation on this theme occurs when the broker learns of favorable news affecting the stock's price and buys ahead of his clients at a more favorable price.

In my experience, I usually don't know that frontrunning has actually occurred until I have filed a claim alleging some other violation, and the frontrunning turns up during the discovery process (discovery is discussed in detail in Chapter 11). I then amend my complaint to include the frontrunning charge. Once I have discovered the frontrunning, the brokerage firm often has more incentive to settle the claim before the arbitration hearing occurs; brokers very rarely engage in frontrunning ahead of only one client.

Establishing damages caused by frontrunning is difficult and expensive. It is perhaps for this reason that you don't see a lot of frontrunning claims.

ORDER FAILURE

Order failure is not a common charge made when you deal with a traditional broker, either full-service or discount. However, it is a frequent problem when dealing with online brokers. Order failure is a violation of NASD Rule 2320, the so-called "best execution rule," which says that every order placed by a client must be executed promptly at the best price possible.

Order failure is not sinister. It is usually due to simple human error or, in the case of online brokerages, to technology problems caused either by temporary system interruptions or by the inability of the system to handle the volume being put through it.

Traditional order failure occurs either when a broker fails to notify you that he or she was unable to execute an order on a trade you had either asked to be made or agreed to, or when a broker fails to implement a "stop-loss" order request and the stock falls below the price at which you had asked the stop to be placed.

A stop-loss order is an order placed to sell a security at a particular price. If the order is placed at a price below which you bought the security, you automatically stop the loss on the investment at a particular place. If the order is placed above the price at which you bought the security, but below the price at the time the order is placed, you automatically lock in a profit. The stop-loss order essentially keeps the price from falling below a particular threshold if you or the broker are not monitoring the price constantly.

There is little motivation for a broker to fail to execute an order, unless the broker is working for a boiler room and simply refuses to execute a sell order. If a broker has explained to you the possibility that because of rapid price movement it is possible a trade will not be executed at the exact price you asked for, if the price moves beyond a reasonable limit, the broker will simply call you back and say you missed the opportunity, or the security will cost a little more or you will get a little less if you are selling.

With regard to failure to execute a stop-loss order, it is difficult to prove that the broker simply did not hear you ask for a stop to be put on the security at a particular price, unless you keep very detailed logs of your telephone conversations with the broker.

SELLING AWAY

Selling away occurs when a broker sells securities outside the scope of his or her work for a brokerage firm employer. It is a violation of NASD Rule 3040, which essentially prohibits brokers from engaging in any private securities transactions outside the scope of their employment with their brokerage firms, unless they have obtained written consent from their employer.

A broker is tempted to sell away because he or she is offered the opportunity by promoters to earn hefty commissions on products the firm refuses to sell. These are often very risky and illiquid securities, such as limited partnerships.

Arbitration tribunals tend to look at whether the transaction at issue was made to appear to the investor that it was part of the ordinary course of the brokerage firm's business. If you can convince the tribunal that it was, the brokerage firm will most likely be held liable for the losses incurred as a consequence of this investment, assuming the investment was unsuitable. If it was clearly apparent that the broker was issuing non-company documentation, it is usually more difficult to win an award against the firm, although it is still possible to win an award against the broker.

David Robbins, in his *Securities Arbitration Procedure Manual,* suggests the following areas of inquiry in a selling away case:

1. Did the broker use the firm's marketing materials (letterhead, etc.) to market the investment?
2. Were meetings concerning the investment held at the firm's offices?
3. Did the firm's management and the investors have contact concerning the investment?
4. Were funds for the investment made payable to the brokerage firm?
5. Would it be reasonable to expect that the customer should have known that the investment was not authorized by the firm?

Obviously, a "yes" to the first four of these questions and a "no" to the fifth should be convincing evidence to an arbitration tribunal that the brokerage firm should be responsible for any losses you suffered making an investment under such circumstances.

FAILURE TO SUPERVISE

Failure to supervise is not a "stand-alone" claim. It is a claim that is made against the administration of the branch in which the offending broker worked. Without necessarily naming the branch manager or the branch's compliance officer, it charges that they were negligent in not supervising closely enough the offending broker and in failing to enforce the firm's internal guidelines, which typically require intense supervision of the activities of their brokers.

It is important to make this claim where it is warranted, in order to insure that the financial resources of the brokerage firm itself, and not just the broker's financial resources, are available to pay any judgment.

Failure to supervise is also a charge the SEC frequently levels against a firm that ties the firm to the particular fraudulent actions of a particular broker whom the SEC is charging with a violation of the securities law. The SEC, as well as NYSE and NASD, which also will bring charges of failure to supervise, have very strict protocols for how branch managers, branch compliance officers, regional managers, and even national managers and national compliance officers are supposed to conduct their supervision of brokers' work, including random audits of how brokers handle trades for clients. In the go-go years of the mid- and late 1990s, many of those supervision mechanisms broke down.

OVER-LEVERAGING IN A MARKET ACCOUNT

Buying securities in a margin account amplifies the potential risk and potential return of the purchase. If you buy a security using "margin," you use the security itself as collateral for a loan given to pay for part of the purchase. In this way, you "leverage" the investment.

The simplest analogy to a margin account for securities buying is the purchase of a house. When you buy a house, you put down 20 percent or more of the purchase price (some lenders allow you to put down less), and the lender uses the house itself as collateral against the loan. You pay the loan back in monthly payments over a set period of time. If the value of the house goes up, you can sell the house and earn a return on your actual cash investment. If the value goes down, you may be "under water" (where the value of the house is less than the amount of the loan) but the lender cannot take back the house unless you fail to make regular payment on the loan.

In the case of a margin loan, the Federal Reserve, under its Regulation T, establishes the "down payment" necessary to purchase a security. Currently, you must put up cash equal to 50 percent of the value of stocks being purchased, 2 to 25 percent for bonds, and 10 percent for U.S. Treasury bonds.

As David Robbins explains, Regulation T only establishes margin requirements for purchases. The requirement for the margin value that must be maintained in the account is set by the NASD and NYSE, and individual brokerage firms can set their requirements at a higher level than these self-regulating organizations (SROs).

If the value of the underlying securities falls below the margin requirement, you face a "margin call." To meet the margin call, you need to put either more cash or securities held elsewhere into the margin account. If you don't, a portion of the securities held in your margin account needs to be liquidated in order to raise your equity in the securities held in the account above the margin loan threshold.

All the time you hold the margin debt, you are paying interest, part of which the firm may be sharing with the broker in addition to any commissions being made. Margin accounts are also considered managed accounts, and a

A Margin Call

Here is an example of a margin call: Mrs. P. agrees to open a margin account with her broker. She then decides to buy 10,000 shares of stock, valued at $20 a share. The total value of the stock is $200,000. To meet the Regulation T requirement, Mrs. P. is asked to put up $100,000. Mrs. P. now has a margin loan, called a debit balance, of $100,000, on which she pays interest. She also has equity in the form of securities of $100,000.

Monthly interest is added to the debit balance.

Her brokerage firm's margin requirement for stocks in an active account is 35 percent of the market value of the stocks (the NASD and NYSE minimum requirements are 25 percent). This means that if her equity falls below 35 percent of the total of the sum of her equity and her debit balance, she needs to put more cash, or other securities held elsewhere, into her margin account, or face liquidation of some of the position.

Six months later, the debit balance has risen to $104,000, and the value of the stock has fallen to $160,000. She now has equity of $56,000, and a total equity plus debit balance of $160,000. Her ratio of equity to equity plus debit is now 35 percent. If the value of the stock falls any lower, Mrs. P. will face a margin call.

A margin call is made at the end of a trading day, when the securities are valued at the current market price (a process known as "marking to the market"). Fulfilling the margin maintenance call must be done by early in the next trading day or liquidation occurs.

Margin accounts are usually set up so an investor can speculate, borrowing money from the brokerage firm in order to buy more securities than he or she can truly afford. If the value of the securities purchased with the loan goes up, the investor makes more than he or she would have if the securities had been purchased with cash. But if the value of the securities goes down, the investor loses more than he or she would have. Because of the volatility of securities, this kind of leverage can be very dangerous.

management fee is charged. Altogether, commissions, management fees, and margin debt can add significant costs to the portfolio, thereby increasing its cost-equity ratio to a point where it may be very difficult to break even, much less earn a positive return.

There are a few technical violations around the issues of margin accounts and margin calls that you may have cause to file a complaint about. These are that the brokerage firm failed to notify you before liquidating your account; that the firm liquidated your account prior to a deadline it had set for you to meet the call or face liquidation; or that the firm didn't allow you to participate in the decision about which securities to liquidate to meet the margin call.

The bigger issues around margin, however, have to do with the suitability of securities held in margin accounts, and with the advice brokers give to clients about the use of margin lending to pay taxes due on the unforced sale of some securities held in the account, a situation that falls into the category of over-leveraging a margin account.

THE OPTIONS AND MARGIN PLAY

From 1999 to 2001, a lot of technology company employees, who received large grants of options to buy their company's stock at a discount as part of their compensation, exercised those options on the advice of stockbrokers, put the stock in margin accounts, then faced continual margin calls as their stocks slid precipitously. Many have filed complaints against their brokers.

Sometimes their brokers urged them to keep all of their assets in their employer's stock. But even when brokers suggested they diversify, the "diversification" was usually into other high-risk stocks in technology companies.

One firm that has faced a host of these over-leveraging claims is Salomon Smith Barney, which managed the options programs for Microsoft and World-Com, among other companies. Employees from these two companies have charged Salomon brokers and the firm with pressuring them into exercising their options so the company could reap financial benefits, then convincing them to borrow money to pay income taxes due on the shares exercised, placing the stock as collateral in a margin account.

When an employee exercises a nonqualified stock option (NSO), the difference between the price at which the option can be exercised and the stock's market value is taxed in that year as ordinary income. For instance, an employee who can exercise 100,000 NSOs at $10 per share must pay $1 million to exercise the options. If the stock is valued at $60 per share, the value of the 100,000 shares is $6 million. The difference, $5 million, is taxable as ordinary income in the year in which the options are exercised.

To exercise the options, all but the wealthiest employees will need to borrow the money. After the options are exercised, the prudent thing to do is to sell enough shares to meet your tax liability (in the case of shares exercised in 1999, 2000, or 2001, 39.6 percent of $5 million, or about $2 million) and put the money away in a risk-free investment until tax day.

Another $1 million of stock, plus a few extra shares, need to be sold in order to pay off the brief loan of $1 million to exercise the option. The remainder, roughly $3 million, should then be allocated over major asset classes (cash, stocks, and bonds) and diversified into a number of passively managed investments in each asset class (asset allocation and diversification are discussed in detail in Chapter 6).

According to the claims of Microsoft and WorldCom employees, however, Salomon brokers urged them to, in effect, put the full $6 million in stock into a margin account, maintain the $1 million loan, and borrow $2 million more to pay the taxes. The $6 million value of the stock is more than enough to carry a margin loan of $3 million.

However, once the prices of these stocks began to fall, the debit balance in the employees' margin accounts rose as a percentage of the underlying value of the stocks held in the account. Eventually, the employees faced margin calls, their stock positions were liquidated with the money going to Salomon to pay off a portion of the margin loan, and, especially for those who exercised their options in 2000 and faced tax bills in 2001, nothing was left to pay their tax bills, which were often larger than their annual salaries. Many had to file for personal bankruptcy.

In an interesting twist, Salomon settled a number of claims with WorldCom employees and fired two brokers who had a number of WorldCom employees as clients.

In August 2003, the NYSE fined Salomon Smith Barney $1 million for failure to supervise the brokers in the Atlanta and other offices who dealt with WorldCom employees and gave them this advice. The NYSE also temporarily removed a Salomon Smith Barney branch manager's license to supervise and charged one of the brokers Salomon had fired in 2002 with recommending unsuitable investments to his clients.

Big Earners Can Cost You Big Bucks

With all the pressure on brokers to produce, you would think it would be brokers in the bottom of the heap who would be committing frauds and violations in an effort to bring their gross commissions up, increase their commission payout, and maybe even hold on to their jobs.

But that is not always true.

In fact, sometimes the biggest producers find it easiest to create a situation where they can take advantage of their clients. They are the brashest, the most confident, the most in-your-face about their success. The size of their book—their client list—is proof of their prowess at selling.

Their book helps them bring in new clients, and it also tells the branch manager and the compliance officer to "lay off." In a world of sell, sell, sell, where the bottom line is all that counts, the big producers are too often given wide latitude, which they use to take advantage of their clients.

RICHARD GREENE

In May 2000, Merrill Lynch signed a consent decree with the Massachusetts Secretary of the Commonwealth's securities regulators to settle charges against one of its brokers. Richard Greene worked for Merrill from 1960 until 1998, when he retired. In the consent decree, Merrill Lynch did not admit any wrongdoing.

At the time of his retirement, Greene had been in Merrill's Boston office for more than 30 years. He was one of the firm's top producers in the country, with 1,400 clients and $1.5 billion in those clients' accounts. He earned well over $1 million a year for himself and had five sales assistants working for him.

Beginning in the mid-1990s, Greene began actively recommending that his clients invest in four thinly traded speculative stocks. Between 300 and 400 did so. Greene continued to solicit investments in these companies (or invested on behalf of discretionary accounts) to the point where, regulators concluded after an investigation, the accounts were overconcentrated in these risky stocks.

The stocks dropped substantially in 1998 and 1999, creating millions of dollars in losses for the clients.

As part of the settlement for failure to supervise Greene's activities, as well as the activities of another broker who misappropriated client funds into his own trading account and lost it speculating on options, Merrill agreed to pay a $750,000 fine, make a $100,000 contribution to the Massachusetts Investor Education Fund, and hire a consultant to monitor the Boston office's compliance activities for two years. The consultant would report to the securities regulators every three months.

In addition, Merrill agreed to set up an expedited mediation process for any of Greene's clients who had a concentration of greater than 50 percent in one or more of the four stocks in question at year-end 1997 or the end of the first quarter of 1998, and whose losses on the stock(s) were greater than $25,000 at the time the mediation claim was filed. A single mediator was appointed by the Securities Division and paid for by Merrill Lynch to handle all claims.

TANIA TORRUELLA

Tania Torruella, another former Merrill Lynch broker, has also cost the firm a bundle of money. Torruella, who was fired by Merrill in the summer of 2001, became party to no less than 139 arbitration claims by disgruntled former clients. As of February 2002, Merrill had already paid out $18.7 million in claims to about 90 of her former clients, including at least seven of her own relatives, who collected nearly $700,000 from Merrill. Her father, Ricardo Torruella, received $250,000 in a settlement from Merrill. Torruella's broker's registration was terminated by the NASD on August 1, 2001. On March 13, 2002, she became the subject of a New York Stock Exchange Division of Enforcement investigation, according to the NASD Regulation Public Disclosure Program.

Merrill lured Torruella and her multimillion-dollar book of business away from the Dean Witter brokerage business of Morgan Stanley Dean Witter in 1999 with a signing bonus said to be almost $1 million. From then until she was fired, her book of business grew from $78 million to $160 million. In her best year, Torruella generated over $2 million in commissions and earned over $700,000. She first became a stockbroker in 1995 in Dean Witter's Orlando office, after 10 years as sales director of a small business she owned with a partner. Her former business partner settled a $257,000 claim against Merrill stemming from Torruella's handling of her account for $45,000.

The 42-year-old broker was an avid networker who was very popular among middle-aged and professional women, especially those facing illness, divorce, or going through other difficult times.

According to the *Wall Street Journal*, one attorney in West Palm Beach, Florida, filed nearly 90 claims in a batch in August of 2001, charging Torruella with overconcentrating her clients' accounts in unsuitable investments, mostly high-tech stocks, and misrepresentations regarding her record as a broker. She claimed to have produced a compounded annual return of over 40 percent for clients since 1986, which was nearly nine years before she became a broker.

Torruella's attorney claims she was given no training or supervision at either Morgan Stanley Dean Witter or at Merrill Lynch. Merrill Lynch is defending these claims, and the charges remain to be proven. In a lengthy interview with the *Orlando Sentinel* in February 2002, Torruella said, "I had no training. I was just fortunate that the stock market was going straight up. . . . I did not know what to do in a bear market. I don't consider myself incompetent, just inexperienced and untrained."

FRANK GRUTTADAURIA

Before he disappeared on January 11, 2002, Frank Gruttadauria, a 45-year-old broker in the Cleveland office of Lehman Brothers, wrote a letter to the FBI claiming that he had been stealing from his clients for more than 15 years.

"I can hardly believe that I could have done this without detection for so long," the Cleveland *Plain Dealer* quoted Gruttadauria as writing to the FBI. "This began as an attempt to make up lost monies for customers and mush-roomed over the course of time."

Gruttadauria surrendered to the FBI two blocks from his Cleveland office a month after disappearing. He was charged with making a false statement to a bank in an attempt to get a $6 million line of credit, and was being held while the FBI continued the investigation of his decade-and-a-half scam. On August 29, 2002, Gruttadauria pled guilty to federal charges of securities and mail fraud and was subsequently sentenced to seven years in prison.

Gruttadauria defrauded at least 50 clients in a number of ways. He mis-appropriated at least $115 million, siphoning it from his clients' accounts into his own or his companies' accounts. In addition, he inflated the value of client funds by over $250 million in order to hide trading activity (much of which resulted in losses to the accounts) and the commissions that were generated by that trading activity. He created a set of fraudulent account statements monthly for some of his wealthiest clients, using company letterhead, while having Lehman mail the actual account statements to post office boxes Gruttadauria set up in the clients' names.

At his peak performance in the late 1990s, Gruttadauria had about 300 clients and generated as much as $6 million in commissions annually. There is no evidence that Lehman or S.G. Cowan, where he worked before going to Lehman, was aware of Gruttadauria's illegal activities. However, both firms had allowed Gruttadauria to be a "producing branch manager," meaning that he had branch management responsibilities as well as responsibilities for managing his own book of business with clients. As branch manager, Gruttadauria was the direct supervisor of the branch's compliance officer. If ever there was a case of a compliance officer being cowed by a big shot, this would be it; not only was Gruttadauria one of Cowan's, then Lehman's, top producers, but the branch manager as well.

The Gruttadauria case was the hook used by the Financial Services Oversight and Investigations Subcommittee of the United States House of Representatives for its hearing of May 23, 2002. In that hearing, some of Gruttadauria's victims testified, as did Lori Richards, the chief of compliance for the SEC, and Marc Lackritz, president of the Securities Industry Association, the trade association for brokerage firms.

In compelling testimony, Carl Fazio, a former client of Gruttadauria's who had parlayed a small fruit stand into the Fisher-Fazio supermarket chain, told the committee that "today, as I stand before you, although I earned and invested a handsome amount of money, I have few liquid assets. I received fictional statements tailored to the investments that I directed. I did not have a clue that Frank Gruttadauria took control of my account and traded the hell out of it. What Gruttadauria did, and I am still learning as the brokerage firms begrudgingly turn over a limited amount of information, was take my funds and generate mind-numbing amounts of commission for the firm while losing money in the market hand over fist. . . . I learned that in 1990 alone in my real account, the one I never saw, I paid commissions equal to more than 50 percent of my average equity and that my account turned over more than 15 times."

Lori Richards, the SEC's compliance chief, told the committee that the SEC investigated Gruttadauria in 1993 for churning, but found no pattern of churning and filed no formal charges. At the same time, the NYSE examined the compliance procedures of Cowan and Company, where Gruttadauria then worked, and found many deficiencies.

In August 2003, the SEC and the NYSE jointly entered into an agreement with Cowan and Lehman regarding the Gruttadauria case. Without admitting or denying guilt, Cowan and Lehman accepted censure from the SEC and NYSE and agreed to pay $5 million (Cowan) and $2.5 million (Lehman) in administrative penalties, to be divided equally by the SEC and NYSE. The NYSE decision separately found that Cowan had "engaged in conduct inconsistent with the NYSE's just and equitable principles of trade by failing fully to implement policies and procedures to which it had committed pursuant to an undertaking imposed in an earlier NYSE enforcement action." In other words, the NYSE had caught Cowan in lax supervision of Gruttadauria and the entire Cleveland office (without actually discovering the extent of Gruttadauria's fraud); Cowan had agreed to tighten its supervision and had failed to do so.

As part of the 2003 consent agreement, both firms agreed to full restitution of all funds stolen by Gruttadauria (much of which had been accomplished already) and to an expedited arbitration procedure for claims against him stemming from the excessive trading and losses to the funds from those trades. Any pending NYSE or NASD arbitration claims were to be automatically pulled into the expedited proceedings. They also agreed to supervision of their compliance policies and procedures through consultants they would pay who would report regularly to the SEC and the NYSE. Cowan, Lehman, and a third brokerage firm which previously owned Cowan's brokerage assets settled criminal charges with local prosecutors in January 2004 and agreed to pay $9.74 million in fines.

Closing the Barn Door

Such enforcement actions by the SEC, NYSE, and state securities regulators always seem like a case of closing the barn door after the horse has escaped. And to a great degree they are.

Unfortunately, too often these agreements result in administrative penalties and fines that are paid to the regulators with little or none of the payment in the form of restitution for aggrieved investors, who must pursue individual claims against brokers and firms through the arbitration process.

In August of 2003, the NASD proposed new rules that would increase the supervision required for brokers whose dealings with clients become the basis for arbitration actions. Any broker who has been the subject of three or more customer complaints or arbitration claims, three or more regulatory actions or investigations, or two or more employment terminations or internal firm reviews involving wrongdoing would be subject to a written plan of supervision. The supervisor writing the plan would have to acknowledge responsibility for allowing the broker to continue working.

This would make supervisors think twice about continuing to employ such problem brokers and would not allow them to evade their responsibility for supervision in any subsequent actions or arbitrations.

TERMINOLOGY

ANNUALIZED TURNOVER: The percentage of a securities portfolio's value that has been turned over each year. A "low" turnover is below about 0.5 times per year, while a "high" turnover is above about 1.2 times per year (based on a study of mutual fund styles). A turnover of more than 2 times is a possible hint of churning.

BOILER ROOM, sometimes called a "chop shop": A brokerage firm that uses high-pressure telephone sales techniques to get investors to buy stocks. Boiler rooms often engage in manipulation in the price and the entire market for thinly traded stocks, unauthorized trading, churning, and other fraudulent practices.

CHURNING: Excessive trading of a securities account for the purpose of generating commissions for the broker and brokerage firm.

COST-EQUITY RATIO: Sometimes called the "break-even" ratio, cost-equity tells what portion of the portfolio's value is being spent on transaction costs and margin interest. Cost-equity shows how much a portfolio would have to generate in investment returns to cover the costs. A cost-equity ratio above 3 percent is a possible hint of churning.

FRAUD: Obtaining money from another party through commission of an act of lying, cheating, deceit, or misrepresentation. Securities fraud involves use of a deliberate "manipulative or deceptive device" including misstatement of a material fact or failure to disclose a material fact during the sale or purchase of securities.

FRONTRUNNING: When a broker or brokerage firm (or investment advisor) buys or sells for his, her, or its own account(s) before doing the same for client accounts. As clients' purchases drive the price higher, the individual or firm reaps profits by selling ahead of clients.

MARGIN CALL: When the ratio of equity to the total of equity plus margin debt falls below a certain level, the brokerage firm requires the investor to bring the ratio back up. This can be done either by putting more cash (or other securities) into the account or by selling some of the securities in the account.

PUMP-AND-DUMP: A classic stock fraud in which a boiler-room firm or group of boiler-room firms manipulates the market and price of a thinly traded stock by selling to a small group of investors. Insiders in the stock sell out their position in the security at the top of the market, causing the price to begin to collapse, which usually sends the stock into free fall.

STOP-LOSS ORDER: An order placed to sell a security at a particular price. If the order is placed at a price below which you bought the security, you automatically stop the loss on the investment at a particular place. If the order is placed above the price at which you bought the security, but below the price at the time the order is placed, you automatically lock in a profit.

4 Not Even Mutual Funds Are Free of Conflicts

Between 1998 and 2000, Robert Ostrowski, a Prudential Securities Inc. broker in the firm's Wilkes-Barre, Pennsylvania, office, sold mutual funds to many of his clients. This is nothing special. But the way in which Ostrowski allegedly sold the funds may have caused him to be fired, and set off a Securities and Exchange Commission (SEC) investigation.

In July 2003, Prudential settled charges of failing to supervise Ostrowski with the SEC, agreeing to pay disgorgement and prejudgment interest of $82,000, to be returned to investors harmed by Ostrowski's sales practices, as well as a civil penalty of $300,000. Ostrowski, just shy of his 65th birthday at the time of his firing in 2001, and the Wilkes-Barre office's branch manager, Rees Harris, faced an administrative hearing before the SEC.

At the height of the bull market in 1999 and 2000, Ostrowski and his two daughters, also Prudential brokers, had approximately 3,500 clients and assets under management of $375 million. For years, Ostrowski had been one of Prudential's top-grossing brokers, often taking home more than $1 million a year.

The SEC complaint alleges that between 1998 and 2000, on 42 separate occasions, Ostrowski sold clients over $100,000 in class B shares of Prudential proprietary mutual funds, which generated a larger commission to him and Prudential than would have been earned had the money been invested in class A shares. According to the complaint, Ostrowski earned approximately $51,500 in excess commissions on the sales, and Prudential earned approximately $63,000 in excess commissions. The complaint states that Ostrowski failed to explain to clients the benefits of purchasing A shares for investors making larger investments.

The SEC complaint states that Ostrowski "knowingly or recklessly concealed the salient characteristics of class A and class B shares that would have been important to any reasonable investor. . . . Ostrowski obtained the customers' approval to purchase a particular fund, but he failed to provide the customers with a prospectus in advance of the sales, and to disclose the existence of multiple classes of shares, breakpoints, rights of accumulation, and letters of intent. As a result, the customers did not understand that they were purchasing class B shares." Ostrowski allegedly often made multiple purchases of B shares in the same fund for the same client on the same day or in a short period of time.

Over 90 million households own mutual funds as part of their investment portfolios. Many of these funds are held in company-provided 401(k) and other retirement plans, but millions own funds in individual accounts as well. The concept of a mutual fund is simple and elegant: A fund is formed to pool the money of many small investors in order to create economies of scale and equalize the playing field between small investors and institutional investors such as pension funds, endowments, and the like.

Oh, that it were so.

As we have come to realize in the last few years, mutual funds are fraught with conflicts, from broker compensation that skews recommendations away from investors' best interests, to fund fees that move from one pocket of the mutual fund's parent company to another, to mutual fund managers granting preferential treatment to some clients, allowing them to trade frequently and often after hours, and thus siphon off profits from long-term mutual fund owners.

The SEC, Congress, the New York Stock Exchange (NYSE), and the NASD have ongoing investigations into whether the mutual fund industry needs additional regulations. And investors have filed class-action lawsuits against mutual funds as well.

As an individual investor, you may have the opportunity to participate in one or more of these suits against particular mutual fund companies. You may be able to be reimbursed by the brokerage firm you used if the firm, its clearing firm, or the mutual fund company you are invested with failed to honor breakpoint commission discounts. But if you have an individual com-

DOES YOUR BROKER OWE YOU MONEY?

plaint against a broker for exploiting the conflicts between brokers' interests and their clients' interests, you will have to go through arbitration.

And investors are doing just that. According to the NASD's statistical analysis of arbitration cases filed, of the 6,074 arbitration cases filed in 2005, 1,348 were about common stocks while 888 were about mutual funds.

Today's World of Mutual Funds

Mutual funds are regulated by the SEC under the provisions of the Investment Company Act of 1940, which was drafted to protect investors from the conflicts of interest inherent when a third party manages a pool of assets. Mutual funds can be purchased through two primary channels. The first is directly from the fund distribution company. The second is through a broker-dealer. When an investor goes through a broker-dealer, he or she pays a load, which is analogous to the commission paid on a stock transaction. This load compensates the fund for distribution costs, the lion's share of which are commissions paid to the broker for his sales efforts on behalf of the fund family. In most transactions made directly through a fund family, the investor pays no load. Until 1980, the only way a broker could get compensated on a mutual fund transaction was through the load.

In 1980, the SEC adopted Rule 12b-1, which allowed funds for the first time to pay distribution expenses directly out of the fund's assets. The 12b-1 fee allowed traditional mutual fund companies that sold their funds through brokers, insurance agents, and other intermediaries to repackage their commissions and internal marketing costs in any combination of front-end, back-end, or annual charge to investors. At that time, so-called "no-load" funds, sold directly to the public by such companies as Vanguard, T. Rowe Price, and Fidelity, were just beginning to appear on the market. Many investors were asking why they should pay a sales charge to buy into a fund if they could buy a no-load fund. By moving away from front-end loads, in effect hiding the sales charge in annual fees over time and in back-end loads, traditional mutual funds were able to continue fighting against the upstart no-loads.

Until 1995, mutual fund companies had to set up new funds if they wanted to move away from a front-end load structure to a back-end load or annual-fee-based structure. Then, in 1995, the SEC adopted Rule 18f-3, which allowed mutual funds to create multiple share classes that represent claims against the same underlying portfolio. This set the stage for the world of mutual funds we have today, where most funds have A, B, and C classes of shares.

Table 4-1 shows a typical expense structure for a mutual fund with three classes—A, B, and C shares. Many funds today also have separate classes for college savings, called 529 shares after the section of the Internal Revenue Code, and some funds have three classes of 529 shares that parallel the A, B, and C shares.

Three things are important about this expense structure:

1. The front-end load for A shares declines as you invest more.
2. The back-end load for B shares, known as a contingent deferred sales charge, declines the longer you hold the shares.
3. The 12b-1 annual fee for B and C shares is 75 basis points (75/100 of a percent) larger than for A shares.

Because of these differences in the expense structure of the share classes, if you are going to buy funds through a broker, you need to do a careful analysis of the total cost to you of owning the fund over the lifetime of your investment. In other words, you need to determine how much you are going to invest in the fund and how long you are going to hold the fund in your portfolio after you buy it. Only then can you determine if A, B, or C shares are the most appropriate investment for you.

DECLINING LOAD (BREAKPOINTS)

The dollar points at which the front-end load on A share purchases declines are known in the industry as "breakpoints." Breakpoints look like they are simple, but like most things in life, they are not. Different "families" of mutual funds have different breakpoints (the breakpoints in Table 4-1 are typical but not always the case). Different mutual fund families also have different rules about how you can achieve breakpoints.

All fund families allow you to get the lower front-end load by investing above the breakpoint in one investment. Most fund families also allow you to submit a "letter of intent" that you will hit a particular breakpoint with a series of smaller investments over a certain period of time (usually 13 months) and pay the lower front-end load on all of the smaller investments. This is helpful, for instance, to a self-employed individual opening a SEP retirement plan who intends to contribute $50,000 and reach the breakpoint between this year's contribution and next.

**TABLE 4-1 Expense Structures of a
Typical Multiple Share Class Mutual Fund**

SHARE CLASS	12B-1 FEES	OTHER EXPENSES	EXPENSE RATIO	FRONT-END LOAD INITIAL INVESTMENT	LOAD	DEFERRED LOAD
A	0.25%	0.75%	1.00%	< $50,000	5.75%	0.00%
				$50,000 - $100,000	4.50%	
				$100,000 - $250,000	3.50%	
				$250,000 - $500,000	2.50%	
				$500,000 - $1,000,000	2.00%	
				> $1,000,000	0%	
B	1.00%	0.75%	1.75%	0.00% Converts to A shares after year 8		5% in year 1 4% in year 2 3% in year 3 3% in year 4 2% in year 5 1% in year 6
C	1.00%	0.75%	1.75%	0.00%		1% in year 1 0% thereafter

Most fund families allow you to aggregate all of your investments in the funds within the family to achieve a breakpoint (e.g., three $20,000 investments in three funds in the same family would achieve the $50,000 breakpoint). Since most fund families offer numerous funds, this allows investors to diversify across funds with different investment goals within the same fund family and achieve the breakpoint.

Most fund families also allow you to aggregate your accounts, regardless of where they are held (e.g., you have a taxable account with one broker and an IRA retirement account with a different broker that are both invested in funds within the same family), to achieve a breakpoint.

Finally, most funds also allow you to "household" to achieve breakpoints (aggregate the accounts held by all members of a household, including the primary account holder, a spouse or domestic partner, children, and sometimes even grandparents). However, fund families may define children in different ways (e.g., up to 18, to 21, to 23 if full-time student, disabled and living with parents or guardians, etc.).

Each of these successively broader definitions of aggregating assets to achieve breakpoints is addressed in a fund family's description of "rights of accumulation" within the prospectus.

Such aggregation sets up a paperwork nightmare, and a situation where individual investors must do a lot of digging to find out if they qualify for particular breakpoints. A study carried out by the SEC, the NYSE, and NASD and released in March 2003 sampled 9,000 mutual fund transactions conducted by 43 brokerage firms. Of 5,515 transactions that qualified for a breakpoint discount, the examiners found that 1,757 transactions (19 percent of the total and 32 percent of those that qualified) did not receive the appropriate breakpoint discount. The study found 12 reasons customers didn't receive the discount:

1. Not linking fund shares held by members of the same household (362 instances)

2. Not linking funds in the same fund family owned by the same customer (330 instances)

3. Customers not receiving the retroactive benefit of a letter of intent (244 instances)

4. Not considering purchases by the same investor of multiple funds in the same family on the same day (241 instances)

5. Not linking multiple accounts held by the same investor at the same firm (205 instances)

6. Brokers purchasing shares in numerous different, though similar, mutual funds (151 instances)

7. Not aggregating the current purchase with previous purchases of the same fund in the same account (114 instances)

8. Not granting waivers for repurchase of the same fund (55 instances)

9. Not receiving a discount on a single trade that exceeded the dollar amount for the breakpoint discount (29 instances)

10. Not receiving the benefit of a letter of intent on file (11 instances)

11. Not receiving a waiver of any fee when a customer exchanged shares in one fund for another within the same family (8 instances)

12. Transactions just below the breakpoint, and where the customer had sufficient funds in the account to meet the breakpoint discount level (7 instances)

The average discount not received was $364 per transaction. The largest single discount not received was $10,289, while the smallest was $2. The total of discounts not received was $637,023.69.

Brokerage firms of all sizes had instances where breakpoint discounts were not provided. Many, if not most, of the instances were due to systems (manual or computerized) and procedures that made it time-consuming (if not difficult) for the individual broker to determine if a breakpoint discount was appropriate. Combine this with a lack of investor education in when they are entitled to a breakpoint (after all, who reads a mutual fund prospectus?) and a lack of knowledge on the part of many brokers as to when breakpoints are applicable.

Finally, there is a total lack of transparency in how mutual fund loads are recorded on confirmation slips. Only the gross investment into the mutual fund is recorded on the confirmation slip, not the amount that is then returned to the distributor and the broker in the form of the sales commission. This means that an investor must look at the net asset value on the day the purchase was made, see from the confirmation slip how many shares were purchased, multiply that by the net asset value, and subtract that total from the total investment made to see how much he or she was charged and if the proper breakpoint was applied.

A small number of instances are clear examples of broker misconduct. Purchasing shares in many similar funds from different families that together would be above the breakpoint, and making a purchase just below a breakpoint level when enough money is in the account to reach the breakpoint are clearly fraudulent activities on the part of brokers.

From these findings, the NASD organized a joint NASD/industry task force to investigate how to improve the system of allocating breakpoint discounts and came up with nine recommendations in its July 2003 report. Among these were better investor education about breakpoints, instructions in fund family prospectuses that clearly outline appropriate aggregation of funds and accounts for breakpoints (e.g., whether grandparents' accounts for the benefit of grandchildren in the household are allowed, multiple holdings through accounts with different firms are allowed, etc.), and how the investor should report these aggregations at the time of a purchase. The task force also recommended standardized checklists for brokers to fill out for order verification to make it easier for processing personnel to track applicable breakpoints, and better systems for linking account information.

The task force also recommended more training of brokers, and the transmission of taxpayer ID number and broker ID number to the mutual funds with every transaction so more linking can be done automatically within the mutual fund's systems. (This is especially important for brokerage firms that keep "omnibus accounts" with mutual fund companies, where in the fund company's records, the brokerage is the fundholder and the fund shares are subdivided at the brokerage firm level into individual accounts.)

In settlements of cases filed in 2004 by NASD and the SEC, brokerage firms paid tens of millions of dollars in fines, penalties, and breakpoint rebates to investors.

DECLINING CDSC IN B SHARES

While the issue with A shares is the size of the holding and the consequent breakpoint discount for any new purchase, with B shares the key is the holding period. As a fund investment is held longer, the back-end load, or contingent deferred sales charge (CDSC), declines. If the CDSC were the only charge imposed on a B share, for long-term investors B shares would clearly be the share class of choice.

And indeed, many brokers have pushed B shares for long-term investors because there is "no sales charge if you hold them long enough." But the CDSC is not the only charge imposed on B shares. As with C shares, B shares carry a higher annual 12b-1 fee, which over time can more than offset the lack of a front-end load.

DIFFERENTIAL 12B-1 FEES

The 12b-1 "distribution" fee is paid by the mutual fund to the distributor and the brokerage firm annually to help them market the fund. It is the same as a residual paid by an insurance company annually to the agent who originally sells the policy. The split between the distributor and the brokerage firm is different depending on the share class, but the 12b-1 fee is paid even if the distributor is owned by the same parent firm as the mutual fund (a common occurrence) and even if the mutual fund company, the distributor, and the brokerage firm are all owned by the parent firm.

In May 2002, the SEC announced that it had opened an investigation into mutual fund 12b-1 marketing fees. When 12b-1 fees were established in the 1980s, they were meant to be short-term fees levied by new and small mutual funds to help them become known in the financial community. However, according to the Morningstar service that rates mutual funds, in 2002, 69 percent of all mutual funds levied a 12b-1 fee.

Although you don't see the 12b-1 fee as a charge at the time you buy the shares, unless the broker explains the nuts and bolts of the prospectus to you (which few do), higher annual fees reduce the mutual fund's annual performance for share classes in which the higher fees are levied.

In addition, the 12b-1 fee is levied on an average-daily-balance basis, not as a percentage of the original investment. So, in a mutual fund that is increasing in value steadily, paying 1 percent a year in 12b-1 charges (the typical charge on a B or a C share) costs more over time than paying 1 percent of an original investment in front-end load charges.

A final word about 12b-1 fees: An academic study in 1997 of 3,861 multiple-share-class funds found that funds with multiple share classes and 12b-1 fees also had higher management fees than those charged by funds with a single share class, and, therefore, were more costly to investors even without considering the 12b-1 fee.

INVESTOR PREFERENCE

Edward S. O'Neal, Ph.D., a professor at the Babcock Graduate School of Management at Wake Forest University, is an expert on mutual fund share classes. His analysis of the preferable share class for investors to own is seen in Tables 4-2 and 4-3. Table 4-2 compares investments in a two-class mutual fund, with A or B shares, while Table 4-3 compares investments in a three-class mutual fund, with A, B, and C shares.

In both tables, the assumptions about expenses are those shown in Table 4-1, and the assumption about return before annual fees is 12 percent. The A-share investor has an annual net return of 11 percent, while the B- and C-share investors have an annual return of 10.25 percent, due to the larger 12b-1 fee levied on them.

As you can see in Table 4-2, the only instance where a purchase of B shares has an advantage over a purchase of A shares is for a small investor (below the first breakpoint) who is going to hold the shares for five years or less. By eight years, when most B shares automatically convert to

TABLE 4-2 Comparison of Redemption Amounts in A and B Share Mutual Fund

INITIAL INVESTMENT	SHARE CLASS	1 YEAR	3 YEARS	5 YEARS	8 YEARS
$10,000	A	$10,450	$12,848	$15,796	$21,533 *
$10,000	B	$10,454 *	$12,925 *	$15,973 *	$21,498
$50,000	A	$52,945 *	$65,093 *	$80,028 *	$109,094 *
$50,000	B	$52,269	$64,624	$79,865	$107,492
$100,000	A	$106,999 *	$131,549 *	$161,731 *	$220,472 *
$100,000	B	$104,538	$129,248	$159,731	$214,983
$250,000	A	$270,270 *	$332,280 *	$408,518 *	$556,891 *
$250,000	B	$261,345	$323,120	$399,326	$537,458
$500,000	A	$543,312 *	$667,968 *	$821,225 *	$1,119,494 *
$500,000	B	$522,690	$646,239	$798,653	$1,074,916
$1,000,000	A	$1,108,800 *	$1,363,200 *	$1,675,969 *	$2,284,682 *
$1,000,000	B	$1,045,380	$1,292,479	$1,597,306	$2,149,833

* Indicates preferred share class for specific holding period and initial investment

A shares, the larger annual 12b-1 fee has offset the front-end load and the B-share owner has paid more in total fees than the investor who originally purchased A shares.

When a third share class, C shares (often called level-load shares, because except for the 1 percent CDSC in the first year, the 1 percent annual 12b-1 fee is the only load), is introduced, as illustrated in Table 4-3, the picture becomes more complex.

But one thing is crystal clear, and somewhat striking: At no investment amount, and at no holding period, are B shares the advantageous share class. Because of the CDSC imposed on B shares usually until the sixth or seventh year of holding, a redemption of B shares at 1, 3, or 5 years is always lower than C shares. For small investments (below the first breakpoint) and for holding periods of 1, 3, or 5 years, a redemption of B shares is higher than a comparable redemption of A shares; but once you hit the first breakpoint, that advantage disappears.

In all instances, for shorter holding periods, C shares are advantageous over A shares. As the investment amount increases above successive breakpoints, the holding period at which the advantageous share class switches from C shares to A shares becomes shorter.

TABLE 4-3 Comparison of Redemption Amounts in A, B, and C Share Mutual Fund

INITIAL INVESTMENT	SHARE CLASS	1 YEAR	3 YEARS	5 YEARS	8 YEARS
$10,000	A	$10,450	$12,848	$15,796	$21,533 *
$10,000	B	$10,454	$12,925	$15,973	$21,498
$10,000	C	$10,894 *	$13,325 *	$16,134 *	$21,498
$50,000	A	$52,945	$65,093	$80,028	$109,094 *
$50,000	B	$52,269	$64,624	$79,865	$107,492
$50,000	C	$54,470 *	$66,623 *	$80,672 *	$107,492
$100,000	A	$106,999	$131,549	$161,731 *	$220,472 *
$100,000	B	$104,538	$129,248	$159,731	$214,983
$100,000	C	$108,940 *	$133,245 *	$161,344	$214,983
$250,000	A	$270,270	$332,280	$408,518 *	$556,891 *
$250,000	B	$261,345	$323,120	$399,326	$537,458
$250,000	C	$272,349 *	$333,113 *	$403,360	$537,458
$500,000	A	$543,312	$667,968 *	$821,225 *	$1,119,494 *
$500,000	B	$522,690	$646,239	$798,653	$1,074,916
$500,000	C	$544,698 *	$666,226	$806,720	$1,074,916
$1,000,000	A	$1,108,800 *	$1,363,200 *	$1,675,969 *	$2,284,682 *
$1,000,000	B	$1,045,380	$1,292,479	$1,597,306	$2,149,833
$1,000,000	C	$1,089,396	$1,332,453	$1,613,440	$2,149,833

Indicates preferred share class for specific holding period and initial investment

WHY BROKERS PUSH B SHARES

So, if most mutual funds have three classes of shares, and A and C shares are always advantageous over B shares, why do brokers push B shares?

Take a guess. Of course, it all has to do with commissions. Table 4-4 on page 91 shows the typical brokerage commission structure for a mutual fund with three share classes and the expense structure shown in Table 4-1.

As Table 4-4 shows, while the initial brokerage commission for A shares declines as the front-end load declines (at each breakpoint), the initial commission for B funds is set at the highest A-fund commission, no matter how much money is invested. The "trailing commission" is the portion of the annual 12b-1 fee that is passed from the fund distributor to the brokerage firm, an issue I'll explore in a moment.

Okay, this seems perverse. The broker gets the best initial commission for selling the least advantageous investment option to the investor. Why is that?

Remember, the three share classes have a claim on the exact same underlying portfolio. The only difference on the annualized return on each share class is the difference in fees. B shares (and C shares) generate more fees, both for the mutual fund company, which is allowed to charge different internal operating fees to different classes of shareholder, and for the distributor (often a corporate sibling of the mutual fund), which collects a hefty annual 12b-1 fee (which is used to offset the hefty up-front commission paid to the broker and brokerage firm for selling B shares, for which the buyer pays no sales charge up front).

Added to the anomaly of the best deal for the broker (short-term) being the worst deal for the investor, if you look at A shares versus C shares, the interests of the investor are diametrically opposed to the interests of the broker. In an A or C choice, the longer an investor can be expected to stay in the investment, the more advantageous buying A shares is for the investor but the more advantageous having the investor buy C shares is for the broker. (Over an eight-year period, the broker would receive total compensation of 7 percent— 5 percent at purchase and .25 percent × eight years in 12b-1 trailing commissions—for an investment of less than $50,000 in A shares, as opposed to compensation of 9 percent—1 percent at purchase and 1 percent × eight years in 12b-1 trailing commissions—for the comparable investment in C shares.) Some brokers do in fact try to get clients they are pretty sure will be long-term investors to invest in C shares (a practice known in the broker community as "annuitizing" one's book of business).

In an analysis of the net present value of all future brokerage commissions for A, B, or C shares Professor O'Neal did in his 1999 article for the *Financial Analysts Journal* entitled "Mutual Fund Classes and Broker Incentives," he found that if the broker's discount rate is 12 percent, A shares provided the broker with the best present value for holding periods of five years or less, at which point C shares provided the broker with the best present value. If the broker's discount rate is increased to 20 percent, the A shares remained advantageous for seven years before C shares became advantageous.

But this prospect of annuitization is offset by the risks to the broker that the client will switch firms, or that the broker will be fired or otherwise have to leave the business. If the broker is nearing retirement, there is no incentive to annuitize. At the end of the day, despite being the least advantageous of all the compensation options in terms of net present value, the B share offers the broker not only a higher initial payout anytime the investor is above the first breakpoint, but far less risk that he or she will not receive the highest payout possible than would moving investors toward C shares.

TABLE 4-4 Broker Compensation Arrangement

SHARE CLASS	INITIAL INVESTMENT	INITIAL COMMISSION	TRAILING COMMISSION
A	< $50,000	5.00%	0.25%
	$50,000 - $100,000	4.00%	
	$100,000 - $250,000	3.20%	
	$250,000 - $500,000	2.25%	
	$500,000 - $1,000,000	1.70%	
	> $1,000,000	1.00%	
B	All Amounts	5.00%	0.25%
C	All Amounts	1.00%	1.00%

In one of the largest investor arbitration judgments on record, a three-member NASD arbitration panel in May 2006 awarded a group of retired Enron employees $22 million from Ameriprise Financial's subsidiary Securities America Inc. for selling variable annuities and B shares for the plaintiffs' tax-deferred Individual Retirement Accounts and failing to inform the plaintiffs of the high fees involved in the investments.

The bottom line of this entire discussion is that for an investor who intends to build a long-term portfolio of mutual funds that are sold by brokers, he or she should:

■ Look to invest in funds within a family that offers broad diversification of fund styles.
■ Always purchase A shares.
■ Be very aggressive about monitoring when he or she reaches breakpoints, and that proper credit is given for reaching those breakpoints.

Proprietary Funds

Another perverse incentive is the higher commission paid to brokers at major firms for selling mutual funds created by and managed by the firm, even when they do not perform as well as competing funds.

Remember the commission structure for a typical A share. The load is 5.75 percent for investments below the first breakpoint. Of that 5.75 percent, .75 percent is kept by the fund distributor (often a corporate sibling of the mutual fund company, and in the case of proprietary funds also a corporate sibling of the brokerage firm your broker works for). Of the 5.00 percent from a third-party mutual fund that goes to the brokerage firm, the broker may get anywhere from 30 to 42 percent of that commission, depending on his or her production.

So, for a hypothetical $10,000 investment, the investor would get a net investment into the mutual fund of $9,425. The distributor would keep $75. The broker would get from $150 to $210 typically, and the brokerage firm would get from $290 to $350.

If the broker sells a proprietary fund, his or her split may be boosted by 3 to 5 percent of the gross commission, or from 33 to as much as 47 percent of the gross commission, depending on his or her production, or from as little as $165 to as much as $235 on a $10,000 investment. In addition to in-house developed and managed funds, most major brokerage firms went on a mutual fund company buying spree in the 1990s, and brokers also get a larger commission for selling these affiliated funds.

Of one such high-profile and highly marketed fund developed in the late 1990s by a major brokerage firm, one former broker I know says, "There were lots of sales calls and plenty of prizes for those who put their clients in it. The fund lost 50 percent the first year. But some brokers put their clients in it to get the prizes, only to take them [clients] back out some time later."

In 1999, the NASD issued new rules against sales contests, bonuses, or other incentive programs based on selling particular investment products. It is still within the rules to create an incentive program based on sales of a class of products (e.g., mutual funds) but not the sale of specific mutual funds or even house-managed mutual funds in general.

Sometimes the carrot is tempered with a stick as well. At some firms, if brokers don't sell the house mutual funds and/or annuities, the branch manager provides the broker with no assistance in meeting his or her targets. This can mean that if another broker leaves the firm or retires, none of that broker's clients are assigned to the offending broker. Or the broker does not act as "broker of the day" ever, with the opportunity to deal with walk-in new accounts. Or the broker does not get any of the myriad other forms of assistance a branch manager can offer to make a broker more successful.

Morgan Stanley ended up in a heap of trouble during 2003 over its mutual fund sales practices. The company is a defendant in a number of investor lawsuits, has agreed to a sanction and fine levied by the NASD, and is the subject of wide-ranging investigations by the SEC and Massachusetts' Secretary of the Commonwealth William Galvin, who along with New York Attorney General Eliot Spitzer has become one of the most aggressive state securities regulators in the country.

In late February 2003, just before the SEC, NYSE, and NASD released the March analysis of brokerage firms' failure to provide investors with breakpoint discounts, a group of investors filed suit in federal district court in Nashville, Tennessee, alleging that Morgan Stanley brokers had sold them class B shares when class A shares would have afforded them hefty break-point discounts. Professor O'Neal, acting as an expert for the plaintiffs, did an analysis of the assets of retail investors in the 24 Morgan Stanley funds introduced since 1997 with a multi-class structure. As of December 31, 2002, using Morningstar Inc. data, he found that 83 percent, or $4.85 billion, of the assets in those 24 funds was held in class B shares; 8 percent, or $460 million, was held in A shares; and 9 percent, or $530 million, was held in C shares.

Almost immediately after the breakpoint study was released, the SEC and NASD began investigating whether brokers were selling investors inappro-priate classes of mutual funds. The SEC's investigation was wide ranging; the SEC asked 10 major brokerage firms for reams of data about the com-pensation structure for its brokers in terms of selling proprietary "house" funds, as well as for incentives for selling "partner" funds of companies that pay the brokerage firm for shelf space, and about the commission split between the firm and broker for different classes of mutual funds, among other data. The NASD's investigation focused more closely on Morgan Stanley and a group of brokers in particular offices.

Effective July 23, 2004, the SEC issued a new requirement mandating enhanced disclosure by mutual funds regarding breakpoint discounts on front-end sales loads.

About the same time, Secretary of the Commonwealth Galvin's office received an anonymous letter from a broker in Morgan Stanley's Back Bay office in Boston accusing branch and regional managers of pressuring bro-kers to sell a new Morgan Stanley fund, the Morgan Stanley Allocator Fund, an asset allocation fund that hoped to maximize return by adjusting its asset allocation as market conditions changed. In his letter, the broker said the branch manager's efforts to get brokers to sell the fund, which included everything from individual and group prizes for the most sales to threats of firing for brokers who refused to participate, were "nothing short of extortion." Sales practices that promoted particular products within a product class over other products in the same class (e.g., house mutual funds over other mutual funds) were explicitly outlawed in the NASD's 1999 consumer-protection regulations.

In a May 8, 2003, letter responding to questions by Galvin's office, Morgan Stanley executives denied that its brokers and branch managers received extra income or other incentives. But Tom Lauricella, who covers the brokerage industry for the *Wall Street Journal*, unmasked Morgan Stanley sales practices in a scathing article in which he detailed how Morgan Stanley was flouting the spirit, if not the letter, of the 1999 NASD regulations.

Using internal Morgan Stanley documents, Lauricella showed some of the biggest carrots Morgan Stanley dangled in front of brokers and branch managers.

Brokers who sold Morgan Stanley funds, as well as those of Van Kampen Investments, a fund family Morgan Stanley bought in the 1990s, were eligible for hundreds and even thousands of dollars in "business development credits." These credits could be used to defray the costs of hosting seminars, a major marketing tool for many large brokerage firms. In many cases, mutual fund companies or insurance companies team up with brokerage firms or individual brokers to host such seminars or pay the cost of booths at professional or business association meetings. Brokers could also choose marketing communications materials, such as holiday or birthday cards for clients and Morgan Stanley logo items such as golf balls or ball caps, from a catalogue, using their credits.

Morgan Stanley, like other brokerage firms, also has arrangements with mutual fund families to showcase their funds (a practice discussed in more detail a little later). At Morgan Stanley, unlike at many other firms, brokers received higher commissions for selling these so-called "partner funds," which number over 800 funds from 14 different mutual fund families.

Finally, Morgan Stanley branch managers received higher bonuses when brokers in their offices sold more proprietary or partnered funds. A Morgan Stanley spokesperson defended the practice to Lauricella by saying that proprietary and partner funds are more profitable to Morgan Stanley than other funds, and branch managers' bonuses are profitability-based, so it is logical that the more of these funds are sold the higher the branch managers' bonuses.

In a suit brought by Galvin's office in Massachusetts Superior Court on August 11, 2003, the Secretary of the Commonwealth's Securities Division charged Morgan Stanley with a violation of the state's antifraud laws by failing to disclose material information to client investors. The specific disclosures Morgan Stanley is accused of failing to make regard branch manager compensation, financial advisor (broker) compensation, partner program compensation, and the potential conflicts of interest created by these various compensation arrangements.

In the complaint, Galvin's staff showed that the Back Bay office was the number-one office in terms of sales of the Allocator Fund in February 2003, during the fund's initial offering period. For the month of February, brokers in the Back Bay branch earned a total of $24,439.41 in commissions for Morgan Stanley funds, $539.71 for Van Kampen funds, $842.82 for funds from the 800+ partner funds, and only $355.64 from sales of all other mutual funds, of which there are more than 7,000.

Galvin asked the court to order Morgan Stanley to cease and desist from violating the state securities laws, pay a $1 million fine, disgorge profits generated by sales of proprietary and partnered sales throughout Massachusetts from the beginning of 2003, when a new compensation schedule went into effect, and allow Massachusetts investors who purchased proprietary or partnered funds during 2003 to rescind those purchases and receive their original investments. He also asked that the court allow his office to censure Morgan Stanley for its conduct (under the Securities Division's powers to censure, suspend, or revoke the license of any individual or business selling securities) for unethical and dishonest conduct in the securities business and for failure to supervise its branch managers and brokers in the Back Bay and other offices throughout Massachusetts.

A month after Galvin's office filed suit, the NASD, which had been investigating the same practices not only in Massachusetts but throughout the Morgan Stanley system, censured the firm and fined it $2 million for violating its 1999 consumer-protection regulations regarding sales contests, bonuses, and other rewards for brokers and branch management for selling proprietary and partnered funds in lieu of other funds. Bruce Alonso, the head of Morgan Stanley's retail sales unit, was also censured and fined $250,000. The firm and Alonso accepted the NASD's actions in a settlement, without admitting or denying the charges.

A Morgan Stanley spokesman told the press, "We're pleased to have put this matter behind us. We recognize that investors must have absolute confidence in the quality of the mutual funds they buy and the integrity of those who provide them. And we are committed to that standard."

But that wasn't the last of Morgan Stanley's problems. In October 2003, Morgan Stanley disclosed in a routine regulatory filing that the SEC had notified the company through so-called "Wells notices" on September 23, and again on October 8, that it was the subject of investigations into inadequate disclosure to customers of broker incentives and its practices of selling certain mutual fund share classes "among other things." Morgan Stanley subsequently paid $50 million to resolve these complaints.

Buying Shelf Space and Sharing Revenue

The arrangement Morgan Stanley has with its mutual fund "partners" is endemic throughout the industry. Fund companies pay hundreds of thousands of dollars to arrange a selling agreement with a major brokerage firm. And that just allows their salesmen (known as wholesalers) to go into the brokerage firm and pitch the brokers on the company's funds. To get on a brokerage firm's "preferred" fund list can cost hundreds of thousands of dollars more. And getting on a preferred list is more important than ever, as brokers have over 8,000 mutual funds they can "put their clients into."

In an *Institutional Investor Newsletter* survey of over 4,000 brokers, 24 percent said they sold mainly funds to their clients, and on average a broker deals in funds from three or four fund companies. And Thomas Miltenberger, mutual fund marketing manager for Edward Jones, a national brokerage firm with 7,500 branches, mostly in small communities not on the radar of the Morgan Stanleys and Merrill Lynches of the world, told *Business Week* magazine in February 2002 that although his firm has arrangements to sell funds from 180 fund companies, 97 percent of the firm's business goes to funds from two companies.

The mutual fund consulting firm Financial Research found in a 2000 survey of fund companies that the industry spent about $1.5 billion in such pay-to-play fees. Guess who pays for all that "marketing" cost? You do, of course, in the form of the annual 12b-1 fees.

In addition, the U.S. General Accounting Office (GAO, since renamed the Government Accountability Office) reported in its June 2003 study entitled "Mutual Funds: Greater Transparency Needed in Disclosures to Investors" that more and more of these arrangements are becoming "revenue sharing" arrangements where the brokerage firm asks the investment advisory firm that actually manages the mutual fund portfolio to give back a tiny percentage of the assets of the fund purchased by its clients. This payment usually comes out of the advisory fee that the mutual fund company pays the advisory company (often a corporate sibling) for operating the investment portfolio. Because the advisory company has its own expenses to meet, it therefore must raise the fee it charges the fund company, which in turn increases the fund expenses paid by investors.

In January 2004, the GAO supplemented its report and recommended additional fee disclosures by mutual funds "that could increase the transparency and investor awarness of mutual fund fees . . . "

Fund Fees and Trading Costs

Within the large category of a mutual fund's annual fees come its trading costs. Obviously, the more actively a fund's portfolio managers trade the account, the more costs the fund incurs in brokerage commissions.

Mutual funds, and other "institutional" investors, pay much lower commissions than you do as a retail investor if you buy or sell shares in an individual stock. However, they don't always pay the lowest commission possible, and they often pay these commissions to yet another corporate sibling.

Often, a fund pays a higher trading commission than necessary and gets some of the money returned in so-called "soft-dollar" credits. Brokerage firms that want the mutual fund's trading business often use these soft-dollar credits as an inducement. Here's how it works:

A mutual fund manager, who often trades in blocks of 10,000 to 100,000 shares of a particular stock at a time, should be able to have that transaction performed for between $0.01 and $0.02 per transaction (a penny or a penny and a fraction), especially if he or she were to use an electronic trading platform. But that manager also wants company research from as broad a spectrum of providers as possible, including independent researchers and brokerage firm researchers. The fund manager also wants access to news feeds and market figures through a service like Reuters or Bloomberg.

So the fund manager strikes deals with brokers at the big brokerage houses (not the brokers you deal with, but institutional brokers). The manager pays $0.04 or even $0.06 per share to trade, and in return the brokerage firm returns a penny or two in soft-dollar credits, with which it offsets its fees for research services, or pays for the mutual fund manager's Bloomberg terminal or other equipment.

In another practice called directed brokerage, a mutual fund pays outsized commissions to a brokerage firm if in return the firm's brokers push the mutual fund to their retail clients.

In January 2004, the SEC issued a report on the prevalence of directed brokerage and revenue sharing. The report included some proposed new regulations regarding these practices. At the same time, the SEC said it was likely to take enforcement actions in the future against firms that failed to disclose these practices to clients.

The SEC has pointed out, and rightly so, that soft-dollar arrangements and directed brokerage potentially increase costs for fund investors (buying the research outright for cash may cost less than it does in soft-dollar credits; as an analogy, think of the dollars that must be spent on a credit card to earn the 500,000 points necessary to pay for a five-day golf holiday). In addition, such arrangements may compromise fund managers' fiduciary duty to investors to find brokers who can provide the best execution of trades when they are choosing brokers on the basis of soft-dollar offerings. Professor O'Neal and another academic estimated in a 1996 study that as much as two-thirds of the cost of brokerage commissions for mutual funds may be attributable to the soft-dollar arrangements between fund managers and institutional brokers.

England's Financial Services Authority (FSA), the analog to the United States SEC, has called for a ban on soft-dollar arrangements. Many brokerage firms have told the SEC that they would not negotiate lower brokerage commissions with mutual fund managers even if soft-dollar rebates were banned. Whether that is true or not can only be tested by, indeed, banning the practice.

Letting the Gamers In

While the practices discussed above are odiferous, and many violate securities regulations in the states, at the federal government level, or those of self-regulatory organizations (SROs), they are not illegal per se.

In September 2003, however, New York Attorney General Eliot Spitzer dropped a hand grenade into the world of mutual funds when he settled a civil case with a hedge fund, and later filed criminal charges against a broker, for conspiring to rig the game through two practices known as "late trading" and "market timing."

The hedge fund initially charged by Spitzer, which settled the civil matter without admitting or denying guilt, was called Canary Capital Partners. Canary's principal, Edward J. Stern, agreed to pay a $10 million fine and $30 million in restitution to investors at four mutual fund families, the mutual fund units of Bank of America and Bank One, as well as Janus Capital Management and Strong Capital Management. Stern also agreed to help Spitzer and the SEC in the ongoing investigation.

Three weeks later, Spitzer filed criminal charges against a Bank of America broker, Theodore Sihpol III, who had worked at the bank's private client group in New York, which catered to wealthy investors. Sihpol was charged with larceny and securities fraud under New York's Martin Act, which gives the state attorney general broad powers to enforce securities laws through both civil and criminal sanctions. Sihpol was also named in a civil suit by the SEC on the same day, charging him with securities fraud and seeking disgorgement of profits, a fine, and a lifetime ban from the securities industry.

Sihpol allegedly acquired Stern as a client for the private client group, then worked with Stern to set up a mechanism by which Stern would be allowed to trade Bank of America mutual funds in a way ordinary investors cannot.

When the New York Stock Exchange and the Nasdaq close at 4:00 p.m. eastern time (let's say on a Monday), all U.S.-based mutual funds close their books and calculate the net asset value (NAV) of shares in the fund. If an order is placed to buy or sell shares any time after 4:00 p.m. Monday, and through Tuesday's market close, that trade will be executed at Tuesday's NAV.

Companies often make announcements after 4:00 p.m. eastern time that will have an effect on their stock's price the next day, such as earnings reports or offers to purchase another company. Sihpol and those above him in the Bank of America chain of command created a mechanism by which Stern could continue to execute trades until 6:30 p.m. at that day's NAV. So he could use after-market information that he knew would affect stocks in the mutual fund portfolios one way or another and act on that information before it was incorporated into the next day's NAV. Spitzer likened this to "betting on a horse race after it has been run."

Market timing in and of itself is not illegal, although most mutual funds say they actively discourage it. Market timing is used mostly with funds that have some investments in stocks that trade in Europe or Asia. Since it takes a day to incorporate the closing prices of stocks in those markets into the fund's NAV, the market timer, who dashes in and out of a fund with quick trades, often gets the benefit of "stale prices" to capitalize on these time-zone discrepancies, buying on overseas closes that will drive the NAV up and selling immediately after those closes become incorporated into the NAV the next day.

Market timing to capitalize on stale prices has two negative effects on buy-and-hold investors.

First, but less important, is the added costs of transactions. When a fund manager is required to buy and sell securities for the mutual fund, the costs of those purchases and sales are spread across all investors in the fund and not levied solely against the individual or institution forcing the fund to trade.

The more important cost to buy-and-hold investors is that the market timers are getting a better price than they should on their mutual fund shares. The difference between the price they are getting and the price they should be getting is borne collectively by all other investors in the fund. If a market timer redeems his shares of the fund for $15 each when in fact they are only worth $14 each, the other investors in the fund are in effect paying the market timer that extra $1 per share.

Eric Zitzewitz, professor of strategic management at Stanford Graduate School of Business, has studied both phenomena. He believes late trading occurs in one of six mutual fund families and costs mutual fund investors $400 million per year in lost profits, and that market timing, which is even more prevalent, costs investors upwards of $4 billion per year. On a $100,000 investment in an international stock fund, Zitzewitz believes an investor can lose up to $2,000 in profits to market timers each year.

Sihpol and his superiors at Bank of America allegedly created a proprietary trading platform for Stern to trade until 6:30 p.m., when the bank sent its daily order to the four fund families named, in the name of the bank. The other fund families may not have been totally willing participants, since they often allow banks and brokerage firms to send omnibus orders after 4:00 p.m., assuming that the firm has aggregated only those trades from before 4:00 p.m. into the order. If the brokerage firm allowed in-and-out trading, or late trading, the fund company may not know about it.

What was in it for Bank of America? Fees. The bank gave Canary a $100 million line of credit for its trading, on which it earned interest. The bank also garnered so-called "sticky assets" from Canary, investments in low-volatility bank-managed bond funds that Canary used as ballast for its high-volatility trading and promised to keep in the funds for a long period of time. The bank earned management fees on that money.

Over the subsequent weeks, a number of Wall Street firms and mutual funds acknowledged that they were also under Spitzer's microscope, and that all of their mutual fund trading activity was not on the up-and-up. Brokerage firms fired brokers for letting market timers in, and mutual fund companies fired traders for colluding with the brokers. In October, a trader with the hedge fund Millennium Partners, Steven Markovitz, pleaded guilty to securities fraud for late-day trading. Brokerage firms Markovitz had used to make his trades fired brokers.

Prudential Securities (which was in the process of being rolled into the Wachovia Securities division of Wachovia Corp.) fired a dozen brokers and managers in Boston. The *Wall Street Journal* reported that Prudential had ignored up to 25,000 written warnings from mutual fund companies that the Boston-based brokers were allowing clients to violate policies regarding market timing. On November 4, both the SEC and the Massachusetts Secretary of the Commonwealth filed civil fraud charges against five of the brokers and two of the managers Prudential had fired. After the charges were filed, the brokers cried foul, alleging in the press that their bosses very high up in the organization had known and approved of their allowing market-timing clients to trade through them.

At the end of October, the SEC and the Massachusetts Secretary of the Commonwealth filed civil fraud suits against Putnam and two of its former fund managers for fraud, alleging that the firm's executives allowed heavy market timing by retirement fund and other clients, and that the two fund managers had used market-timing techniques to trade the firm's funds for their own accounts. The tip about the market timing came from a low-level Putnam employee at a suburban call center who, after getting the cold shoulder from his managers at Putnam and even from the Boston office of the SEC, went to the Secretary of the Commonwealth's office and told his story. The Putnam employee, Peter Scannell, kept a tally of rapid-fire trading by, among others, members of the Boilermakers Union, Local 5, in New York. Over a six-month period in late 2000, 10 members of the union made over 5,300 trades involving $657 million in shares; their total gains amounted to as much as $2 million. After the charges were filed, Putnam funds began hemorrhaging money as pension fund managers and others withdrew millions of dollars from the funds in question. Within days of the charges being filed, both the CEO of Putnam, a subsidiary of Marsh and McLennan, and the head of the SEC's Boston office had resigned.

In early November, Stephen Cutler, the SEC's head of enforcement, told a U.S. Senate committee that an SEC study found that 25 percent of brokerage firms had business arrangements with investors to allow them to market-time mutual funds.

Throughout 2004, New York Attorney General Spitzer reached settlements involving payments of well over $1 billion with a number of well-known mutual-fund companies that had wrongfully engaged in market-timing activities. On March 15, 2004, Spitzer announced a $675 million settlement with Bank of America and FleetBoston Financial Group. At the time, this was the largest mutual fund settlement ever negotiated.

Of course, investors can easily avoid all of these problems and conflicts involving mutual funds. All they have to do is avoid using a broker to purchase mutual funds and, instead, buy only index funds directly from the fund manager (like Vanguard: www.vanguard.com) or use a fee-based registered investment advisor to purchase passively managed funds managed by Dimensional Fund Advisors (www.dfaus.com), which are only available through certain investment advisors.

5 Unsuitability: What's a Good Investment Strategy for You?

I have a client I will call Sally, a resident of New Zealand who went through a bitter divorce and received a large settlement. She placed about $2 million with a large American full-service brokerage firm and told the broker she needed this money for her retirement.

The broker invested her assets in an aggressive mix of stocks, with a high proportion in technology stocks. The account was poorly diversified, consisting of only about 20 different stocks. Over three years, the account lost $1.5 million.

During the arbitration hearing, Sally testified that she did not know a stock from a bond, and that she relied entirely on the advice of her broker. The broker testified that he never computed the account's standard deviation and that he did no objective assessment of the risk inherent in her portfolio.

After hearing all the evidence, a New York Stock Exchange (NYSE) arbitration tribunal awarded Sally $600,000.

Claims of unsuitability are among the most common in securities arbitration. And there should be more of them. Thousands—maybe even millions—of investors who are not suing their brokers have valid claims that their brokers have either made unsuitable investments for them or encouraged them to invest in unsuitable securities.

The biggest reason these unsuitable investments were made is not broker fraud or overt abuse of customers, although there are many examples of this type of conduct. It is not even the perverse incentives of the broker compensation system. The biggest reason so many brokers "put their clients" in unsuitable investments is simply that brokers do not understand the basic mathematical concepts available to measure historical volatility (risk), or how to mitigate investment risk through the techniques of asset allocation and diversification.

In this chapter, I'll outline the current state of suitability theory in investment arbitration law. Chapter 6 will discuss the specifics and the importance of Modern Portfolio Theory (MPT). In Chapter 7, I'll show how you may be able to use your knowledge of MPT and your broker's lack of knowledge to make a valid unsuitability claim (and other claims as well) based on what I call, for lack of a better term, The Solin Theories for Recovering Losses from Your Broker.

Investment Objectives

What are your broker's goals when he or she asks you to define your investment objectives?

When you open an account with a brokerage firm, you are commonly asked to define your investment objectives. Unfortunately, there are no definitions of investment objectives that are agreed upon across the brokerage industry.

In 1993, Seth C. Anderson and Donald Arthur Winslow studied the issue in an article in the *Kentucky Law Journal* titled "Defining Suitability." They wrote:

> *An analysis of several major firms' new account forms shows a high degree of variation in the section . . . addressing [investment] objectives. For instance, Firm A's form asked the customer to rate in priority one or more of three objectives: (1) Income, (2) Growth, or (3) Speculation. It then asked the investor to rate his or her investing experience as: (1) None, (2) Low, (3) Moderate, or (4) High. Firm B's form asked whether the customer sought: (1) Appreciation with risk, (2) Speculation, (3) Income with safety, (4) Income with risk, or (5) Tax reduction, without specifying a priority requirement or a limitation on the number of boxes to be checked. Firm C asked whether the investor sought Income, Growth, or Total Return, and whether he or she preferred Aggressive, Moderate, or Conservative risk, with one goal apparently to be matched to one risk factor. Finally, Firm D offered four alternatives—Income, Investment Grade, Capital Gains, and Speculative—with all four to be prioritized in accordance with the client's investment objectives.*

It is not unusual for brokers to have a client sign an account-opening application that is blank, then fill in the client's supposed investment objectives themselves (the consequences of this have been discussed in previous chapters). When this occurs, the broker frequently writes in the most aggressive investment objective (speculation), recognizing that this designation affords him or her maximum protection in the event of an arbitration proceeding where unsuitability is alleged.

In any event, these terms are so vague that they can easily mean different things to the broker and the client. In addition, if the client indicates that his or her investment objectives are, for example, "growth" and "income," the precise mandate to the broker may be subject to differing interpretations of those terms in the event of an arbitration.

Finally, as Anderson and Winslow state, "it is not uncommon for a customer to be unclear as to his or her own objectives. But the broker has the best chance to control the issue by thoroughly questioning the new customer to ensure that the broker will not misunderstand the customer's expressed intent."

Brokers really need to start by asking their clients how much risk the client wants to assume. A good start would be to ask the question: "How much of your portfolio's value could you lose in a single year before you begin worrying?" In order to assess whether the client's response to this question is reasonable, the broker should also obtain full and complete financial information about the client.

In practice, however, this is rarely done, leaving the determination of suitability of investments to an interpretation of the vague and ambiguous investment objective terms used on the new-account forms.

It Would Suit Everyone if Brokers Followed the Suitability Rules

Brokers have a clear obligation to only recommend investments that are suitable for each particular client. A number of rules of the exchanges and professional organizations (collectively known as self-regulatory organizations, or SROs) state this very clearly.

NASD Rule 2310 of the Rules of Fair Practice and New York Stock Exchange (NYSE) Rule 405, the so-called "know-your-customer" rules, admonish brokers that they must understand their client's financial condition and investment objectives before making investment recommendations.

The NASD has interpreted Rule 2310 to require brokers to have reasonable grounds for believing that a recommendation is suitable for their customers, taking into consideration their other security holdings, their financial situation, and their expenses. Moreover, Rule 2310 applies to investors who are wealthy and sophisticated with the same force that it applies to investors with a low tolerance for risk. Any investment recommended to any investor must be determined by the broker to be suitable for that investor.

In a similar vein, NYSE Rule 405 requires:

> . . . *every member organization . . . to (1) Use due diligence to learn the essential facts relative to every customer, every order, every cash or margin account accepted or carried by such organization . . . and (2) Supervise diligently all accounts handled by registered representatives of the organization.*

American Stock Exchange (ASE) Rule 411 places a duty on brokers "to know and approve customers."

The Chicago Board Options Exchange (CBOE) has its own set of suitability requirements, which mandate a determination by the broker that the proposed options transaction is suitable, that the customer understands the risks associated with options trading, and that the customer has the financial resources to withstand those risks.

Similar suitability rules govern the purchase of municipal bonds.

Finally, there are comprehensive rules governing the purchase of "penny stocks"—those that trade for under $1 a share via the "over-the-counter" and "pink sheet" informal markets, and which are subject to fraud and manipulation. The primary rule dealing with penny stocks is the Securities Exchange Act Rule 15g-9, which was issued as part of the Penny Stock Reform Act of 1990.

This rule requires brokerage firms, prior to approving an account for penny stock transactions, to obtain detailed financial information from the client, determine that penny stocks are suitable for the client and that the client understands the risks inherent in trading penny stocks, and provide the client with a written statement describing the basis for its suitability determination.

Suitability is also discussed in more colloquial publications provided to brokers as part of their training. In its booklet "Understanding Your Role and Responsibilities as a Registered Representative," the NASD writes under the heading "Obligations to Your Customer":

The foundation of the securities industry is fair dealing with customers. Whether your work is with individuals, institutions, or business entities, your obligation in this profession is to serve your customers with honesty and integrity by putting their interests first and foremost.

The first step in serving your customers properly is to obtain a clear understanding of each customer's financial condition. You will obtain some of this information when opening a new customer's account with your firm. You may learn other information through conversations with your customer or checks your firm makes with credit agencies or other financial institutions. Because a customer's financial status is constantly changing, account records should be updated whenever necessary.

The second step in serving your customer properly is for both you and the customer to have a clear understanding of the customer's investment objectives. As a professional, you will be trained to recognize the risks of various types of investments and to discuss with your customer which strategies are most suitable. Once you determine these objectives and record them in your customer's account records, you must make certain that specific recommendations for that customer fall within these objectives and would, therefore, be suitable. Just as your customer's financial position may change, your customer's investment objectives may change as well. You should, therefore, review your customer's investment objectives periodically, and make a written record of any changes as they occur.

These suitability rules are designed to counteract the natural conflict of interest in the broker/client relationship and recognize that most retail investors utilize brokers for investment advice. Unfortunately, they have not had the effect of deterring some brokers from recommending to their clients investments that are clearly unsuitable.

Suitability Violations Can Result in Big Suits

The suitability rule can be violated in two ways.

First, a broker can violate the suitability rule if he or she fails so fundamentally to comprehend the consequences of his or her own recommendation that the recommendation is unsuitable for any investor, regardless of the investor's wealth, willingness to bear risk, or other individual characteristics.

Second, a broker can violate the suitability rule if he or she makes a recommendation that may be suitable for some investors but is unsuitable for the specific investor to whom the recommendation is directed.

The first type of violation is more common than you might imagine. For instance, in March 2002, the *St. Petersburg (Florida) Times* reported that an NASD arbitration panel had awarded $3.4 million to 14 investors who had purchased promissory notes backed by car loans issued by First American Capital Trust from a Fort Lauderdale broker. The investors alleged that the broker misrepresented the safety of the notes, which turned out to be worthless when the company went bankrupt in 1999. Clearly, such unsecured promissory notes were unsuitable for most investors, and the broker should have been more diligent in his investigation of the securities.

Cases where there is a high turnover rate and high cost-equity ratio also fit into this category. One way to look at these situations is to compare them to mutual fund returns in comparable categories. If the data indicate that only a tiny percentage of the relevant mutual funds (those making investments in the same types of securities) would have been able to achieve the returns necessary for a portfolio to simply break even, given the turnover and cost-equity ratio of the portfolio in question, there is a compelling argument that the portfolio should be deemed unsuitable for any investor.

The more common instances of unsuitability, however, require an individual assessment of an investor's unique situation. These violations occur because the broker does not take the time and put out the effort to truly understand his or her client's financial condition, investment objectives, and tolerance for risk. Or, having gained this knowledge, the broker disregards it, driven by the mandate from managers to "sell, sell, and sell some more," and sometimes by the client's desire for the kinds of outsized returns they hear that others are making by investing.

In order to establish that this type of unsuitability occurred, it is necessary to demonstrate that the broker "controlled" the account by showing that the broker either had discretionary authority over the account or what is known as de facto control, meaning that the broker made recommendations that the client routinely followed without questioning them.

The same brokerage firms that tout their expertise and ask clients to trust them frequently take the position in arbitration proceedings that even if the broker made unsuitable recommendations that the client followed, the broker should not be responsible for any ensuing losses because the client had the intelligence and understanding to make the ultimate decision. This is like saying, "We did you wrong, but you should have been smart enough to catch us earlier."

The Securities and Exchange Commission (SEC) has rejected this position in at least one case, and many arbitration tribunals have done so as well, recognizing that clients rely on their broker's presumed expertise. If the broker makes an unsuitable recommendation, it seems unfair and disingenuous for the brokerage firm to try to excuse that conduct by blaming the client for not being astute enough to figure out at the time that the investment was inappropriate.

For example, in January 2002, an NASD arbitration panel awarded $500,000 to a former professional football player, Chris Dishman. The panel agreed with Dishman that his financial manager, another former football player named Sean Jones, had engaged in unauthorized trades in unsuitable investments. Dishman said he had asked Jones to invest only in low-risk investments, but that Jones had made a number of investments Dishman did not understand, including a $450,000 investment in a hedge fund.

Once the issue of "control" is established, each case turns on its unique facts. Tribunals scrutinize cases involving low-priced, speculative securities more carefully than those involving a blue-chip portfolio. And even investors who consent to a speculative investment strategy are entitled to the protection of the suitability rules. Clearly, not all investments are suitable, even for those investors willing to take very aggressive positions.

In the bull market of the 1990s, the fact that most investments were making money shielded brokers from the fact that their disregard for the overall risk in their clients' portfolios (as well as the tendency to trade) was hindering portfolio performance.

Had brokers not been recommending that their clients invest so aggressively and trade so frequently, those accounts very well might have earned more in net terms (they might have had less in gross gains, but more in net gains after subtracting transaction costs and taxation on any gains). The bull market also hid the fact that many investments and the resulting portfolios that brokers recommended were highly risky and therefore clearly unsuitable to their clients' financial conditions, investment objectives, or tolerance for investment risk. This was only discovered after the market fell and many investors lost enormous sums and large percentages of their portfolios.

Inadequate Diversification

Overconcentration is a form of unsuitability. Overconcentration is what happens when the funds in an account are invested in a narrow group of securities, which does not afford the investor enough portfolio diversification to guard against risks that the stock or bond of any one company or group of companies in the same industry "sector" or asset class will decline in value. (The case of Richard Greene, discussed at the end of Chapter 3, is a classic case of overconcentration.)

The number of stocks necessary for adequate diversification of a portfolio is a matter of debate within the community of finance scholars and experts. However, recent studies have suggested that even as many as 60 individual stocks in an equity portfolio may only achieve 90 percent of full diversification.

During the last years of the bull market, brokers were increasingly recommending to their clients that they invest (or investing themselves for clients' discretionary accounts) in technology stocks, both large, well-known companies and small, speculative companies. While the failure of dot-coms and other new and small companies was a significant factor in the market decline, many more investors were hurt by the crashing stocks with large capitalization such as Cisco, JDS Uniphase, Lucent, and Enron.

For a time in the 1990s, these stocks may have even been seen as "prudent" investments. And in appropriate concentrations it may be, in fact, prudent to have some risky investments in a portfolio. But such investments are not prudent if they represent the bulk of a portfolio.

This focus on a risky and volatile market sector placed many investors in portfolios that were far too risky for their investment objectives and their ability to withstand a meaningful downturn in the market. The problem was exacerbated by the tendency of many brokers to fail to diversify adequately, thereby increasing volatility and risk. This practice is fertile ground for an unsuitability claim based on lack of diversification.

The Churned Account

Churning, or excessive trading, is another form of unsuitability. If you can establish that your account was churned, you can often also establish a violation of the suitability rule. (For a detailed description of churning, see Chapter 3.)

For example, in 1997, an NASD arbitration panel awarded the estate of a former Worcester, Massachusetts, businessman $30,000 after finding that an A.G. Edwards broker in that city had churned two accounts he had discretion over and made unsuitable investments for the accounts. The estate of Howard Brown, who had been in a nursing home from the time he suffered a stroke in 1983 until he died in 1994, sued the broker and Edwards, alleging "a pattern of unsuitable, high-risk investments, excessive trading, and reckless mismanagement."

According to the claim, the two accounts plus a modest home were all Brown and his wife owned. The accounts were supposed to be invested for income with which to pay Brown's nursing home expenses and Mrs. Brown's living expenses. Instead, beginning in 1990, and becoming more apparent in 1993 and 1994, the account was invested in speculative stocks, and both the stocks and options were traded heavily. Attorneys for the estate had sought $123,333 in damages, the amount the account declined in the six months prior to Brown's death.

Surviving Financial Suicide

"Financial suicide" cases refer to those instances where the customer directs the trade, receives no advice from the broker, but seeks to recover his or her losses because the broker should have known that the trade was "financial suicide" for the investor. The concept of broker responsibility to keep investors from committing financial suicide is sometimes compared to the bartender's duty under state "dram shop" laws not to serve a drink to a drunk, who might then leave the bar and kill someone in an auto accident.

It is not surprising that it has traditionally been very difficult—but not impossible—for investors to win these cases.

For example, an arbitration tribunal awarded a customer partial compensation for losses sustained when the customer traded options actively on his own initiative and the brokerage firm did not stop him when losses mounted.

Another tribunal held that a brokerage firm was required to monitor the account of a compulsive trader on an ongoing basis and was required to attempt to stop his trading, even though it gave him no advice and made no recommendations to him.

Finally, a third tribunal found a firm liable for losses in one of its customer's accounts because it knew that the customer's trading patterns were not suitable for him.

Investors relying on the financial suicide theory have an uphill climb, but it might be one worth carefully evaluating.

An interesting twist on the financial suicide argument is the one undertaken by the Salomon Smith Barney brokers who were fired and sued the firm in early 2002. (I discussed this case in Chapter 3.)

The brokers had a number of clients who were employees of WorldCom.

The clients exercised their options in WorldCom stock and used the stock to open margin accounts to borrow money to pay taxes. After WorldCom tanked, these clients lost a lot of money and filed arbitration claims against Salomon and the brokers. The firm settled and fired the brokers.

The brokers turned around and sued Salomon, claiming that they had counseled their clients to diversify rather than keep their entire portfolios in WorldCom stock and leverage their portfolios with margin borrowing. They argued that the financial suicide committed by their clients through overconcentration in WorldCom stock was caused by the firm's bullish telecommunications analyst and not by them; they said that they in fact counseled their clients against these actions. Salomon has denied any wrongdoing and is defending against these claims.

There Is E-Suitability

What happens in a world where investors do their own trading over the Internet, without any intervention—let alone recommendations—from a broker? Can there be such a thing as unsuitability in such a world?

In fact, there can.

As would be expected, most online broker-dealers argue that suitability rules should not exist for Internet trading. They make two main points:

1. The conflict of interest in the broker-client relationship is absent because the investor is trading without using a broker.
2. The research and analysis available online to customers does not constitute a recommendation. If online brokers needed to remove all the information that could be argued constituted a recommendation, this would in fact hamper online investors by greatly reducing the information available to them.

The counterargument is that suitability rules should be more stringent for online trading, since online trading is, in and of itself, a risky endeavor for many (if not most) investors. In addition, those who seek to maintain or even strengthen the suitability rules for online trading argue that the conflicts of interest between the firm (if not an individual broker) and the client still exist.

There may have been a time early in the era of online brokerage firms when most investors who invested online had, indeed, severed the traditional broker/client relationship.

In 1996, there were approximately 1.5 million accounts with online brokerage firms. Most of these firms had started as discount brokers, who offered inexpensive trade execution with no investment advice. The Internet offered discount brokers a way to reduce their staffs of order takers and a way to offer account holders even lower execution costs.

But by 2000, there were over 23 million online accounts, and most traditional broker-dealers had established online divisions or subsidiaries. Many offered their customers account management, trading, and the entire panoply of firm research services online, with commissions on orders discounted for clients who conducted their own orders online.

Clearly, for many online account holders today, the Internet is a different communication channel to maintain what they consider to be a traditional broker/client relationship. Online customers of large and well-regarded brokerage firms still trust in the firm's name and reputation, even if they don't trust in an individual broker's presumed expertise.

For instance, in 1998, the online brokerage Ameritrade liquidated a margin trading account held by Lael Desmond, a medical student, in order to meet a margin call. In January 2001, an NASD arbitration panel awarded Desmond $40,000. Desmond had sought $225,000, claiming negligence, misrepresentation, unauthorized trading, and breach of contract.

Desmond claimed that Ameritrade should not have allowed him to continue investing in highly speculative securities when it realized he was overextended in his margin account. He also claimed that no one at Ameritrade had explained to him the possibility of or mechanics of a margin call, and that he had signed the margin account agreement without reading it closely. He told the website *Web Finance* that Ameritrade had "breached its suitability obligations by allowing me to continue investing on margin when I was financially unable to meet the commitment of the margin investment."

Ken Kolaski, a securities arbitration attorney, told *Web Finance* that "online brokerage doesn't change anything. A brokerage firm's legal duties are the same. . . . One of the NASD member rules is know your customer, their age, net worth. This applies equally to the Internet."

ONLINE RECOMMENDATIONS

As Nancy C. Libin and James S. Wrona note in their 2001 *Columbia Business Law Review* article "The Securities Industry and the Internet: A Suitable Match?": "To date, the term 'recommendation' has not been defined."

In the context of Internet communications, they write that online communications can, under some circumstances, be considered "recommendations."

> *Because of the variety of ways in which a firm can present information to its customers, determining which electronic communications are recommendations can be difficult. . . . Because the determination is [objective] . . . , an important consideration is whether the communication—given its content, context, and presentations—would be reasonably viewed as a "call to action," or suggestion that the customer engage in a particular transaction.*
>
> *In addition, the more individually tailored a communication to a specific customer or targeted group of customers about a security or group of securities, the more likely the communication will be viewed as a recommendation that triggers suitability obligations.*

Professors Libin and Wrona also believe that online firms can be liable under suitability rules in cases of "self-churning," where online investors engage in excessive trading. They write:

> *One can imagine this scenario in the online context. A firm could use information about customers' investing habits to target e-mails about specific securities to particular customers in an effort to induce those customers to trade. A firm could be vulnerable to a quantitative suitability claim if a customer routinely acts on this information and trades excessively as a result.*
>
> *As long as brokerage firms depend on transaction-based fees as a source of revenue, they arguably will have a profit incentive to encourage customers to trade frequently, which is often not in the customers' best interest.*

Perhaps the way online investors put themselves at greatest risk is through use of margin accounts. Without benefit of a discussion with a broker, who should explain how margin investing works, online investors can become mired in margin debt and wiped out through margin calls.

The bottom line is that you may have a claim for unsuitability (or some other basis for a claim) even though you traded through an online broker.

Unseemly Responses to Unsuitability Charges

Brokers and brokerage firms have two major counters against a claim of unsuitability. The first is that the investor is "sophisticated" and therefore understands the risks involved in investments recommended by the broker. The second is the "you asked for it" defense: that the trade was not solicited by the broker but rather requested by the client.

YOU KNEW WHAT YOU WERE DOING

The first way brokers try to duck out of unsuitability claims is by arguing that the investor was "sophisticated" and therefore knew the risks inherent in an aggressive portfolio. The word "sophisticated" has two meanings in the context of investing; one is specific within SEC regulations and the other is colloquial.

The SEC exempts certain kinds of securities from registration under the terms of what are known as Regulation D offerings. Regulation D exemptions are granted to "private placements" of stock, usually in smaller companies. Stock issued under Regulation D exemptions is owned by a small number of people or other companies such as venture capital firms, and as such is illiquid (i.e., there is no open market in which the stock trades).

Regulation D defines a sophisticated investor as an individual with $200,000 in annual income (or $300,000 if filing jointly with a spouse), or over $1 million in net worth. The theory is that such an investor can tolerate losing his or her entire investment in an illiquid, highly speculative investment.

In the colloquial sense, the term "sophisticated investor" is used to mean an investor who is savvy, who understands the ins and outs of investing. Brokerage firms commonly abuse this notion, arguing that an individual who owns a lot of securities, or who has been investing in stocks, bonds, and other investments, is by definition sophisticated about investments. The reality, of course, is that many of those people only have all those different kinds of investments—many highly speculative—because their brokers have been pushing them into high-risk, high-commission investments for years.

In any event, even sophisticated investors rely on their brokers for advice. Why else would they use a broker and not just conduct their own trades with a discount broker? While this reliance is often misplaced, it seems ironic that in arbitration proceedings brokers reverse their normal position and imply that their clients really did not rely on them at all.

YOU ASKED FOR IT

The second way brokers try to dodge unsuitability claims is by saying that not only did the investor know the risks, but that he or she asked that the investment be made.

As I've noted earlier, whenever a broker executes a trade, he or she fills out an order slip. One piece of information on this slip—along with the security, the number of units, the price per unit bid or asked, and whether the order is to buy or sell—is whether the transaction was solicited or unsolicited.

If you ask your broker to buy you shares of stock, he or she marks the ticket unsolicited to make it clear that the transaction did not come about as the result of a recommendation or solicitation. If that stock tanks, you probably don't have any recourse (there are exceptions, discussed in the next section).

One way that brokers try to take the onus off themselves for getting clients to buy speculative stocks is to mark order tickets unsolicited even when the transaction was, in fact, solicited. When you receive a confirmation, make sure to confirm that it is correct about whether the trade was solicited or not. If a trade that was solicited is marked unsolicited, call the broker immediately. If he or she says it was a mistake, ask for a new confirmation statement marked "corrected" or a letter acknowledging the mistake. Ask that the corrected confirmation or letter be cosigned by the branch manager.

What Broker Violations of Suitability Rules Can Mean to You

Let's assume that your broker has violated the suitability rules in your account. What does this mean to you?

You could complain directly to the appropriate SRO (the NASD, NYSE, AMEX, or CBOE) and ask the SRO to institute disciplinary proceedings. This can get your broker sanctioned, fined, or even—if he or she has shown a pattern of this behavior—barred from the securities industry. But it does not put any of your money back in your pocket.

What could give you financial redress is filing a claim for an arbitration proceeding against your broker and his or her brokerage firm. In all likelihood, you would allege a violation of Section 10(b) of the Securities Exchange Act of 1934 and SEC Rule 10b-5 (the so-called antifraud provisions), as well as breach of fiduciary duty, in addition to citing the legal theories that are subsumed within a claim of unsuitable trading.

As I've indicated, these kinds of claims are among the most common filed in arbitration against brokers and brokerage firms. The parameters of suitability violations described in this chapter are the traditional ones (the world is moving so fast that Internet suitability issues have become traditional), over which lawyers representing investors and those representing brokers and brokerage firms duel all the time.

However, as you'll see in the next two chapters, an untold number of claims are not filed because investors and their lawyers are ignorant of systemic practices in the securities industry that put many (perhaps even most) investors into investments in securities that are unsuitable, thereby giving those investors the possibility of recovering their losses.

The analysis necessary to uncover and prosecute those claims is not new or controversial. However, the ramifications of using the analysis are extremely significant to many investors who had previously given up on the possibility of ever recovering their losses from their broker.

This is why The Solin Theories for Recovering Losses from Your Broker (the subject of Chapter 7) add such an important dimension to the traditional theories of unsuitability. However, before you can understand those theories, you have to understand a little of the history and mathematics of risk, and of the modern theories of finance and portfolios that utilize that math.

TERMINOLOGY

FINANCIAL SUICIDE: An investor is said to be committing financial suicide if he or she directs a broker to execute a trade in an unsuitable security. Courts and arbitration tribunals have ruled that brokers have an obligation not to execute such a trade, in much the same way that a bartender has an obligation not to serve a drink to an obviously intoxicated person, then let that person drive.

"KNOW-YOUR-CUSTOMER" RULE: The New York Stock Exchange (NYSE) rule that requires brokers to know their client's investment objectives and financial condition before making any investment recommendations. The NASD has a similar rule, as do other exchanges.

ONLINE SUITABILITY: The concept that, even when investors trade online with no interaction with a broker, the firm has some responsibility to know the customer's objectives and financial condition, and to not allow the investor to make investments that are incompatible with those objectives and conditions, and thus unsuitable.

PENNY STOCK: A stock that trades for under $1 per share. Penny stocks are highly risky. They do not trade on an exchange, but rather on the "pink sheets" or the "over-the-counter" broker-to-broker marketplace. The Securities and Exchange Commission (SEC) has special regulations regarding to whom penny stocks may be sold.

SOLICITED/UNSOLICITED ORDER: A solicited order is a securities transaction that results from a broker's recommendation. An unsolicited order is one that results from an investor's request.

SOPHISTICATED INVESTOR: Under SEC guidelines, an investor is defined as "sophisticated" if he or she meets certain income and net worth requirements. Being classified as a "sophisticated" investor allows the investor to purchase unregulated securities such as private placements of stock.

6

Boring Theories, Big Bucks

My client Miriam was 60 when I met her, a widow who had invested $1.4 million in proceeds from her husband's life insurance with a small regional brokerage firm. This money was essentially all of her assets. She told her broker she needed to preserve capital and generate enough income to pay her monthly expenses.

The broker she worked with invested 100 percent of her portfolio in stock mutual funds, all of which had greater volatility than the Standard & Poor's 500 index. Over a little more than a year, Miriam's account lost almost $300,000, more than 20 percent of the portfolio's value.

At the arbitration hearing, Miriam's expert testified that this allocation was completely unsuitable for Miriam, and that an appropriate allocation would have been in the range of 40 percent stocks and 60 percent bonds. The brokerage firm defended the case by demonstrating that Miriam's two sons were a lawyer and an accountant, that the sons were aware of the allocation made by the firm, and that they should have complained if they didn't think the account was managed appropriately.

The tribunal agreed with this defense and awarded Miriam nothing. Fortunately, I had entered into a "high/low" agreement with the opposing counsel, who was obviously concerned about losing. Under such an agreement, the defendant's counsel agrees to a minimum payment to the plaintiff, and the plaintiff's counsel agrees to an upper limit for the payment. Even if the tribunal returns a decision for a payment larger than the upper limit, the plaintiff agrees to accept the upper limit. If the tribunal returns a decision for a payment below the floor (or no payment at all, as in this case) the defendant agrees to make the floor payment.

In 1952, a University of Chicago graduate student named Harry Markowitz presented his Ph.D. thesis to his dissertation advisors, the economists Milton Friedman and Jacob Marschak. Although the dissertation represented brilliant analytical thinking, it didn't fit into any of the traditional categories the professors were used to dealing with: economics, business administration, or applied math.

What Markowitz had done was, in essence, to invent a new avenue of academic inquiry, which we know today as Modern Portfolio Theory (MPT). In 1990, Markowitz, William Sharpe, and Merton Miller shared the Nobel Prize in economics for their work in defining and continually refining MPT.

Remember the key question from Chapter 5: How much of your portfolio's value could you lose in a single year before you began worrying?

Keep this question in mind as you read the rest of this chapter, because concepts of risk and volatility, and the mathematical calculations that can be used to help you measure risk and volatility, really get to the heart of that question.

I would be practicing some other kind of law if brokers educated themselves about risk, volatility, and the portfolio construction techniques that can be used to mitigate risk and volatility, helped their clients to understand those concepts, then gave their advice to clients on how to properly construct portfolios (and properly documented that advice).

But many don't do that, so you need to educate yourself. Armed with the information from this chapter, you can then go toe-to-toe with your broker using The Solin Theories described in Chapter 7.

MPT—The Mother of All Finance Theory

Modern Portfolio Theory is grounded in a disarmingly simple concept: An investor's desire is not simply to maximize the return on his or her portfolio; rather, an investor desires to maximize the portfolio's return while maintaining the risk level with which he or she is comfortable. This simple, intuitive, yet elegant economic theory led to what we now know as portfolio management, which in turn has spawned a multibillion-dollar industry of professional advisors, managers, and securities analysts, all intent on outperforming the market.

However, as you'll see, it is very unlikely that they will be able to do that over the long term. This isn't because they are incompetent. It is because the market is an incredibly efficient entity at processing all available information and incorporating it into the prices of securities (stocks and bonds). Each analyst, in his or her attempt to uncover undervalued stocks, is competing against this market that consists of all other individuals participating in the market. In other words, in order to beat the market, an analyst must be better than all 10,000 other analysts in the market collectively. Each individual may be very good, but he or she certainly isn't better than all other analysts put together.

While simple in theory, portfolio management is complex in practice. Dozens of books have been written about Modern Portfolio Theory and how to use its principles to construct the ideal portfolio. It is a highly technical subject (most of the books are written by professors of finance), and I will only scratch the surface of the topic in this chapter. The point is not to be all-inclusive (I'll provide you with suggestions for further reading on this topic in the bibliography) but rather to give you some basic tools with which to measure your portfolio's risk and volatility, to spur conversation with your broker, and to determine if you have an unsuitability claim against your broker because investment decisions were made without regard for these concepts.

There are four important investment concepts that extend directly from Modern Portfolio Theory:

- Asset allocation
- Diversification within asset classes
- Risk
- Costs

Allocate Your Assets or Compound Your Losses

The term "asset allocation" refers to the mix of investments among the various classes of financial assets. The goal of asset allocation is to create an "efficient" portfolio that provides the highest return for a given amount of risk. In doing so, it attempts to reduce risk by placing portions of the portfolio in asset classes that move up and down in value out of sync with one another (this is called having less than perfect correlation) and that have different inherent levels of historical volatility (risk).

You can think of financial assets in a simple form of the three major asset classes—stocks, bonds, and cash. In this sense, an asset allocation asks: How much of the portfolio should be invested in stocks, how much in bonds, and how much in cash? Although each of these asset classes typically performs its own unique service (i.e., stocks for growth, bonds for income and volatility control, and cash for short-term liquidity needs), the combination of these assets creates a portfolio that provides an investor with a way to understand the overall expected (historical) return and the associated risk (volatility). This historical return and risk cannot be used to guarantee the portfolio's future performance, but it can be used as a gauge with which to predict parameters within which the portfolio can statistically be expected to behave.

Or you can discuss asset allocation at a more granular level, as the percentage of a portfolio that should be invested in each of the many subclasses within those different asset classes (e.g., for stocks, U.S. large-capitalization stocks, growth, or value, U.S. mid-cap stocks, U.S. small-cap stocks, international large-cap and small-cap stocks, emerging market stocks, etc.). Some people include "hard" assets such as gold, as well as real estate, in their asset allocation breakdown.

ASSET CLASSES
■ Stocks (equities)
U.S. Large Capitalization (Large-Cap)
U.S. Mid-Cap
U.S. Small-Cap
International Large-Cap
International Small-Cap
Emerging Markets

■ Bonds (debt)
U.S. Treasuries
Municipal
Asset-Backed (e.g., Ginnie Mae mortgage bonds)
Corporate

■ Cash
Certificates of Deposit
Money Market Funds

■ Real Estate
Direct ownership in land and buildings
Real Estate Investment Trusts (REITs)

Many investors give short shrift to asset allocation, as do many brokers. Not many investors understand the concept, and the brokerage industry has up until now had no real incentive to educate investors. This is a major reason for my writing this book, to educate you so you can force your broker to utilize these academically proven tools and possibly recover market losses from brokers who have neglected these tools in the past, to your detriment.

Academics who study Modern Portfolio Theory and practitioners of modern portfolio management have shown consistently in study and in practice that asset allocation accounts for by far the greatest proportion of a portfolio's behavior.

In 1986, three finance professors, Gary P. Brinson, L. Randolph Hood, and Gilbert Beebower, published a study called "Determinants of Portfolio Performance" in the *Financial Analysts Journal*. The three looked at investment results of 91 pension funds with between $100 million and $3 billion in assets over a 10-year period from 1974 to 1983. They updated their study in 1991 with additional data.

They used mathematical calculations to determine the percentage of each portfolio's behavior attributable to each of four factors:

■ Investment policy
■ Selection of individual securities
■ Market timing
■ Costs

They found that investment policy, what most people think of as asset allocation, was responsible for about 92 percent of a pension fund's variability over time. The particular securities within each asset class were responsible for about 5 percent of the variability. Market timing—digressing from the "ideal" asset allocation to take market conditions such as a generally overvalued stock market or high interest rates into consideration—was responsible for about 2 percent of variability.

Costs in this context refer to annual management fees. Since fees typically do not change much over time, they have little impact on variability of returns over time for a particular fund. However, other studies have shown that costs have an extremely large effect on return levels across funds (not for one fund over time). These studies suggest that costs matter greatly and that minimizing annual fees is extremely important in portfolio management. Consider the importance of these statistics. Do you believe the value of working with a broker is that he or she can pick undervalued stocks and time the market better than you? As I'll show later in the chapter, there is precious little research to support this supposition. And even if a broker could time the market and pick stocks better than you, research has shown that market timing and stock picking have little effect on your portfolio's overall value. If your broker could actually reliably beat the market, it is as likely that he or she would be working as an "account executive" at a brokerage firm's local branch office as it is that Michael Jordan would be playing pickup basketball at the court in the schoolyard.

Diversify Your Risks or Consolidate Your Losses

Diversification is the process by which an investor can eliminate certain risks. In today's financial world, it means two different things. First, it means the spreading out of investments within one asset class among a number of different securities. The goal of diversification is reduction of risk within an asset class. Second, it means holding assets in a number of different (preferably negatively correlated or not highly correlated) asset classes.

In order to effectively manage risk, it is necessary to be properly diversified within the stock and bond asset classes, so if one security experiences a dire loss of value (Enron or Global Crossing, for instance, or Argentina for those who held that country's bonds), the entire asset class within your portfolio does not go in the tank.

The ideal amount of diversification is an issue that is argued by finance scholars and professionals. However, as one recent study suggests, "even 60-stock portfolios achieve less than 90 percent of full diversification. . . . The implication of an increased volatility of individual stocks, combined with unchanged volatility within the S&P 500, is that correlation between stocks has declined." This reduced correlation suggests the need for an ever-more-broadly diversified equity portfolio.

UNDERSTAND RISK OR RISK BIG LOSSES

Too many brokers, and too many of their clients, focus on one measure of a portfolio—return—while failing to put enough thought into the other side of the equation—risk. While you may perceive returns as the only reporting issue that matters, in reality you should also be worried about your portfolio's risk and costs.

Risk, according to Ron S. Dembo and Andrew Freeman, authors of *The Rules of Risk: A Guide for Investors*, is "a measurement of the potential changes in value that will be experienced in a portfolio as a result of differences in the environment between now and some point in the future."

But risk can also be seen as the answer to the question "How much of your portfolio can you stand to lose in one year without getting worried?" Professional financial advisors call this the "stomach acid" test.

If you say the answer is zero, that you always want to see your portfolio grow, that is not impossible. But a "zero-risk" portfolio has other potential pitfalls. While it is possible to construct a portfolio that contains little in the way of market risk (entirely or almost entirely in cash or risk-free Treasury securities), the nominal gains in such a portfolio may be largely eaten up by inflation. In other words, though your portfolio may be growing at what seems like a reasonable rate, your purchasing power is growing much more slowly or not at all.

For most investors, this is not a path they want to take. And MPT shows that adding appropriately sized investments in even very risky securities can actually lower the portfolio's overall risk, if those securities have a less-than-perfect correlation with the majority of the portfolio.

Creating the appropriate asset allocation for your portfolio, then properly diversifying within each asset class, can greatly reduce your investment risk, as I'll demonstrate later in the discussion on portfolio construction.

There are a number of different risks you face as an investor, but the four most important are:

- Business/market risk
- Credit risk
- Interest rate risk
- Inflation risk

Business/Market Risk

This is the major risk you take on when you make an investment in a stock (an equity security).

If you own stock in an individual company, you take on the risk that the business conditions will deteriorate for that company, for whatever reason, and the perceived value of the stock in that company (the price a potential buyer would be willing to pay to buy the stock from you) will decline.

Market risk is the risk that the entire stock market, or the segment of the market in which the company does business, will lose value.

Credit Risk

This is one of the risks you take on when you invest in a bond (a debt security). It is the risk that the company or government entity you loaned money to by buying the bond will not be able to repay the bond when it comes due.

Interest Rate Risk

Interest rate risk is another risk that affects bond investors. Remember, you don't have to hold a bond until it matures; there is a market for trading bonds. In this market, the value of a bond at any time is determined by the relationship between the interest rate the bond carries and the prevailing interest rate on other similar fixed-income securities.

If interest rates are rising, bond values go down, since an investor can purchase a newly issued bond at a higher interest rate, and in order to compensate for the lower interest rate, one will pay a "discount" off the face value of a lower-interest-bearing bond. If interest rates are declining, bond prices increase, since investors are willing to pay a "premium" for bonds that have a higher interest rate than those currently being issued.

Inflation Risk

Inflation risk is faced by every investor, regardless of whether investments are in stocks, bonds, or cash. If the return on your investments is less than the rate of inflation, the value of your portfolio in real terms is declining, even though nominally it may be growing.

RISK PREMIUM—RISKING LARGER
LOSSES TO INCREASE RETURN

The risk premium is the amount of extra return an investor wishes to receive above the risk-free return (usually considered to be the rate on short-term U.S. Treasury bills) in order to compensate for the various forms of investment risk being taken (either business and market risk for stocks or credit and interest rate risk for bonds).

The risk-free rate of return actually means the investment is free of market risk and credit risk. This risk-free rate includes an inflation premium, which is the aggregate market's overall expectation for inflation over the remaining period of time before the security matures. It also includes what we call the real risk-free rate. This is the rate the market rewards you in the absence of any inflation for simply forgoing the use of money and delaying your consumption to some time in the future.

Risk-free assets do contain inflation risk. The risk is that the level of inflation that actually happens is significantly higher than the market expected when you purchased the security. If that scenario plays out, your growth in purchasing power can be seriously eroded (or even completely nullified) in a risk-free investment. Of course, such erosion occurs for risky investments as well. However, the severity is more extreme with risk-free investments because the realized level of inflation is a much larger percentage of the expected risk-free return than the expected return on a risky investment.

Using historical data, an investor who owns a portfolio entirely in stocks, but diversified across the entire universe of U.S. stocks, would have earned a risk-free rate plus 6.42 percent annually. There is no guarantee that such a risk premium for equities will continue over time. Recent data suggest that this premium may be overstated. However, the idea is that investors must be compensated for taking the additional risk of being in the market, or they would never make the riskier investment.

The entire universe of U.S. corporate bonds returns less of a risk premium than does the universe of stocks (in case of a bankruptcy, bondholders are ahead of stock holders in the creditors' queue, making bonds "safer" than stocks), while different subcategories of stocks return more of a risk premium than the entire universe of U.S. stocks. For instance, an investor who put his or her entire portfolio in small-capitalization U.S. stocks would have had a historic risk premium of 9.8 percent above the risk-free rate of return annually. He or she would also assume much more risk (volatility) than would the investor who invested in the entire universe of U.S. stocks.

This brings us to the next issue. Now that you know that there are risks, and that various investments that carry more risk pay, historically, a higher rate of return (a larger risk premium), how do you go about measuring risk and determining which risks are appropriate and which aren't?

YOU CAN MANAGE RISK, BUT FIRST
YOU NEED TO MANAGE YOUR BROKER

Risk is about the future, and about mathematically calculating the probability of one outcome or another occurring at various points in time.

The first attempt to calculate—and hence manage—risk occurred in 1654, when a French gambler named Chevalier de Mere and his mathematician friend Blaise Pascal determined that they could predict the future outcome of a game of chance. Working with another mathematician, Pierre de Fermat, they developed the theory of probability.

It is this theory of probability that underpins all thinking of risk management, and which allowed mathematicians and economists to take Harry Markowitz's basic Modern Portfolio Theory and convert it into a set of rules that guide portfolio construction. It is also the theory of probability that allows for "card counters" to beat the odds of losing at the blackjack table.

Financial risk management appeared first in England in the 1680s. Using the theory of probability developed by the French gambler and mathematicians a generation earlier, the English government, with the help of the mathematician and astronomer Edmund Halley (discoverer of Halley's Comet), drew up a set of life-expectancy tables which defined the probability of a person of any given age living to another age.

Using these tables, the government sold life annuities, which promised a set annual payment for life to a person who purchased one. The annuity, and its cousin the life insurance policy, are still staples of financial investments today. Actuaries calculate how long the "average" person of a given age should live, the rate of return the annuity or insurance sponsor can expect to receive on its investments over that time, and what the desired profit to the sponsor is. These calculations are used to determine the proper price of the annuity contract, or the annual premium for the life insurance policy.

In England, these same theories and calculations of probability were soon used to create marine risk insurance, the first "property and casualty" insurance sold on the Lloyd's of London insurance exchange. The notion of probability and risk are the underpinnings of the entire insurance industry, and indeed of many of the decisions we make in life.

For instance, if I eat better and exercise more, the probability increases that I will live longer (by reducing my risk of heart disease). If I buckle my safety belt, the probability increases that I will survive a serious auto accident. These relationships are fairly obvious to most people. However, such an objective relationship is more difficult to draw when we are talking about investment strategies. For example, what is the relationship between, say, the risk level of my retirement portfolio and the probability that I will have enough to live on in my old age? The answer to this question lies in the measurement of risk and our estimates of how risk and return are related. But how do I figure out how risky an investment really is? And is the issue really how risky a single security is, or how risky the entire portfolio is?

The trick to reducing risk in investing is to understand what your investment objective is and the time horizon you have in which to meet that objective. Knowing these two factors, you can then construct a portfolio that first defines the level of risk you wish to undertake in the portfolio as a whole, then seeks to maximize your expected return given that level of risk.

Calculating Brokers Don't Often Calculate Risk

Simple probability calculation can help define the proper premium for a single insurance policy against a known risk. But this simple probability must be enhanced in order to determine the risks that exist in an investment portfolio.

For the purpose of this discussion, I will focus on calculating risk in stocks (and, by extension, stock mutual funds), because research shows that well over 50 percent of American households own either individual stocks or stock mutual funds, either in taxable portfolios or in tax-advantaged retirement portfolios (IRAs, Roth IRAs, 401(k) plans, 403(b) plans, 457 plans, or SEP/Keogh plans). Some of these risk calculations are just as valid for bonds or bond funds.

I'm going to define four different calculations. A couple of these are specific measures of risk, while the other two are important in analyzing the performance of investment portfolios:

- Standard deviation
- Beta

- R-squared
- Sharpe ratio

There are other measures important to defining risk, but these are the ones most frequently used.

THERE IS NOTHING STANDARD ABOUT STANDARD DEVIATION

Standard deviation measures "dispersion" from an average. The concept was discovered in 1730 by Abraham de Molvre. It can be used to estimate how far on either side of the expected return (a mean) one must travel to capture most (two-thirds) of the possible returns. Standard deviation is often used in describing probabilities under a bell-shaped curve, also known as the "normal distribution." Many variables, but certainly not all, are characterized by a normal distribution. Portfolio returns are best described by a log-normal distribution, which is similar to the normal distribution.

The bell curve and standard deviation can be used to measure the statistical dispersion of any group, from the weight of infants to the grade-point average of a high-school graduating class; from intelligence to family income. The larger the number of items in the group being studied, the more chance that the curve will "normalize" into the classic bell curve.

In the realm of investment, standard deviation compares a range of expected returns for a particular security (for instance, a stock or mutual fund) to the security's historical mean return.

For instance, if a mutual fund has a mean (average) return of 12 percent and a standard deviation of 8, two out of every three years the fund can be expected to return between 4 percent (12 – 8) and 20 percent (12 + 8). The other one year (in every three), its return can be expected to be either lower than 4 percent or higher than 20 percent. In about 95 of each 100 years, the security can be expected to have returns within two standard deviations of the mean (between –4 percent [12 – 16] and 28 percent [12 + 16]).

Standard deviation is an absolute measure of the volatility of a security. A security with a lower standard deviation is one where most of the returns for any given time period are closer to the historic mean, while a security with a higher standard deviation is one where most of the returns are more widely dispersed from the mean. A lower standard deviation means less volatility, and hence less risk.

Investors can use standard deviation to understand the historical range of returns that an investment has provided. A higher standard deviation means that a stock or stock fund has exhibited a wider range of returns, both positive and negative, from the mean than a stock or fund—or a market index—with a lower standard deviation.

It is important to note that standard deviation measures historic returns only. It is not a measure of future performance. Indeed, since investment returns often demonstrate non-normal patterns (so-called "fat tails"), the fact that extreme volatility occurred only rarely in the past does not mean that it might not occur more frequently in the future.

YOU HAD BETTER KNOW YOUR BETA

Beta is a measure of an investment's sensitivity to market movements. By definition, the beta of the entire stock market (often thought of as the Standard & Poor's 500 index, which is commonly used as a proxy for the U.S. stock market) is 1.0. If a mutual fund has a beta of 1.25, this means that historically the investment performed 25 percent better than the market (the S&P 500) in up markets and 25 percent worse in down markets, assuming all other factors remain constant.

When trying to use beta to compare a potential investment's risk (or a portfolio's risk) against market risk, it is important to define what market you are measuring the potential investment or portfolio against. Beta is predicated on comparison to a particular index, most often the S&P 500, but not always.

IT IS NOT SQUARE TO UNDERSTAND R-SQUARED

In order to properly view a stock or fund's beta, you must also consider the R-squared. R-squared tells how much of the ups and downs of the fund or stock are caused by the ups and downs of the market. Highly diversified funds often have high R-squareds. Single stocks often have low R-squareds. The lower the R-squared, the less reliable your calculation of beta.

R-squared is closely related to correlation. If a stock or fund has a low R-squared, it has low correlation. This can be good when considering stocks to add to a portfolio—lower correlation provides diversification benefits. It is probably not good when looking at a fund, since it may suggest that the fund is not well diversified.

R-squared is measured on a scale of 100. If a stock fund has an R-squared of 97 to the S&P 500 and its beta is 1.25, the statement that the fund is 25 percent more volatile than the S&P 500 would be correct. However, if it has an R-squared of 47 to the S&P 500 and a beta of 1.25, we must look on the 1.25 beta with some skepticism. While 1.25 is our best estimate at this time, it is likely that the fund's riskiness may at times be far more than 25 percent greater than the market or it may be far less.

DON'T GET CUT ON THE SHARPE RATIO

The Sharpe ratio, named for the Nobel Prize–winning economist William Sharpe, measures an investment's risk-adjusted return and is calculated by using the investment's return minus the risk-free return (the return on the short-term U.S. Treasury bills) as the numerator and the investment's standard deviation as the denominator.

Sharpe used Markowitz's MPT as the starting point for creation of the capital asset pricing model (CAPM), which defines the risk and volatility relative to the market. The CAPM states that a stock's expected return is proportional to the stock's risk relative to the entire universe of stocks. The CAPM model shows that, as Markowitz implied with MPT, increased return can only occur in the presence of increased risk.

Asset Allocation and Diversification Reduce Risk

Now, if your financial advisor asked you, "How much of your portfolio can you stand to lose in one year before you start worrying?" you might say, "I can tolerate occasional years of a negative return of perhaps 10 percent but would prefer to do so only if I am being compensated for such risk." This answer should then drive you and the advisor to use risk measurement calculations, along with asset allocation and diversification techniques, to construct a portfolio that conforms to your definition of risk and investment goals. In reality, most stockbrokers would not understand what you were talking about.

Markowitz's first flash of brilliance—that investors seek to maximize returns while simultaneously reducing risk—was possibly not as important as its corollary: that just as you can minimize risk for a given level of return, you can also maximize return for a given level of risk. In effect, you can build a portfolio that conforms to a level of risk you are willing to tolerate.

Markowitz showed that by constructing a properly diversified portfolio, you can reduce the inherent risk in any single security by offsetting it not only with risk-free investments but with equally risky investments in different asset classes, which often have low or negative correlation to one another. So, while some risky investments may be losing value in any given time period, other equally risky investments may be gaining a lot of value, and risk-free assets are working as ballast to keep the portfolio's value stable or growing.

Despite the ability to measure risk and simply construct portfolios that start with the desired level of risk and increase return without increasing risk and with minimal trading costs, the vast majority of brokers continue to counsel their clients to chase short-term portfolio return with little understanding of the risks involved or the likelihood that it can be consistently profitable. During the 1990s, too many brokers focused their clients' investments in risky and volatile market sectors, such as technology (including biotech and telecommunications).

This focus placed a significant portion of many investors' portfolios in investments that were far too risky for their investment objectives and their ability to withstand a meaningful loss of their portfolio's capital. This problem was exacerbated by the tendency of many brokers to chase "hot sectors," continually ramping up allocations to recent high flyers, thereby increasing volatility and risk.

One common piece of investment wisdom is that the shorter your time frame, the more difficult it will be for any portfolio to produce the expected results. This typically means that investors with short time frames should be more conservative, as these portfolios are less likely to suffer losses. For instance, for a 40-year-old investor, it is okay to take on more risk in a retirement portfolio (which has a 25- to 30-year time horizon) than in a fund for his or her children's college education (which probably has a five- to 15-year time horizon).

The reason for this is again mathematical. As the time period under question becomes longer, the annual standard deviation for any security becomes smaller.

That's because standard deviation measures the probability of dispersion of a given result around the mean. If you measure the heights of a 20-child fifth-grade class, two very tall children or very short children can cause the standard deviation to stretch far from the mean (together they make up 10 percent of the class, and must fall within the second standard deviation from the mean height). If you measure the 130 children in the fifth-grade classes throughout the city, two very tall or very short children now fall outside the second standard deviation.

The same is true with time. The S&P 500 standard deviation for one year for all years from 1945 through 1999 was 16.4. But the five-year standard deviation was only 6.2, and the 20-year standard deviation was only 3.1.

This means that if you bought an S&P 500 index fund at any point and held it one year (index funds didn't actually exist for the general public until about 1975), you would have had an expected return of between roughly –4 percent (the S&P mean return for those years was roughly 12 percent) and roughly 28 percent for the year. But if you bought that index fund and held it for five years, your expected (historical) return would have been between roughly 6 percent and roughly 18 percent annually for five years.

Consider Costs or Have Costly Losses

Costs can have a large impact on your portfolio's performance. When you look at your portfolio's return against any benchmark, you have to look at your net return, after accounting for all costs.

When the mean expected returns and standard deviations from those returns are calculated for particular market indexes, those returns are based on a zero-cost assumption (i.e., owning all of the stocks in the S&P 500 for 20 years). Of course, in the real world of investing, it is impossible to do away with costs completely. Whether you buy individual securities or mutual funds, you or the fund have some transaction costs when securities are bought or sold. Mutual funds also have administrative costs associated with managing the portfolio and providing customer service, as well as legitimate marketing costs.

Even the most cost-efficient S&P 500 index mutual funds have some transaction costs. That's because the S&P 500 index undergoes changes. Remember, the S&P 500 index is an index of 500 of the largest U.S. companies, as measured by their market capitalization (number of shares outstanding multiplied by the current market price per share).

Natural growth of some companies allows them to overtake other companies in size and become eligible to be placed in the S&P 500 index by the Standard & Poor's index committee. When this happens, S&P 500 index funds must sell their shares in the former S&P 500 member company and buy shares in the new index member company. A similar thing happens when two S&P 500 index member companies merge; the index now needs to take on as a member a new company.

Costs for index mutual funds in other indexes (e.g., S&P mid-cap 400 and

S&P small-cap 600) are higher, because companies of this size are growing more rapidly, or ceasing to exist, or being purchased more frequently, than the companies with the largest market capitalization. This forces the mutual funds to conduct more transactions.

For an investor who buys shares in individual companies to try to properly diversify within the stock asset class is an expensive proposition. Many academics today believe that it takes upward of 90 separate stocks (some say as many as 200) to create a portfolio that is appropriately diversified to significantly reduce risk. Because your transaction costs for purchases of individual stocks are far higher than are the same costs for institutional investors and mutual funds, most investors have found since the 1980s that the lowest-cost way to create a diversified portfolio is through mutual funds.

When you think of costs, remember this calculation. If you were to invest $10,000 today in a fund that returns 12 percent a year and incurs no expenses at all, in 30 years your investment would be worth $300,000. If the fund has a 1 percent expense ratio, your 30-year return would be $229,000. If it has a 2 percent expense ratio, your 30-year return would drop to $174,000. Expenses are as susceptible to the law of compounding as are returns.

Remember the concept from Chapter 3 of cost-equity ratio? Now that you understand the trade-off between return and risk, let's look at how this all plays out between you and your broker.

Historical data indicates that a long-term investor (at least 10 years) who is willing to take a very substantial risk as measured by standard deviation can expect a mean annual return of no more than 15 percent above the risk-free rate of return (let's assume the U.S. Treasury bill yields 3 percent, so this "high-risk" return is 18 percent). Such a portfolio would be heavily weighted in small-cap value stocks, and the three-year-weighted standard deviation might be as high as 30.

If you incur a cost-equity ratio of 5 percent (which I believe is difficult to justify), your high-risk return has just dropped to 13 percent, not very much over the mean return of the S&P 500, which would have a significantly lower standard deviation. Why take that extra risk and receive no extra reward for doing so?

If your broker told you that by listening to his or her suggestions and buying dot-com stocks and biotech stocks and broadband stocks (and paying commissions on each transaction), you were taking a meaningful chance of losing a significant portion of your portfolio, but the long-term upside was

The Gurus Who Couldn't Beat the Market

Your very rich uncle calls to offer you the opportunity to invest in a fund managed by a former partner at Salomon Brothers, who put together a team generally regarded as the finest bond arbitrage group in the world.

It gets better. The fund's management includes Robert C. Merton, a professor of finance at Harvard Business School and an outstanding academic in the financial world; Myron Scholes, one of the creators of the famous Black-Scholes formula used for determining the value of stock options (Merton and Scholes together won a Nobel Prize in economics); and David W. Mullins, vice chairman of the Federal Reserve and widely considered to be a possible successor to Alan Greenspan.

Let's say these men have created a formula for investing against the grain of prevailing wisdom (after all, the fund was a so-called "hedge fund"). Perhaps even an article in *Business Week* chortled: "Never has this much academic talent been given this much money to bet with."

The fund's managers find undervalued securities, play the odds on currency fluctuations, and engage in other techniques to create above-average returns.

What's more, your uncle tells you that among your fellow investors would be the Bank of Taiwan, the Kuwaiti state pension fund, the foreign exchange office of the Italian central bank (a $100 million investment), Sumitomo Bank (another $100 million investment), Phil Knight of Nike footwear fame, the partners of McKinsey & Co. management consultants, St. John's University, Yeshiva University, PaineWebber (another $100 million investment), and the pension fund of Black & Decker. The list seems endless and could not be more impressive. A very exclusive opportunity, indeed.

There's more good news. The mathematical wizards who started the fund have calculated precisely the risk of losing money in the fund: You could expect to lose 5 percent or more about one month in every five, and 10 percent or more about one month in 10. Despite this high volatility in very short time frames, you could only expect to lose 20 percent of your investment in one year out of 50. The risk of losing more than 20 percent in one year was so low that the fund's mathematical geniuses felt it was not even worth calculating.

So you invest ....

Things start out well. The first year, the fund racks up a 28 percent return. In its second (and record) year, the return is 59 percent. In its third year the fund earns 51 percent. In its fourth year it earns 25 percent. What a track record! More than 160 percent growth in just four years.

But then the unthinkable happens. The fund, which has $3.6 billion in capital—and is highly leveraged with borrowed funding—tanks. Its $100 billion debt (essentially the world's largest-ever margin call) almost causes a worldwide financial panic. In the end, a group organized by the U.S. Federal Reserve Bank must bail out the fund. The partners in the fund take personal losses of almost $2 billion.

The fund, of course, was Long Term Capital Management. After its downfall, every dollar invested in the fund at its inception was worth only 23 cents. During the same four-year period, a dollar invested in a broad-based U.S. stock index fund would have increased to two dollars.

The best and the brightest could not beat the market. Do you still think your broker can?

a return of about the same as an S&P 500 index fund, would you approve of such a trading strategy?

PORTFOLIO CONSTRUCTION: THE EFFICIENT FRONTIER

So how do you go about constructing a portfolio that conforms to the amount of risk you wish to undertake while seeking the highest return? The answer is by discovering the place you wish to occupy along Harry Markowitz's greatest invention, the efficient frontier.

"Efficient" is a term economists use to describe something that is objectively preferential to something else. Markowitz's theoretical efficient frontier ran from the origin (all cash, with no risk) almost along a 45-degree angle (implying that additional risk equaled additional reward) for a period; then the line steepened to show that additional return could be generated without taking on equal additional risk.

In the 50 years since Markowitz, empirical evidence has described how the efficient frontier ought to look in a vacuum. The curve shows that return actually goes up more than risk early on as you allocate assets across asset classes, then it becomes harder to add return without also adding risk (think of the portfolio study that showed that 92 percent of portfolio behavior is determined by proper asset allocation).

Let's look at how this works in practice. For this section, I refer to work done by Dimensional Fund Advisors (DFA), a money management firm that invests over $100 billion for many of the country's largest institutional investors, including endowments and pension funds. Individuals cannot invest in DFA funds through stockbrokers but can through designated investment advisors.

DFA uses a technique called passive investing, which means investing to mimic stock and bond market indexes. (Vanguard does the same thing for retail customers through its index mutual funds. DFA has created funds using many more asset classes than has Vanguard.)

I'll discuss indexing in more detail in a little bit, but the first issue in portfolio construction is allocation and diversification.

If an individual created a portfolio that was 40 percent in a bond fund that held all of the bonds in the Lehman Government/Corporate Bond Index and 60 percent in a fund that held all of the stocks in the S&P 500, that portfolio would have earned an annualized return (mean return) of 11.60 percent, with an annual standard deviation of 11.18 percent. This means that in two of every three years during the history of these indexes, that portfolio's return was between 0.42 percent and 22.78 percent.

By diversifying part of the portfolio into other asset classes, you may be able to either reduce the standard deviation while maintaining approximately the same return, or increase the return while maintaining approximately the same standard deviation. This can be done either through a different diversification scheme within an asset class, or by more finely tuning the investments in an asset class within subclasses.

For example, by changing the 40 percent invested in bonds from the Lehman Government/Corporate Bond Index (which holds bonds of different length maturities) to the DFA one-year fixed-income fund, you would have reduced the portfolio's standard deviation from 11.18 to 9.92, while only sacrificing 0.10 percent of return.

In addition to switching the bond investment, by splitting the 60 percent stock investment across six different indexes (7.5 percent in the S&P 500, 7.5 percent in DFA's U.S. MicroCap portfolio, 7.5 percent in DFA's US 6-10 Value portfolio, 7.5 percent in DFA's Large-Cap Value portfolio, 15 percent in DFA's International Value portfolio, and 15 percent in DFA's International Small Company portfolio), you would have increased the annual mean return to 13.00 while actually reducing the annual standard deviation from the 11.18 of the original 60/40 portfolio to 10.49.

This is equivalent to finding the Holy Grail! A portfolio with a higher expected return with lower risk! Of course, as mutual fund prospectuses are quick to point out, "past performance is no guarantee of future results." These are historical results, based on rigorous mathematical calculations by some of the brightest people in the world of finance, including at least three Nobel Prize winners. But that still doesn't guarantee that this strategy will continue to work in the future.

Active Management: The Myth of Picking Winners

Asset allocation accounts for over 90 percent of a portfolio's behavior, and you can reduce the risk in your portfolio by diversifying broadly across securities within each asset class. The best way to do this is by investing in mutual funds, which perform the diversification for you and don't subject you to a high relative transaction cost for every purchase of a new stock (assuming you can only afford to buy small amounts of each stock).

So why do you hear so many stories about people who made a killing on one or two stocks? And why do you feel like a coward for buying and holding a few broadly diversified mutual funds?

Blame it on Gerald Loeb. Loeb was a leading Wall Street pundit in the 1930s and one of the founders of a brokerage firm that bore his name and is now part of Smith Barney, a division of Citigroup. In his 1935 book *The Battle for Investment Survival,* Loeb wrote that "diversification [is] an admission of not knowing what to do and an effort to strike an average," and that "competent investors will never be satisfied beating the average by a few small percentage points."

Loeb, we need to remember, was writing before Markowitz. But the spirit of Loeb lives on in the training materials used by brokerage firms to train their sales staffs (brokers).

Someone I know asked the plan administrator for his wife's 403(b) non-profit organization retirement account why there were no index funds available in the plan. The administrator said the reason was that index funds didn't allow the investor to beat the market.

Has this man never heard of the term "efficient market"?

The first rule of MPT is that markets are too efficient to allow any kind of "trading system" to provide long-term returns in excess of the market's overall rate of return.

One of the true beauties of an open, transparent market for securities is that, in theory at least, all investors have equal access to all information about the market and the individual securities that make up the market. That means that the "true value" of a security is, in fact, the price it has in the marketplace at that moment in time, since the price reflects the desires of all those who have the same information and what they are willing to pay to buy the security or what they are willing to receive for the sale of the security.

James Tobin, a Yale professor and Nobel Prize–winning economist, outlined this concept.

The idea behind stock trading (the foundation of most brokers' business today) is based on the notion that, for some reason, the market has "mispriced" a particular security.

Now, in truth, we do not all have equal access to information. Every investor does not spend all day long poring over market data and market information. And that's only the public data; that doesn't take into account

Times of London Investment Dartboard

In March 2002, the *Times* of London reported that a five-year-old girl from the Camberwell neighborhood of South London had won the "Pounds Fantasy" investment game. Tia Laverne Roberts chose the stocks for her portfolio at random from 100 pieces of paper each representing a company in the *Financial Times* Stock Exchange (FTSE, pronounced Footsie).

The girl's portfolio gained 5.8 percent in the year-long contest period. Her two competitors were Mark Goodson, 40, a financial analyst, whose portfolio lost 46.2 percent, and Christeen Skinner, 50, a "financial astrologer" who chooses stocks by studying the movement of the planets and lost 6.2 percent. The girl had beaten the same two contestants in a month-long competition before the year-long competition began.

During the year-long contest period, the FTSE 100 index lost 16 percent. The analyst got creamed, while the astrologer and the child beat the market.

---

the "aggressive accounting" shenanigans, insider trading, and rampant self-dealing that came to light in 2001 and 2002 about companies such as Enron, Global Crossing, WorldCom, Adelphia, or Tyco.

It is precisely the imperfection of the information average investors have that allows them to fall victim to the myth that they (or more likely a stockbroker, who somehow ought to be "in the know") can pick winners.

But markets are efficient enough so that over the long term, stock picking is a loser's game. For such "active management" of a portfolio to succeed, stock pickers must consistently predict the future based on the same public information all other investors have.

As early as 1968, academic studies of active management performed by professional mutual fund managers showed that most actively managed funds failed to match the returns of the indexes they compared themselves to. "Very little evidence [was found] that any individual [mutual] fund was able to do significantly better than that which we expected from mere random chance," wrote Michael Jensen, another University of Chicago economist, in the May 1968 *Journal of Finance* article "The Performance of 115 U.S. Equity Mutual Funds in the Period 1945–1964."

Burton Malkiel brought Markowitz, Jensen, and MPT to the masses in his 1973 book *A Random Walk Down Wall Street*. In the book, Malkiel argued somewhat tongue-in-cheek that "a blindfolded chimpanzee throwing darts at [the stock tables in] the *Wall Street Journal* can select a portfolio that performs as well as those managed by the experts." Although facetious, the point is important to you: You can do as well as your broker at "picking winners," and neither of you can probably do very well in the long term.

Since Jensen's initial look at the fallacy of stock picking, dozens of other academic studies have shown that, as would be statistically expected, the mean gross return of all actively managed mutual funds was just about the mean of the appropriate indexes the funds compared themselves to. On a net basis, of course, most funds' returns were lower than the comparative index, due to the cost of trading and the funds' other internal costs. If you add the cost of taxes on winning stock picks for taxable accounts, the results would become even worse.

Given all of this statistical proof that returns will tend to be grouped around the index mean return; that most actively managed portfolios do worse than their comparative index once costs are taken into account; that transaction costs eat up much of the gains of those portfolios that do better than the index . . . why do people continue to try to pick winners?

In his essay "The Active Versus Passive Debate: Perspectives of an Active Quant" in *Selected Topics in Equity Portfolio Management*, Robert C. Jones suggests two reasons.

One is the catch-22 argument. If the market was truly efficient, where the true value was the price, there would be no incentive to try to gather information and no profit to be gained by using that information to estimate "fair value." But if no one gathered and evaluated that information, how would price (and hence true value) change over time?

For a marketplace to exist at all, there need to be investors with "heterogeneous expectations" of what the price of a security will be in the future.

The second reason is psychology, and it gets back to Gerald Loeb. People are not perfectly rational. Behavioral psychologists have shown that people make what these psychologists call "systematic errors in judgment" and probability assessment.

Studies show that most people consider themselves to be better-than-average drivers and more than 90 percent of American men consider themselves to be better-than-average athletes. Of course, this can't be, since the average is the point at which half are better (or more) and half are worse (or less).

In short, investors (and especially brokers) seem to live in Lake Wobegon, that mythical place in northern Minnesota depicted by the radio personality Garrison Keillor where "all the women are strong, all the men are good-looking, and all the children are above average."

But at the end of the day, trying to pick winners in the stock market is nothing more than gambling. Stock markets are essentially costly casinos, where the transaction costs and taxes on any gains from trading take a larger cut than the house in Atlantic City or on a Native American reservation. As Paul Samuelson, another Nobel Prize–winning economist (this one from MIT), once said, "It is not easy to get rich in Las Vegas, at Churchill Downs, or at the local Merrill Lynch office."

The Fallacy of Picking Active Managers
By Edward S. O'Neal, Ph.D.

Imagine yourself in front of your computer at the end of June in 1998 attempting to pick an actively managed large-cap mutual fund. You decide to undertake an analysis of which funds are most likely to outperform in the future. The first step is to rank all 494 funds that are available based on their performance over the last five years. Your ranking system gives the best fund a rank of 1 and the worst fund a rank of 494. In order to make the comparison easier to digest, you measure each fund's annualized percentage return relative to the annualized percentage return of the average fund. For example, if Fund A returned 9 percent per year, and the average fund returned 13 percent per year, then the relative return of Fund A would be −4 percent. You put together the first graph.

This graph shows that the fund that was ranked number one outperformed the average fund by 14.2 percent per year! An incredible number—if only you'd had the luck or foresight to buy that fund. The fund ranked 494 underperformed the average by 15.9 percent. An even more incredible number—pity the poor saps who held that fund for the last five years.

In any case, your job now is to use this information to buy a fund for the future. You could decide to purchase the fund ranked number one. However, there may be some constraints: It may not be available in your 401(k), it may be closed to new investment, you may have to go through a broker, etc. Suffice it to say, though, that you would probably concentrate on the funds on the left-hand side of this graph. And you would expect that if we ran the same analysis for the next five-year period, those funds ranked the highest in the first five years would likely deliver better than average returns over the next five years. You'd be wrong.

How did the funds that you ranked and graphed as of June 1998 perform over the subsequent five years ended June 2003? The second graph tells the story:

Note that on this graph we still have funds ranked along the horizontal x-axis according to their earlier-period performance. Their relative performance over the subsequent period is shown on the vertical y-axis. Remember the great fund ranked number one? It under-

Relative fund performance from July 1993 through June 1998:
All large-cap mutual funds

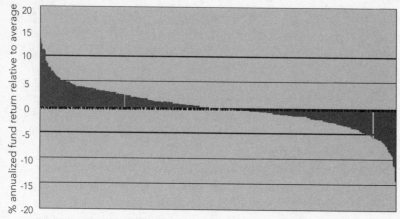

% annualized fund return relative to average

Fund ranking from July 1993 through June 1998 period

Relative fund performance from July 1998 through June 2003:
All large-cap mutual funds

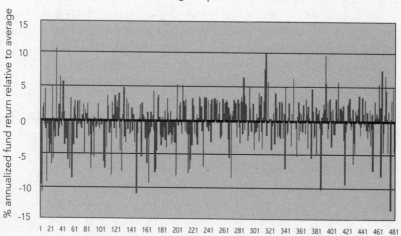

% annualized fund return relative to average

Fund ranking from July 1993 through June 1998 period

performed the average fund in the next five years. In fact, each of the top four funds from the first period underperformed the average fund in the next five years. Remember the pathetic fund number 494? It continued to stink, underperforming by an average of 8.6 percent per year over the next five years! Just a look at this graph is enough to tell you that a fund's performance over one period has absolutely no predictive power in forecasting performance over a subsequent period.

What can we take away from the analysis of this hypothetical situation? To attempt to select managers that you think are going to beat the market based on their recent performance is a fool's game. If these fund managers had skills that would allow them to outperform, the second graph would resemble, at least vaguely, the first graph. It's not even close.

What about performance against a relevant index? A second way to approach this analysis is to tabulate how frequently these large-cap fund managers are beating a large-cap stock market index. If stock picking and market timing is all a matter of luck, we would expect approximately half of all managers to beat the index and half to lose to the index in any given period. The graph at the top of the next page illustrates how funds fared against the S&P 500 index in the first five-year period.

In this period, 46 percent beat the index while 54 percent failed to beat the index. These numbers suggest that active management does not add value since fewer than half of the funds actually beat the index. The results, however, get worse for fund managers in the next period. The second graph on the next page shows the same analysis for the second five-year period, July 1998 through June 2003.

Over this period, only 8 percent of fund managers beat the S&P 500. If anything, this suggests that managers have great skill at underperforming the market.

Finally, the question should be asked, "How many managers beat the S&P 500 in both periods?" These results are sad indeed. The number of funds that beat the market in both periods is a whopping 10—or only 2 percent of all large-cap funds.

Investors, both individual and institutional, and particularly 401(k) plans, would be far better served by investing in passive or passively managed funds than by trying to pick more expensive active managers who purport to be able to beat the markets.

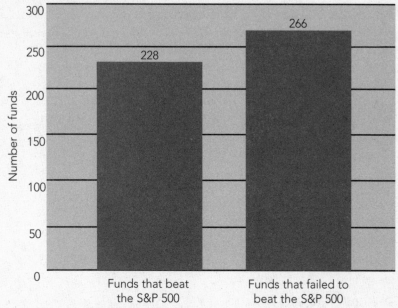

Number of funds that beat the S&P 500 in the five-year period July 1993 through June 1998

Number of funds

- 300
- 266
- 250
- 228
- 200
- 150
- 100
- 50
- 0

Funds that beat the S&P 500

Funds that failed to beat the S&P 500

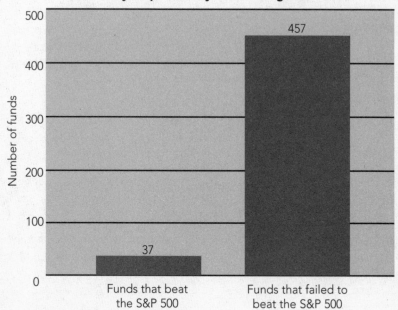

Number of funds that beat the S&P 500 in the five-year period July 1998 through June 2003

Number of funds

- 500
- 457
- 400
- 300
- 200
- 100
- 37
- 0

Funds that beat the S&P 500

Funds that failed to beat the S&P 500

TERMINOLOGY

ASSET ALLOCATION: The mix of investments among the various classes of financial assets. The goal is to create an "efficient" portfolio that provides the highest return for a given amount of risk, and reduce risk by placing portions of the portfolio in asset classes that move up and down in value in inverse relation to one another.

BETA: Beta is a measure of an investment's sensitivity to market movements. By definition, the beta of the entire stock market is 1.0. A diversified portfolio with a beta of less than 1.0 is less volatile than the market, while a beta of greater than 1.0 is more volatile.

DIVERSIFICATION: The process by which an investor can eliminate certain risks by spreading investments across asset classes and among many securities within each investment class.

EFFICIENT FRONTIER: The two-dimensional graph that shows the highest potential return from a diversified portfolio for any given level of risk an investor is willing to assume.

EFFICIENT MARKET: The efficient market concept posits that all information about a security is available to all interested parties, and that the market price of the security factors in all of that information. Hence, the "true value" of a security is, in fact, the current market price.

INDEX FUND: A stock mutual fund that holds all or substantially all of the stocks that make up a particular market index, in their appropriate weighting. Index funds are sometimes called "passive funds" because they do not seek to improve investment returns over the index's expected return through any kind of trading strategy.

MODERN PORTFOLIO THEORY (MPT): The underlying theory from which portfolio management concepts are derived: that investors seek to maximize investment return while simultaneously minimizing risk.

RISK: A measure of the probability of potential outcomes, and of the potential changes in portfolio value as a result of differences in the economic environment between now and some point in the future.

RISK PREMIUM: The excess investment return above the risk-free return an investor hopes to obtain in exchange for taking on investment risk.

RISK-FREE RETURN: The investment return available from a risk-free security, usually considered to be the rate paid on U.S. Treasury bills.

R-SQUARED: A measure of how closely the return characteristics of a security or portfolio match those of a particular market index. R-squared is measured on a scale of from 1 to 100, with 100 being closer to the market index in question. In order to properly understand the meaning of an investment's beta, you need to know how closely it correlates to its comparative index by measuring the R-squared.

SHARPE RATIO: The Sharpe ratio measures an investment's risk-adjusted return, using the investment's return minus the risk-free return as the numerator and the investment's standard deviation as the denominator.

STANDARD DEVIATION: A statistical calculation that measures the "dispersion" of all individual data points in a set from the mean (average). In the world of investments, standard deviation is a proxy for the "volatility" of a security; a security's expected return over a given period of time (e.g., annually) falls within one standard deviation above or below its average return approximately two-thirds of the time, and within two standard deviations 95 percent of the time.

7

The Solin Theories for Recovering Losses from Your Broker

After Don Zabawa was hit by a car while riding his bicycle, he turned over $125,000 to a stockbroker at FAS Wealth Management in Delray Beach, Florida, and asked him to invest the money in "safe investments," hoping to use income from the investments to support his family while he recuperated and could not work.

Unfortunately, his broker didn't heed his request.

In February 2002, an NASD arbitration panel awarded Zabawa $125,000 in damages, as well as $56,250 in attorney fees and the NASD filing and hearing fees. Zabawa had alleged in his claim that the broker, the firm's owner, and the branch manager all contributed to his loss by churning his account, placing his money in unsuitable investments, and pressuring him to buy securities on margin.

The NASD tribunal found the three individuals jointly and severally liable for the award, meaning that one individual might have to pay the entire award if the others can't or won't.

William Bernstein, author of *The Intelligent Asset Allocator* and a principal in the money management firm Efficient Frontier Advisors, has said: "There are two kinds of investors, be they large or small: those who don't know where the market is headed, and those who don't know that they don't know. Then again, there is a third type of investor—the investment professional, who indeed knows that he or she doesn't know, but whose livelihood depends upon appearing to know."

Those who manage money for pension funds and institutional endowments realize that no one knows where the market is headed. Academics know that no one knows where the market is headed. Why don't brokers know it?

Brokers Are Trained to Manage Clients, Not Portfolios

Brokers don't know these basic truths because they are not trained to know them. They are trained to sell. They are trained in cold calling and in deal closing.

Despite brokerage firm marketing, which has changed the titles under which stockbrokers work from "account executive" to "financial consultant" and "financial professional," stockbrokers are still basically salespeople.

"The firm hires us to sell stocks or bonds or whatever," says a former broker who has left the industry. "Brokers are not meant to be financial people, and that is the problem in the system."

The vast majority of brokers are not trained in how to work with a client to establish the client's realistic expectations for a portfolio's return and risk, and how to create a portfolio that tries to derive that return while maintaining that risk.

Another former broker says, "Often, the broker's failure comes from not 'listening' to the client. Understanding how a client thinks about risk versus reward is a fascinating study in human psychology. The exceptional (financial) advisor will take the time to really understand the client and assure him that you are both on the same page and speak the same language."

One former broker, in answering my question about whether she used Modern Portfolio Theory to help her clients construct portfolios, answered:

> To this day, I don't know if real asset allocation in a portfolio means large-cap, small-cap, etc., or individual sectors like technology, cyclicals, banking, etc., or if it means both.
>
> [Actually, asset allocation means allocation across the asset classes of stocks, bonds, and cash. Diversification means owning a number of different securities in one asset class, and also owning different asset classes.]
>
> As for standard deviation, etc., I worked for two [major brokerage] firms over almost five years and I can tell you what I learned

about beta and standard deviation I learned on my own by asking questions. None of that—absolutely none of that—is taught in our training. Training for a new broker goes something like this: study and take the Series 7, 63, 65, and insurance exams.

I spent three weeks in [class] learning about products, mutual funds, and learning to sell. If a broker wants to learn about [asset allocation and diversification], it has to be done on the broker's own time. Most would never take the time because for the first three to five years you are building your business.

As much as I was a student of the market, I never considered what "risk" meant because I didn't have the experience or the training to understand how volatile a market could be.

When you are young and starting out, you go where the market is hot. If you don't, you simply don't have the strength or wisdom to argue with a client about why asset allocation works. As a matter of fact, for a broker starting in the mid-'90s, asset allocation did not work. And if you are a new broker building a business, you can't afford to lose a client. I can't tell you how many times clients would say to me, "How come we don't own Amazon or Yahoo?"

Sometime in 2000, [the firm's strategist] wrote a piece on why asset allocation was dead. No kidding. Boy, did that reinforce what I already had come to believe. Boy, should that guy be fired and pay back a lot of money to my clients.

Another former stockbroker, who read the first edition of this book over Christmas 2003, sent me the following e-mail:

I was a trainee in the broker-training program [of a major brokerage firm] for approximately two years before I left. I spent Christmas reading your book and found it fascinating. You are absolutely correct in your assessment of the retail brokerage industry. My former office was no exception. I left [the company] for many of the same reasons of conflict of interest that were outlined in your book.

The type of investing I did [for my clients] was very different than the norm. I built asset-allocation models for my clients using Modern Portfolio Theory, then completed the model using ETFs [Exchange

Traded Funds]. All of my clients were explained their standard devia-
tions, as well as required rates of return to reach their objectives. Your
book simply reaffirms the type of investing that I do. Thank you.

In several parts of your book you describe the typical training process
for brokers. I think in general you gave the training programs more cred-
it than they deserve. Everything I've learned about investing I had to
learn on my own. We were told by our branch manager about the way we
should attract new dollars. This scheme is clever, but less than ethical.

We were told that one effective way of attracting new clients was to
take 1,000 names and call them with a stock recommendation; 500 of
the calls were told that the stock would go up in the next month, the
other 500 were told that the stock would go down. One month later, we
were to call the group that we were correct with and give them another
stock recommendation, also splitting this group in half. At the end of
this process we should have about 75 people that we have spoken to
four times and been correct every time. Then we were to bully those
people into opening accounts.

Once the accounts were open and money deposited, we should offer
these new clients every syndicate deal that came along. I found this un-
believable given that I was working at one of the largest, most reputable
firms in the world.

Now, I am simply fee-for-advice without conflicts of interest. What a
relief it is to be able to wake up in the morning and look forward to
going to work.

This is the training many of your "trusted advisors" receive, and the support they get from the analysts, market strategists, and other professionals in
the firm who are supposed to assist brokers to do the best they can for clients.
In reality, they are trained to do what is best for the company.

No wonder when you file an arbitration claim citing unsuitability, fraud,
misrepresentation, and/or breach of fiduciary duty, the first thing the brokerage firm does is say, "Hey, you're a grown-up, you shouldn't take what we
say that seriously that you don't use your own judgment."

I reject this argument. Brokerage firms have to come to the realization
that in the twenty-first century, with the increase in education for investors
(of which I hope this book is a major part), their very existence depends on
doing what is right for their clients.

Brokerage firms need to work harder to make sure brokers don't provide poor advice to clients. This doesn't mean that all clients will always listen to advice. After all, we all know that some people will always take less-than-prudent risks, even with their own money. But if clients expect brokers to be professionals who look after their (the clients') best interests, brokerage firms should have an obligation to provide brokers with the training they need to help clients.

Then, if a client chooses not to follow the broker's advice and later encounters a heavy loss, the firm could legitimately say, "We tried to help you, but you would not listen." Unfortunately, that is a far cry from where things are today in the brokerage industry.

Brokers, unfortunately, often don't know what they don't know; or if they do know, they don't care. And they are too lazy or too scared or too greedy to find work selling goods or services in some other industry where the standard of care is merely buyer-seller and not fiduciary.

The Solin Theories for Enhancing Your Chances of Establishing That Your Broker Does Owe You Money

So, how do you use the knowledge you gained in Chapter 5—and the understanding that by and large brokers do not use MPT in helping their clients to construct appropriate portfolios because they have no understanding of the concepts—to make a legitimate claim that your broker owes you money?

I have developed three theories under which you can proceed, and am beginning to argue these theories in arbitration proceedings, where appropriate and necessary. (Remember, there are so many brokers who engage in egregious activities [as demonstrated in Chapter 3] that you don't often need to use these theories to make a compelling case.)

A caveat: It is by no means certain that, even if these theories are persuasively argued, arbitration tribunals will accept them. The makeup of these tribunals tends to be older men, who are very set in their ways and unaccustomed to dealing with anything that they have not heard many times before. It could take a serious effort on the part of a number of investors and attorneys, and a protracted period of time, to convince some of these tribunal members that since the rest of the financial world has long since accepted these theories, they should as well.

In addition, these theories are only applicable if the broker is deemed to be your "fiduciary" (see the discussion of the fiduciary relationship in Chapter 2). So, before you can begin to argue one of the Solin theories, you need to firmly establish a foundation at the tribunal that the broker met the conditions under which he or she would be considered a fiduciary.

Theory 1: Failure to compute or disclose standard deviation, beta, or some other reasonable and well-understood measures of risk may give you a claim for unsuitability.

Let me state the obvious. It may well be that computing the standard deviation and beta of your investments will show that there is no liability. However, since stockbrokers don't understand it and don't run the calculations, a finding of no liability would be a random event. In all likelihood, given their need to generate commissions and their instinct to follow the pack into the market's "hot areas," a computation of standard deviation and beta are likely to be powerful evidence of unsuitability when they show unacceptably high levels of portfolio risk.

My experience with clients (both investors and brokers) is that it is a rare broker who has any idea that these measurements exist, let alone how to properly use them.

The failure to understand and utilize Modern Portfolio Theory (MPT) and its attendant measurements of risk is inexplicable and indefensible, since except for the brokerage industry, the entire financial and academic finance world relies so heavily on them.

In an article in the *Ohio Northern Law Review,* Robert Rapp summarizes the widespread use of MPT as follows:

"MPT is used and endorsed by many in academia, in practice, and in government. Not only is MPT used by individual investors and mutual fund managers, it has also been applied to managing consumer loans, thrift institution investments, real estate, pension investments, international investing, and for insurance companies. Thus, today MPT is a central theme to many high-level investment strategies. The prime question however is whether it can be meaningfully applied at the basic retail level and, just as importantly, whether those who sit in judgment of broker conduct can apply it."

The answer to this question is: Why not?

Every investor case I take begins with an analysis by an expert in forensic accounting and portfolio management. Part of that analysis is to run the standard deviation and beta for the portfolio. If they are out of whack, I use them as evidence of unsuitability. Why shouldn't all brokerage firm clients have the benefit of this analysis (i.e., understand the risk inherent in their portfolio) so they can avoid becoming my clients?

The key question in using standard deviation and beta as proxies for suitable or unsuitable investments is to establish thresholds that permit you to determine whether the standard deviation is indicative of unsuitability.

While each case is unique and depends on many factors specific to the individual investor(s), there is a general rule I have found useful in this analysis. A standard deviation 1.5 times the standard deviation in the market is suspicious, and a standard deviation 2.0 times the standard deviation in the market is strong evidence of the portfolio's unsuitability.

For example, for the 20-year period from 1979 to 1999, the Standard & Poor's 500 index (a proxy for the U.S. stock market) had an average annual return of 17.88 percent and an annual standard deviation of 15.35 percent. When we look at a portfolio with an R-squared that correlates well to this benchmark (as many equity portfolios do), we go on heightened alert if the standard deviation is 23 or over, and we become reasonably confident that we have a valid claim for unsuitability if the standard deviation is 30 or higher. Of course, this is the standard deviation that should apply to the portfolio in its entirety.

This is true even if the client needed or desired the risk of an all-equity portfolio. An all-equity portfolio just isn't an appropriate portfolio for most clients. But I am at least trying to be somewhat conservative.

This does not mean that brokers should not or cannot recommend "risky" investments to clients. Remember that we are looking at the standard deviation and beta of the client's entire portfolio, not just individual investments.

One thing MPT illustrates to investors is that you can add a risky investment or class of investments to a portfolio and actually reduce the portfolio's overall risk. So it is all right to add securities that are, in and of themselves, very risky, so long as they don't cause the entire portfolio to become overly risky. This is accomplished by making sure the risky security has a less-than-perfect correlation with the rest of the portfolio, and the investment in the risky security is of the proper proportion and does not cause the portfolio to become overconcentrated.

However, few brokers understand this concept, and even fewer implement it successfully within client portfolios.

The same is true with beta. Again, assuming a correlation with the S&P

500, there are many investors (like most widows, disabled people, retirees, and others who cannot easily replace losses) who have portfolios on which the beta should be significantly less than 1. For investors with a capacity for greater risk, it might well be that a beta as high as 1.25 would be appropriate, as long as the investor knows that his or her portfolio is 25 percent more volatile than the S&P 500.

A beta of 1.5 or higher is a cause for concern and would lead me to believe that the portfolio's volatility may well be too great for the investor to bear. If this is the case, the investor (who in all likelihood was never informed of the beta or its significance) may have a valid claim for unsuitability against the broker and the brokerage firm for any losses incurred by the portfolio.

The bottom line is that since these risk tools are validated by overwhelming Nobel Prize–winning academic research and used by virtually every professional manager of institutional funds, your broker's failure to advise you of them and use them on your behalf (or at least explain them to you so you can make an informed decision) may well give you the keys to the arbitration forum door.

Theory 2: Failure to disclose that there is no data indicating that brokers or anyone else can consistently time the market or pick winners may give you a claim for fraud under Rule 10(b)-5, misrepresentation, or breach of fiduciary duty.

Brokers can't time the market or pick stocks any better than you can. It has been proven time and again through rigorous academic research. Extensive study has shown that asset allocation accounts for over 90 percent of portfolio behavior, while market timing and security selection together account for about 7 percent of the behavior.

The evidence of the efficiency of markets and the inability of anyone to successfully and consistently pick winners is so overwhelming that it is a mystery why brokers continue to be successful in convincing their clients that they (or the firm's analysts, market strategists, and economists) can do so.

When I say no one can successfully and consistently pick winners, I always get the question: What about Peter Lynch (who managed Fidelity's Magellan Fund so successfully for years) or Warren Buffett? What I mean is that, statistically, the number of people who "beat the market" for any period of time (one year, five years, ten years) is, according to all research, about the number you would expect mathematically to do so purely by random chance.

If more people could beat the indexes and consistently pick winners than you would mathematically expect, you would think it would be those highly paid professionals who make decisions for mutual funds that invest hundreds of millions of dollars. Yet numerous studies have shown that the majority of mutual funds underperform their relevant benchmark index each year. One comprehensive study of pension fund managers (whom you would assume would be extremely sophisticated managers) concluded that "pension fund equity managers seem to subtract rather than add value relative to the performance of the Standard & Poor's 500 index."

Yet brokers (most of whom do not have the background or experience that would permit them to be hired by a mutual fund, much less manage a portfolio of hundreds of millions of dollars) make the claim every day that they can choose the right stocks for your portfolio to outperform the market.

They do this without weighing the risks of these individual securities for their client portfolios. They do it without understanding the dispersion of possible returns (the standard deviation) the investment might generate, or how the particular security's standard deviation might affect the portfolio's overall volatility. And they do it without any support whatsoever that they have the ability to do so with any consistency.

Brokers pick up the phone and make recommendations to their clients to buy specific securities for specific reasons.

As one former broker puts it:

> *Here is how it goes. You come out of training, you are inundated with stock reports, mutual fund wholesalers, products out of the behind.*
>
> *How do you choose? Then, after a few years, oh my God here come the charts and graphs. The whole thing is a never-ending game, and it is a game no broker can ever really win for very long.*
>
> *How do we decide what to do? Well, I would pick the [mutual fund] manager who had the best track record and do large-cap growth, mid-cap growth/value, etc. . . . until a few years went by and I realized the best track record means nothing for the future and the stocks in my mid-cap fund had all grown to be large-cap so I wasn't really allocating anything.*
>
> *I would read my stock reports (believe me, no matter how you understand the bias, even the most seasoned brokers believed them) and buy a bunch of stock . . . mostly in technology because CNBC said the*

Nasdaq was going to catch up with the Dow and [the firm's market strategist] told me asset allocation was dead anyhow.

But no one told us when to sell. We all sat there just watching and believing things couldn't fall the way they fell because they never had before. No one told us because our job is to sell. How could we do our job if we sat in cash? Most seasoned brokers, well, their accounts didn't look much better than mine.

If you knew that this was how your broker was going to carry out research, pick stocks, and time the market to try to help you manage your portfolio, would you invest with him or her?

Theory 3: Failure to disclose that the overwhelming academic/historical data indicate that passive funds with low expense ratios typically perform better over time than actively managed funds may give you a claim for fraud (Rule 10[b]-5), misrepresentation, or breach of fiduciary duty.

Don't let actively managed funds make you passive about recovering your losses from your broker.

The sum of all the buyers and all the sellers in the market is, de facto, "the market."

The mathematical laws of probability and large numbers say that over time and a large number of transactions, the mean expected return will be, you guessed it, about the mean return of the Standard & Poor's 500, which is most often used as the proxy for the U.S. stock market.

In any one year, some investors, mutual fund managers, and investment managers can and do "beat the market" in terms of gross returns. But, after you factor out management costs (for funds), transaction costs, bid-ask spreads, and finally the taxes on any gains taken (especially short-term gains from trading, which are taxed at your ordinary-income tax rate and not the long-term capital gains rate), it becomes that much harder to actually have a net return higher than the market average. And as you extend the time horizon over which this performance is measured, it becomes even harder.

Let's look at the math:

1. The mean return on all stock portfolios is essentially the S&P 500 return (about 11 to 12 percent a year historically since the Second World War).

2. The returns of all investors fall in a bell-shaped curve (and, since this is a very large sample, it should be close to a "normal" or perfect bell curve).

3. The standard deviation of these returns for a one-year period is 8 percent. (This means that about one-third of investors earn between the mean and 8 percent less than the mean (between about 4 and 12 percent in real terms); another one-third earn between the mean and 8 percent more (between 12 and 20 percent); another one-sixth earn a return less than the mean minus 8 percent (less than 4 percent); and the final one-sixth earn a return greater than the mean plus 8 percent (above 20 percent).

This assumption of a perfect bell curve, where 50 percent of all portfolios beat the market each year, is actually a bit generous. Academic studies of mutual fund managers show that about 45 percent of actively managed mutual funds actually beat the market in any given year. But I'm willing to be generous in order to simplify the equation, smooth the bell curve, and make two important points—the first about cost and the second about beating the market over time.

First, if the average cost-equity ratio for an actively traded account or mutual fund is 2 percent, the number of investors and managers who "beat the market" on a net-cost basis is greatly reduced, probably to about 25 percent of all actively managed funds.

Do you like those odds?

Imagine that your broker had said to you, "Mathematically, you have about a one-in-four chance of beating the market net of your costs this year through a strategy of active stock trading or buying actively traded mutual funds."

Do you think you can be in the 25 percent of all investors who beat the market this year (either making your own investment decisions, allowing your broker to recommend stocks, or buying actively managed funds)? Maybe you do. Maybe you live in Lake Wobegon, with all the other strong women, good-looking men, and above-average children. And remember, if your portfolio costs go from 2 to 4 percent (which can easily happen if you use a broker and actively trade individual stocks), your mathematical chances of beating the market go to maybe 15 percent.

But there's a second piece to what your broker would have had to say to you in order to be truthful, since, to use the mutual fund industry's standard disclaimer, "past performance is no guarantee of future results."

"Oh, and by the way, the odds of doing it two years in a row are much less—and the odds of doing it for 10 years running are infinitesimal." (Actually, statistically, without factoring in any costs, the odds of beating the market 10 years running are about 10 percent.)

Would you have invested that way?

Why don't they disclose this? Let's listen again to what one former broker has to say:

> *If a client wanted to buy an index fund . . . he or she certainly could. Of course, if a client wanted to buy an index fund, what good would a broker be? A client could go to Vanguard and buy it a lot cheaper. [My firm] had some index funds, as I am sure all firms do.*
>
> *No one showed us the difference between index and actively managed funds. A few years ago, you could show a client an example of the Fidelity Magellan fund where the active manager hands down beat the indexes.*
>
> *Honestly, no one ever asked me about index funds (until the market began to fall apart in 2000), and the reason probably was that if people come to a broker, they want to do better than an index. I would have offered no value in a client's eyes if I said, "Hey, let's use indexes."*

Remember the discussion in Chapter 2 about brokers having a fiduciary duty to their clients?

Doesn't this mean they have an obligation to you to disclose the overwhelming data that support the superior long-term returns of low-cost index funds over higher-cost actively managed funds sold by brokers to their clients?

Doesn't this mean they have an obligation to you to disclose that 50 percent or more of assets in U.S. pension funds are invested passively (i.e., buying and holding all of the stocks in a group of indexes, or index mutual funds)?

Significantly, the standard for other fiduciaries—those who manage trust accounts—supports the view that the failure to disclose these facts violates this fiduciary duty.

Investment of trust assets is governed in many states by the Prudent Investor Rule, issued by the American Law Institute. In 1995, the Uniform Prudent Investor Act was adopted by many states. This act sets forth the guidelines that should be followed by estate-planning attorneys, trustees, and investment advisors who make decisions for hundreds of millions of dollars in trust assets. The Reporter's Notes to the Prudent Investor Rule state the following:

Economic evidence shows that, from a typical investment perspective, the major capital markets of this country are highly efficient, in the sense that available information is rapidly digested and reflected in the market prices of securities. As a result, fiduciaries and other investors are confronted with potent evidence that the application of expertise, investigation, and diligence in efforts to beat the market in these publicly traded securities ordinarily promises little or no payoff, or even a negative payoff after taking account of research and transaction costs. Empirical research supporting the theory of efficient markets reveals that in such markets skilled professionals have rarely been able to identify underpriced securities (that is, to outguess the market with respect to future return) with any regularity. In fact, evidence shows that there is little correlation between fund managers' earlier successes and their ability to produce above-market returns in subsequent periods.

Translation: There is no one, including your broker, who can demonstrate that he or she can beat the market with any consistency, notwithstanding all of their research and diligence in an effort to do so. What's worse, fund managers have no greater success than individual brokers. Therefore, from a purely economic point of view, you would be better off with low-cost index funds. No doubt it is for this reason that the majority of all trust accounts are invested in index funds, aggregating hundreds of billions of dollars.

If these are the standards that govern the management of trust funds in many states, and if this is the way smart, sophisticated money is invested, is there any reason why your broker, who is also a fiduciary (or, at the very least, holds him- or herself out as your "trusted advisor" and "financial consultant"), should not disclose these undeniable facts to you so you can decide whether or not to invest in the same manner?

If your broker has sold you actively managed funds without disclosing these facts to you, I can think of no reason why you should not be able to recover your losses from him or her.

So, Does Your Broker Owe You Money?

I have often said that I believe a very large percentage of all investors have valid claims against their brokers and brokerage firms, if they choose to pursue them. The reason I say this is because the use of one of these three theories can vastly extend the range of broker conduct worthy of your filing a claim for relief where you have lost money in your investments.

In January 2002, I used the list-serve of the Public Investor Arbitration Bar Association (PIABA) to poll my colleagues on what percentage of people who inquire about the option of filing a claim have a legitimate claim. The results were quite stunning.

Of the 54 responses I received, more than two-thirds (37 respondents) said 40 percent or fewer potential clients have a claim. One respondent said only 5 percent have a claim, and an astounding 14 said only 10 percent have claims. Only five respondents (about 10 percent) believed that 70 percent or more of their potential clients have a claim.

Now, I must admit this was a nonscientific, one-question pop survey, and some of those who responded made it clear that their responses indicated how many clients they believe have a "winnable" claim as opposed to a legitimate claim. Others made it clear that many potential clients have a legitimate claim, but that their losses are too small to make it economically viable for an attorney to take such a case on a contingency-fee basis.

But I'm convinced many attorneys who practice in this area still believe that any claim without a clearly fraudulent practice is not a legitimate claim, or at least not one that is likely to get a favorable response from an arbitration tribunal. I'm equally convinced that if attorneys educated themselves about MPT and its uses as an offensive tool in investor arbitration proceedings, and properly presented the overwhelming data on these issues to a tribunal, we could, over time, get arbitration tribunals to accept the argument.

What does this all mean for you?

What I am saying is that, yes, there are a number of traditional theories under which you can recover money from your broker if he or she has committed a clear fraud or violation of the professional standards of one of the self-regulating organizations such as the NASD (formerly the National Association of Securities Dealers) or the New York Stock Exchange (NYSE).

However, historically, these traditional theories have affected only a small fraction of investors who have lost money in the stock market. But now, with the wide dissemination of knowledge about MPT, and with the ability of every investor (even those with modest portfolios) to find professional money managers who use MPT to their clients' advantage, the brokerage industry must begin using it as well.

When you add these new theories to the traditional theories, the vast majority of investors who have lost money in the largest market downturn in history (in terms of cumulative value lost from investment portfolios, over $7 trillion from March 2000 until the end of 2002, when the stock markets began to move up again) have a possibility of collecting some of that lost wealth from brokers and brokerage firms.

These theories provide vast numbers of investors with the keys to the arbitration hearing-room door, and the opportunity to recover their market losses from those who mislead them (either deliberately or out of ignorance) or who actively place them in investments that can be proved mathematically to be too risky (too volatile) for their investment objectives and risk tolerance.

These theories can (and should) be as significant for investors seeking to recover their losses from brokers and brokerage firms as Modern Portfolio Theory was for the world of finance. They would be of even greater import if they could be presented to an impartial tribunal or tried in a court of law before a jury of your peers.

8 Mandatory Arbitration— A National Disgrace

I represent a group of immigrants who were convinced by a broker for a second-tier brokerage firm that he had figured out a day-trading "system." They each invested a modest amount—$5,000—in a pooled account. In the 2½ months the broker managed their account, he turned it over at an annualized rate of 173 times and generated so much commission income for his firm that my clients would have had to earn 31 percent a year just to break even.

While the case seemed like the proverbial slam dunk, even before an NASD arbitration tribunal, this was not to be.

During the hearing, the "nonpublic" arbitrator—an individual chosen from within the securities industry—a man who was himself a broker at another firm, was openly hostile to my clients. Worse yet, the chairman of the tribunal, one of the two "public" arbitrators chosen because they supposedly don't have a connection to the securities industry, shared this hostility.

On doing some investigation of the panel chairman, we found that he had made some significant omissions in his arbitrator profile. We brought this to the attention of the director of arbitration of the NASD and asked that the chairman be disqualified. Our application was denied. Prior to our learning of the chairman's omissions, the other public arbitrator had resigned due to ill health, and we had agreed to proceed with only two arbitrators.

With nothing to lose, I petitioned the New York Supreme Court, which rarely intervenes in pending arbitration matters. The court refused to intervene, but in a stinging rebuke to the NASD director of arbitration wrote: "This court firmly suggests that the NASD reconsider its position as it is clear that the disclosure document was wrong, and therefore, the NASD itself may have induced petitioners to make an improvident decision. The NASD should make every effort to ensure that the integrity of its arbitration decisions is beyond reproach."

With few practical options, the director of arbitration disqualified the chairman but refused to disqualify the industry arbitrator. Two new arbitrators were appointed. But the new arbitrators refused to start the hearings again; instead, they said they would rely on the tape recordings of the previous hearing sessions. The obviously biased industry arbitrator again refused to disqualify himself.

Faced with this clearly rigged tribunal, I refused to participate in any further proceedings. The tribunal issued a decision finding no liability. I have petitioned the New York Supreme Court to vacate the decision. I can only hope that this sheds some public light on the biased mandatory arbitration system.

On March 17, 2004, the U.S. House Subcommittee on Capital Markets, Insurance, and Government-Sponsored Enterprises held hearings on the fairness of the mandatory arbitration system imposed on all investors who deal with NASD or NYSE brokerage firms. I testified at these hearings, as did William Frances Galvin, the highly regarded Massachusetts Secretary of the Commonwealth. Mr. Galvin's testimony was chilling:

> The term "arbitration" as it is used in these proceedings is a misnomer. Most often, this process is not about two evenly matched parties to a dispute seeking the middle ground and a resolution to their conflict from knowledgeable, independent and unbiased fact finders. Rather, what we have in America today is an industry-sponsored damage containment and control program masquerading as a juridical proceeding.

Welcome to the world of mandatory securities arbitration. It is a system that takes away two fundamental rights of American citizens: access to the courtroom and to a trial by a jury of their peers. Investor plaintiffs in this system are in the position a criminal prosecutor would be in if trials were before juries of three, and one member had to be a convicted felon.

It is a world of almost complete autonomy for the arbitrators, who hold their hearings behind closed doors, with the public barred. The arbitrators have no obligation to explain the reasoning behind their decisions, and they rarely do so. It is exceedingly difficult to overturn their decisions on appeal.

Only approximately 17 percent of the panel members for the NASD (formerly the National Association of Securities Dealers) are women and very few are minorities. A 1994 study conducted by the U.S. General Accounting Office (GAO, since renamed the Government Accountability Office) found that 89 percent of securities arbitrators were white men over the age of 60. The same study found that 97 percent of the arbitrators whose race could be ascertained were white, 0.9 percent were black, 0.6 percent were Asian, and 1 percent were "other"—hardly representative of a cross section of Americans.

The pool of arbitrators eligible to serve on arbitration tribunals is carefully screened and appointed by the director of arbitration of either the NASD or the New York Stock Exchange (NYSE). Each organization's director is an employee of the organization, and his continued employment depends upon a favorable assessment of his performance by higher-ups within these industry-controlled self-regulatory organizations (SROs).

The director of arbitration has significant power over the process, which includes not only the initial screening and appointment of arbitrators deemed qualified to serve on these tribunal panels, but also decisions concerning whether adjournments should be granted and whether or not an arbitrator should be disqualified for bias.

As I found out in the case involving my immigrant clients, refusal by the director to disqualify an obviously biased arbitrator can have a devastating effect on an investor seeking a fair hearing.

Similarly, the classification of an arbitrator as "public" or "nonpublic" (a euphemism for a person strongly affiliated with the securities industry who is unlikely to have any sympathy for the plight of all but those investors who have been the victims of really outrageous broker misconduct) is left to the discretion of the director. In my experience, many "nonpublic" arbitrators are a lost cause when it comes to fairness in evaluating claims against brokerage firms, and even some "public" arbitrators are really wolves in sheep's clothing, with a strong pro-industry, anti-investor bias.

Moreover, for a large number of public and nonpublic arbitrators alike, serving on these tribunals represents a welcome break from endless golf outings and is a significant retirement perk, as well as a nice source of supplemental income. These arbitrators fully understand that a history of anti-industry awards, or even a few large awards, may be enough to cause them to fail to be selected for future panels by attorneys representing brokerage firms, even if they remain on the list of eligible arbitrators. If an arbitrator gets on the bad side of the relatively few defense firms that handle matters for the brokerage firms, his career as an arbitrator, with all of its attendant perks, will quickly end. As a consequence, even when investors prevail and obtain an award, they often are given only a fraction of their otherwise compensable losses.

Adding insult to injury, investors pay a hefty premium for the privilege of giving up their constitutional rights and submitting to this unfair system. A study by Public Citizen published in April 2002 demonstrated that the cost of arbitration in general is almost always higher than the cost of instituting a lawsuit, thereby undermining one of the most frequently cited benefits of arbitration. The authors singled out securities arbitration as an example of how expensive it can be for plaintiffs seeking redress through the arbitration process.

The study pointed out that, because investors are required to submit their claims to either the NASD or the NYSE, these organizations have a monopoly on the process and can pretty much set their fees at any level they choose, without being concerned about the fees of competitors for this business.

The study documented two cases to illustrate this point. In the first case, the investor was awarded damages of $23,750, but the total cost to the parties to resolve the dispute was $19,300, of which the NASD assessed the investor a whopping $7,500.

In the second case, the investor's dispute was resolved before a hearing was held, but the NASD still billed the investor $4,000 for eight hearing sessions that were scheduled but never held.

I believe this system is a national scandal. Others are starting to agree.

The spectacle of Richard Grasso, the chairman of the NYSE, receiving a $140 million pay package was too much for even the usual apologists of the system to defend. As a quasi-regulatory organization, the NYSE has broad disciplinary powers over its members. In addition, it runs the NYSE's security arbitration program. As the tawdry facts came to light, it turned out that some of the members of the compensation committee who approved Grasso's obscene compensation were officers of brokerage firms under active investigation by the NYSE. This obvious, shocking conflict of interest caused Grasso to resign and raised cries from the investing public and members of Congress for a complete overhaul of the NYSE.

In a December 30, 2003, story on the events leading to Grasso's ouster, a team of *Wall Street Journal* reporters noted the frustration of the former NYSE chief of arbitration, Robert Clemente. While the number of arbitrations filed with the NYSE roughly doubled from 2000 to 2002, Clemente said, his budget remained flat. While the NYSE's marketing offices looked like "The Rainbow Room" restaurant, Clemente told the *Journal*, his offices resembled "a hot-dog stand."

"Each year I went and asked for more resources and more money and each year they said no," Clemente told the *Journal*. Clemente was eased out of his job in October 2003, shortly after Grasso's resignation as chairman and chief executive.

The overhaul of the NYSE should include removing the NYSE and the NASD from any involvement in the arbitration process. (The NASD has taken the first step, carving out NASD Regulation—NASDR—as a separate entity, so that those who run operations of the marketplace for Nasdaq stocks are not the same people as those who manage the investigations of member firms or individuals. But this is not enough; the system of investor arbitration should be removed entirely from the umbrella of NYSE and NASD.)

However, there are hopeful signs that even if this system remains in place, some courts may simply refuse to enforce mandatory arbitration clauses. In the most significant of these rulings, the Supreme Court of Montana held that a broker with Edward D. Jones & Co. failed to explain the significance of the arbitration clause to his client, a 95-year-old widow. The court found that it would be unjust to deprive this client of her constitutional rights of access to the court process and a denial of a jury trial under these circumstances.

Another court, this one in Alabama, viewing the practice of inserting mandatory arbitration clauses in a wide range of consumer agreements, pulled no punches in showing its disdain for this practice:

> *Ask any reasonable man on the street, i.e., a consumer, if he thinks it is fair that he is barred from access to the courts when he has a claim based on a form contract which contains an arbitration clause and he will respond with a resounding "No!" . . . The reality that the average consumer frequently loses his/her constitutional rights and right of access to the court when he/she buys a car, a household appliance, insurance policy, receives medical attention or gets a job rises as a putrid odor which is overwhelming the body politic.*

Investors who have been victimized by broker misconduct should not be revictimized by this mandatory arbitration system. It is impossible to understand why Congress and the SEC do not require that investors be given the option of arbitrating their disputes before a totally neutral tribunal, with the arbitration administered by an impartial organization like the American Arbitration Association, or going to court and having their grievance resolved by a jury of their peers.

At least one member of Congress has been convinced of the lack of impartiality of the NASD and the NYSE for quite some time. Testifying before the Senate Banking, Housing and Urban Affairs Committee on July 31, 1998, on the issue of mandatory arbitration agreements in employee contracts in the securities industry, Representative Edward Markey (D-MA) said: "At best, such a setting has the appearance of unfairness; at worst, it is a tainted forum in which an employee can never be guaranteed a truly fair hearing. Like forcing employees to buy goods at the company store, the price of such so-called justice is just too high."

Subsequent to this testimony, both the NASD and the NYSE changed their rules. The NYSE now requires arbitration of discrimination cases only when the parties involved agree to arbitrate after the dispute occurs. The NASD will arbitrate employment discrimination cases based on agreements entered into between employees and firms before or after a dispute occurs. All claims made by investors, however, are still subject to mandatory arbitration administered by these industry organizations.

It seems indefensible that the mandatory arbitration system is so tainted that some protection from the process is deemed necessary for victims of discrimination, yet it remains in place to resolve all disputes of aggrieved investors whose hard-earned savings have been plundered by their brokers.

I can only hope that investors are so mad that they will not take it anymore and will write their Congressional representatives and the SEC and insist that the mandatory arbitration system be abolished and that investors be guaranteed a right to a fair hearing of their disputes with their brokers. You may be assured that the securities lobbyists are hard at work in the halls of Congress. The voice of the people has been no match for them so far.

Of course, the best recourse for investors would be not to do business with brokers at all, following the investment principles I have set forth in earlier chapters. This is the surefire way to avoid becoming twice victimized—first by the broker and then by the biased mandatory arbitration system.

9 Making Your Claim: Alone or with a Lawyer

In March of 2001, an NASD arbitration panel awarded over $500,000 to Elizabeth Sipe Bartolini in her claim against her former brother-in-law, Martin Smith, and his brokerage firm, World Securities. The tribunal found that Smith and World committed fraud in obtaining $300,000 from Bartolini, the proceeds from her late husband's life insurance policy.

Bartolini was not the only investor Smith and his business partner, Gregory Fears, allegedly fleeced. Working out of Joplin, Missouri, starting in 1992, the two formed three corporations: an investment firm called Ozark Financial, the brokerage firm World Securities, and a hedge fund called World Capital Management. Then Smith and Fears went about persuading retirees and elderly widows to let the two men invest their money for them.

Telling their would-be investors that they would invest the money in conservative investments such as Treasury bonds, the two actually put the money into risky stocks and private businesses such as hotels and car dealerships, most of which went bankrupt.

The two pled guilty to criminal charges ranging from securities fraud to wire fraud, bank fraud, and tax fraud in U.S. District Court in Fort Smith, Arkansas, in late 2001.

Smith and Fears set up living trusts for each of their clients, which gave the pair complete control over the clients' money. Under the trust arrangements, Smith and Fears had no obligation to provide any reporting to their clients.

The SEC began investigating the scheme in 1997 and was later joined by the FBI, the IRS, and the Missouri Attorney General's office. Among the victims was the widow of one of the earliest store managers for the Wal-Mart chain, who was bilked out of $59 million by the pair. A number of victims have filed civil suits in state court seeking to recoup their losses.

Now that you understand a little about the potential claims you might have against a broker and/or brokerage firm for your investment losses, it is time to make a decision. Actually, it is time to make three decisions.

The first decision is whether you want to file a claim for arbitration. To properly weigh this decision, it's important to understand what arbitration is. It is a method by which people knowledgeable in the area(s) of controversy resolve conflicts between two or more parties without resorting to litigation in court. Arbitration and its cousin, mediation, are often referred to as "alternative dispute resolution" mechanisms.

The second decision, if you do want to file a claim, is whether you want to hire an attorney to represent you in that claim, or whether you want to handle the claim yourself. These two questions are the subjects of this chapter.

The third decision, again assuming that you want to file a claim, is: Against whom do you file the claim? That is the subject of Chapter 10.

As with all decisions, you need to weigh the potential rewards of taking action against the costs involved (in money, time, and the emotional toll it will take on you) in taking that action. In the case of securities arbitration, if you decide to pursue the claim, you have to weigh the costs of engaging an attorney against the potential advantages an attorney could bring.

Potential Rewards of Filing a Claim

The largest potential reward of filing a claim for arbitration is that you may recover part or all of the money you lost in the market because of your broker's misconduct. In rare cases, it may even be possible to recover more than the amount you actually lost.

A claim is a demand for money or some other relief from a person or organization who has done harm to you in some way. It is sometimes possible to recover more than your out-of-pocket losses in appropriate cases, because the arbitration tribunal has the ability to compute your damages in such a way that you not only recover your actual losses, but you receive any gains your portfolio would have earned if it had been managed prudently. (I'll discuss computation of damages in detail in Chapter 12.)

If the broker's or firm's misdeeds were especially egregious, you may even be able to receive punitive damages—damages assessed by the tribunal as punishment and to deter future misconduct—above your actual damages. You should know, however, that punitive damages are rarely granted in securities arbitration.

Finally, the tribunal has the power (which is also rarely exercised) to grant as part of the award payment of your filing fees, arbitration costs, and even your attorney's fees. (You can expect to pay an attorney between 33 and 40 percent of any award received at arbitration or any settlement.)

Costs of Filing a Claim

The costs of filing a claim include more than just money. In addition to financial costs, there are also costs in terms of your time and your emotional energy. These should not be discounted.

Any kind of legal dispute takes time, includes much frustration, and can be emotionally taxing. Securities arbitration claims generally take between 12 and 18 months to work their way through the system. Smaller claims often get moved on a "fast track" and are decided in less than one year, and complex cases can take two years or more. This is still generally faster than moving civil suits through the federal or state court systems.

During the pre-hearing process known as discovery, you will be asked to provide all kinds of documentation to the attorney(s) representing the broker and/or firm. Some of these required documents involve very detailed information about your personal finances. (I'll discuss the discovery process in more detail in Chapter 11.)

If the dispute reaches an arbitration tribunal and you testify, you will undergo questioning by those attorneys that seek to shift the blame for your market losses onto you, and seek to position you as a predator trying to harass an innocent stockbroker simply trying to make a living. (The hearing itself is the subject of Chapter 12.)

There are also out-of-pocket cash costs to pursuing a claim before an NASD or New York Stock Exchange (NYSE) tribunal. Initially, both organizations charge filing fees and a hearing deposit. Total initial fees charged by the NYSE can range from $45 for claims under $1,000 to $1,800 for claims over $5 million. Initial fees at the NASD range from $75 for claims under $1,000 to $2,250 for claims between $5 and $10 million.

In addition, the arbitrators can assess additional hearing and forum fees against the customer or the brokerage firm, based on the length of the hearings. These fees can be substantial.

You may also incur costs for the services of expert witnesses to analyze your account statements and testify at the hearings. Expert fees vary widely, depending on who they are and how much time they spend. In my experience, expert fees usually run over $2,500, and I have had cases involving extensive expert testimony where the fees have exceeded $20,000.

These fees and related costs deter many customers from pursuing claims against brokerage firms. This seems patently unfair, since the brokerage firms require their customers to agree to arbitration and give up the right to sue in court (and thus their right to a jury trial) as a condition of opening an account. The U.S. Supreme Court has expressed some concern over this issue, hinting that arbitration clauses that impose a heavy financial burden on a party may not be enforceable.

Finally, you will have to pay your attorneys, if you are successful, a contingency fee that usually ranges from 33 to 40 percent of the total award. If the tribunal awards attorney's fees, punitive damages, or both, the amount of such an award is typically added to the award intended to reimburse you for your losses, with the attorney getting the amount agreed to in the contingency-fee arrangement from the total award.

Ultimately, you have to decide if the investment you must make to pursue your claim is a prudent one. As a guideline, annual statistics made available by the NASD show that customers prevail in approximately 43 percent of cases decided in its arbitration forums. However, even when customers prevail, they are frequently awarded only a portion of the damages they sought to recover.

These odds should first cause you to question whether making a claim is prudent; but more importantly, they should cause you to think seriously about accepting any reasonable settlement offer that may be forthcoming. (The topic of settlements is discussed in detail in Chapter 11.)

Potential Rewards of Using an Attorney

If you decide to go forward with a claim, you then need to determine if you want professional representation. I believe it is becoming almost imperative for an investor to be represented by an attorney (and that's not just because I make my living representing investors).

While the securities arbitration process is an "informal" dispute resolution model, since it became "the" method of settling client/broker claims, it has come to look more and more like courtroom litigation. If brokers and firms are unable (or unwilling) to settle before a tribunal is impaneled, they throw a lot of legal muscle into the process.

And in the pre-hearing phase, if an attorney representing a broker or firm knows he or she faces an investor acting pro se (without counsel), the attorney is likely to see this as an opportunity to squash the investor by engaging in every stalling tactic available and burying the investor in a blizzard of legal paperwork.

The 1992 GAO report found that investors who were represented by attorneys prevailed in about 58 percent of all arbitration cases. (The report studied arbitrations at the NASD and the NYSE, as well as the American Stock Exchange and the Chicago Board Options Exchange. It also found that investors represented by an attorney were 1.6 times more likely to receive an award in excess of 60 percent of their claim than were investors who represented themselves at the hearings.)

Nevertheless, there are some distinct advantages to pursuing a claim without counsel. If a claim is less than $25,000, it does not make economic sense to pay counsel to handle it. Indeed, this may be true for larger claims as well, up to as much as $50,000. In addition, if you decide to pursue a case on your own, you will find that both the NASD and the NYSE provide useful guidance to investors representing themselves. You may also find that the arbitrators themselves will bend over backwards to be helpful to an investor who is outgunned by the brokerage firm's professional counsel.

While the decision on whether to use an attorney is based on many factors, if a claim is large enough (involving losses in excess of $50,000), you should give serious consideration to the benefits an attorney experienced in securities arbitration can provide.

COSTS OF USING AN ATTORNEY

As I've said, attorneys represent investors in arbitration work almost exclusively on a contingency-fee basis. This means there is no legal fee paid to the attorney unless you receive payment of an award based on your claim. However, some attorneys handle these cases on a straight hourly basis or a hybrid basis, where they cap their hourly fees and accept a lower contingency fee.

However, many attorneys, including me, insist before taking a case that an expert in the securities industry perform an analysis of the potential client's account(s) to see whether there is a valid basis for a claim. As brokerage firm lawyers are fond of saying, "Not every loss means there is a claim."

In the box below is a sample report from a forensic account analyst. This is a template of the report I routinely receive from the expert I use to analyze all possible claims for prospective clients.

This report computes profits and losses in the account, analyzes the account(s)' asset flows, turnover, and cost-equity ratio (looking for potential churning and unsuitability claims), and compares the performance of the account to the relevant index.

The report also computes the portfolio's volatility and risk, using standard deviation and beta calculations as discussed in Chapter 6. Based on the results in the report, it is fairly easy for me to determine if there is a claim worth pursuing.

Daniel R. Solin Esq.
Address

Dear Mr. Solin,

Per your request, we have completed an initial review of the multiple brokerage account statements you provided for Mr. & Mrs. Smith. This report examines the investments made on behalf of Mr. & Mrs. Smith for the period of March 2000 through May 2001 (one account was examined through June 2001). It seeks to determine the performance of the accounts over this time frame. Our report is based solely upon the information you provided to our office for analysis.

I. Factual Overview

We analyzed monthly/quarterly brokerage statements for five separate accounts for the period March 2000 through May 2001. The five (type of accounts; e.g., cash, margin, IRA, Keogh, wrap, etc.) were handled by (brokerage firm, Inc.). A copy of the Margin Account Application dated May 11, 2001, indicates the Smiths' annual income was in excess of $100,000, liquid asset holdings of approximately $60,000, and approximate net worth of $750,000.

The records provided to our office indicate that Mr. & Mrs. Smith signed a client agreement with (brokerage firm, Inc.) on February 12, 1999. The agreement indicates the account had a negotiated wrap fee of 1.25 percent on the first $500,000, with a $750 minimum annual fee. In January 2000, the Smiths signed a separate replacement client agreement illustrating an applicable fee of 2 percent annually, allowing for 25 free annual trades.

The Smiths signed three separate, but basically identical, Investment Policy Statements indicating their general investment objective and risk tolerance as growth, expecting to earn an average nominal rate of return of 12 percent (9 percent over inflation), and a client understanding that an appropriate target mix of assets would be 100 percent domestic equities. The statement for the Smiths' main account (#XXX-XXXX) showed three separate investment objectives: growth, short-term growth, and speculation.

The attached analysis reviews the monthly asset flows and monthly profit/loss, and analyzes account performance as compared to the Center for Research in Security Prices (CRSP) 1-10 All Equity Index (the comparison index) for each account. We have summarized the results.

II. Monthly Asset Flows

An examination of the time frame mentioned above indicated that $88,539.17 was deposited in cash and/or securities during the periods examined. The records examined indicate a total of $10,000 cash was withdrawn during the same period. It is assumed for our calculation purposes that all asset inflows or outflows occurred at the beginning of each month.

III. Profit/Loss Analysis

The aggregate accounts experienced a total loss of $69,059.04 on a total investment of about $78,539.17. This represents a loss of approximately 88 percent during the period examined.

IV. Account Performance

The actual account performance was compared with an account invested in the CRSP 1-10 All Equity Index during the same period. The CRSP Index was chosen as an example of what the equity market would have returned during the period of our analysis.

During the period examined, the Smiths' five (5) accounts indicated losses of approximately $69,060, while the CRSP 1-10 Index accounts (not taking into account fees) would have indicated a loss of approximately $8,974. The Smiths' accounts, if they had been invested in the CRSP Index, would have shown an ending value as of May 2001 of approximately $69,565 vs. the actual accounts that indicated a total ending value of $9,480.13. This analysis assumes similar, but not exact, cash inflows and outflows.

The Smiths' accounts experienced losses in excess of $60,084 as compared to an All Equity Index account (the index account had no fee withdrawals, so in reality the actual difference would have been less than illustrated).

V. Turnover Analysis

We performed a turnover analysis on the joint Smith account (#XXX-XXXX). The analysis illustrated that during the period examined, the Smiths' account experienced an average monthly turnover rate of 94.4 percent, indicating an annual turnover rate of approximately 1,133 percent.

VI. Risk Assessment

We performed a Morningstar risk assessment of the same Smith portfolio account (#XXX-XXXX) for the month of December 2000. The analysis is attached separately.

The analysis illustrates that the portfolio had a much greater three-year standard deviation than the S&P 500 (103.72 vs. 19.82) and, therefore, would have exhibited much greater volatility.

The portfolio appeared highly weighted toward speculative growth investments during the time periods examined.

There are limitations on the above risk analysis as the Morningstar analysis is using data as of June 30, 2001, which may not accurately reflect the nature of the holdings as of December 2000.

VII. Summary of Conclusions

The analysis indicates that the Smiths' investment accounts experienced poor overall performance. The following is a listing of the potential causes of resulting poor performance.

1) The account had little diversification within the equity market.

It appears that many of the investments were growth-oriented. There was little investment in value and international investment classes. These types of asset classes, although risky alone, have been shown to reduce the overall risk of a portfolio that is comprised of numerous asset classes.

2) The account was invested in highly speculative investments that exhibited poor performance during the period examined relative to the broad market.

3) The use of margin debt increased the leverage, and therefore the losses, in the account.

4) The turnover rate for the main Smith account was high. Given that most professionally managed mutual funds will exhibit annual turnover in the 90 percent rate, the Smith portfolio turnover appears excessive.

5) Margin interest and portfolio costs exceeded $3,700 during the year 2000. This represents a cost of approximately 4.7 percent of the net invested amounts. To achieve the expected return of 12 percent, the accounts would have had to achieve a return of almost 17 percent to offset the fee and interest charges.

6) Although we do not have information about other investments the Smiths may have had, given the net worth and liquid asset amounts listed on the margin application by Mr. & Mrs. Smith, we would question whether an all-equity account was an appropriate investment mix. This is especially true if the accounts we examined represented most, if not all, of their liquid investment holdings. This is further clouded by the conflicting investment objectives listed on the statements and the Smiths' investment policy statements.

A fully diversified equity portfolio account during the same period would most likely have experienced a loss of approximately 11.4 percent, vs. the 88 percent loss experienced by the Smiths' accounts. In our estimation, based upon the information provided to us and examined as explained above, these accounts in the aggregate were not prudently invested to achieve a growth investment objective.

I trust the above analysis and the attached information assists you in your review.

If You Go It Alone

If you believe you have a viable claim against a broker and/or firm and wish to handle the matter yourself, I suggest you do the following:

- Get an accountant or other expert to analyze your account.
- Review the report and determine if you really have a valid claim.
- Decide if you want to file your claim with the NASD or the NYSE (assuming that you have a choice). You can only file a claim before a self-regulating organization if the firm you are filing against is a member of that organization. (All brokerage firms are members of the NASD, but not all are members of the NYSE. You must pick your forum; you can only file one claim against each party.)
- If you believe you have a valid claim, file it.

GET AN EXPERT TO ANALYZE YOUR ACCOUNT

Many accountants are undergoing training and certification as registered investment advisors (RIAs), certified financial planners (CFPs), or other professional designation. Some are doing fee-based financial planning; others are selling financial products; and still others are using this education and training to offer investment portfolio analysis and "second opinions" as both a value-added service to current clients and a way to increase their client base.

Ask your own accountant if he or she (or someone else in the accounting firm) provides this service, or if he or she can refer you to an expert who does this kind of analysis. It should cost you somewhere between $1,000 and $2,500 to have all of your brokerage accounts analyzed, depending on the number of transactions involved.

REVIEW THE REPORT AND DETERMINE
IF YOU HAVE A CLAIM

Many attorneys suggest that you file a formal complaint letter with the broker and/or brokerage firm. I disagree. I don't think it adds value to the process at all. In my experience, these letters get little positive response.

In any event, if you are going it alone, you should not send any complaint letter until after you have had an expert analysis done. Any statement you make in a complaint letter prior to the time when a careful analysis of account records has been done can come back to haunt you when it is used against you at an arbitration tribunal by counsel for the brokerage firm.

Finally, the process of sending such a letter and waiting for a reply can take considerable time, which can be better spent completing an analysis of your potential claim and, if appropriate, filing a Statement of Claim. As a general rule, to paraphrase Rodney Dangerfield: I don't get no respect until I file a claim.

If you hire an attorney, you should follow his or her advice on this matter, and if your attorney thinks a complaint letter might be productive, he or she can help you draft it.

NASD OR NYSE

You may not have a choice. Virtually all brokerage firms (but not investment advisory firms) are members of the NASD. But not all of them are members of the NYSE. You can find a list of NYSE members at www.nyse.com/members. To confirm that a brokerage firm is a member of the NASD, go to www.nasdr.com and follow the links to "investor protection."

If you do have a choice, there are a number of factors to consider. Here are the ones I believe are most important. This is not an exhaustive list, and attorneys differ over what weight to give each of these factors in the final decision.

■ Filing fees, hearing fees, pre-hearing conference fees, and forum fees are lower at the NYSE than at the NASD.

■ The NYSE handles far fewer cases than the NASD (about 10 percent of claims are filed with the NYSE and 90 percent with the NASD). As a consequence, the NYSE is more "user-friendly." Staff counsel at the NYSE are more responsive and there is less staff turnover. However, in response to complaints from attorneys representing investors in NASD claims, the NASD has made significant progress in improving its responsiveness and customer service.

■ The "win" rate for investors is higher at the NASD (43 percent in 2005) than at the NYSE (39 percent in 2005). However, there is evidence that this difference is related more to the geographic location where a significant number of NYSE cases are heard (New York) and does not indicate that investors generally have less of a chance of prevailing in an NYSE arbitration than in one filed before the NASD. In other words, in cases heard by NASD or NYSE tribunals in the New York area, claimants have a lower win rate than they do in cases heard by tribunals in other parts of the country. Nevertheless, there are a number of my colleagues who strongly believe that the NYSE is a less favorable forum for investors and who refuse to file cases there for that reason.

■ Cases move more quickly before the NYSE than at the NASD.

Both the NASD and NYSE provide for simplified arbitration for small claims.

At the NASD, any dispute with a dollar amount of under $25,000, exclusive of costs and interest, goes through the simplified process (Rule 10203). It is heard by a single (nonpublic, meaning industry) arbitrator, appointed by the director of arbitration.

Unless either party asks for a formal hearing within 10 days of the filing of the final documents in the case (known as pleadings), the ruling is made solely on the basis of the paper filings. The arbitrator has 30 days after reviewing all of the documents to make a ruling.

The NASD also has a provision for a single arbitrator to hear cases where the amount in dispute is between $25,000 and $50,000, unless either party requests a three-arbitrator panel.

The NYSE has a simplified arbitration procedure (Rule 601) for claims by public customers for under $25,000, exclusive of costs and interest. At the NYSE, a small claim is heard by a single (public) arbitrator, who rules based on the documentary evidence unless the public customer demands or consents to a hearing, or the arbitrator calls a hearing. (The brokerage firm cannot demand a hearing.)

IF YOU KNOW YOU HAVE A VALID CLAIM, FILE IT

The claim has three main parts to it:

■ A statement of the facts and circumstances of your situation
■ A recitation of the legal theories that explain your view of the alleged misconduct by the broker and the brokerage firm
■ A request of the arbitration tribunal for specific amounts of monetary damages

All of the different people or organizations named in the claim are known collectively as "parties" to the claim. You are referred to as the "Claimant."

Those you are accusing of committing frauds and/or violations are known as "Respondent(s)."

Within your claim, you need to state clearly the chronological order in which the events took place. You need to state clearly why each respondent named is a legitimate respondent, and when possible tie each event to a particular respondent or respondents.

After you have drawn up your claim, you deliver it, together with a "Submission Agreement" and the filing and hearing fees, to the director of arbitration at the appropriate self-regulatory organization. This is known as "filing" the claim. The claim remains on file as a matter of record and reference. To find out how to acquire the proper paperwork, go to the NASD or NYSE website (www.nasd.com or www.nyse.org).

No matter how the claim is ultimately closed out—by a judgment of an arbitration panel, by negotiated settlement, by mediation, or by the claim being dropped—the claim goes on the broker's permanent record maintained by NASD.

In order for your claim to be deemed proper, it must meet the "Eligibility Rules." As a general rule, both the NASD and the NYSE will not hear claims relating to transactions that occurred more than six years prior to the date of filing. However, state statutes may have shorter time periods within which claims must be brought. (At the House Financial Services Oversight and Investigations Subcommittee hearings in May 2002, some of the alleged victims of Frank Gruttadauria, the Ohio broker, argued that these rules should be changed. In this case, Gruttadauria allegedly maintained his fraud for over 15 years, sending out phony monthly statements to wealthy investors he was ripping off. One victim, Carl Fazio, said that by 1996, six years before the fraud was uncovered, his account had already been essentially wiped out, meaning that even if he filed for arbitration against Gruttadauria and the firms he worked for over that time, actual damages since 1996 would be little.)

For more on the mechanics of filing a claim, go to the website of the applicable organization. The American Arbitration Association rules for securities matters (which are now administered under the Commercial Arbitration Rules) can be found at www.adr.org. Because so few claims are filed before the AAA, I won't discuss these rules in any detail here. But if you hire an attorney, he or she may wish to pursue your claim through the AAA, if you have a choice of doing so.

These websites provide documentation to take you through the steps of filing a claim.

MOVE TO MEDIATION IF POSSIBLE

Mediation is a nonbinding, confidential process where a mediator meets with the parties and assists them in negotiating a settlement. The parties generally share the cost of the mediator. The mediator in securities cases is an impartial lawyer with experience both in securities disputes and mediation techniques.

A good mediator can help the parties settle the vast majority of claims before him or her. For this reason, it is generally a good idea to ask for your claim to be mediated. Mediation takes a lot less time to work through the process than does arbitration. It is a less formal procedure.

Mediations are usually concluded in one day or less. And mediators generally try to find some common ground, a compromise, which affords the investor a reasonable settlement.

A relatively high percentage of cases that are mediated are settled. But only a small percentage of cases are mediated. In 2005, 910 cases were settled by mediation at the NASD.

Apparently, the brokerage industry has found that it can wear down most customers by refusing to participate in mediation proceedings and playing hardball by engaging in extensive discovery and taking many cases to a hearing. Unless you are prepared to weather this kind of a storm, you should not institute a claim even though your broker may owe you money.

If You Decide to Use a Lawyer

Securities arbitration is not rocket science. But it is a specialty, with many traps for the unwary. Therefore, if you decide to hire a lawyer to help you with the process, it is important to hire someone with experience in this field.

Finding the right lawyer to handle your claim is important. You should always speak to a few lawyers before hiring one. As it is with any other professional service provider and advisor, it is important that you and your attorney be able to work together in a cordial and professional manner.

The first place to look is to your own attorney or accountant, for a referral to someone he or she knows who specializes in securities arbitration. You can also solicit recommendations from any friends who have brought similar claims and had a good experience with the attorney they hired.

Neither the NASD nor the NYSE makes attorney referrals to individuals as part of the arbitration process. The Securities and Exchange Commission (SEC) website offers information about bar associations and directories of attorneys who specialize in securities arbitration complaints.

A good resource for finding attorneys who specialize in securities arbitration is the website of the Public Investors' Arbitration Bar Association (PIABA). Go to www.piaba.org and click on "find an attorney" on the navigation bar on the left-hand side of the home page.

PIABA is an organization of over 500 attorney members (I am one) who specialize in arbitration on behalf of public investors. One condition of PIABA membership is that neither the attorney nor any other attorney in his or her firm can have spent more than 20 percent of his or her securities practice in the past year representing industry clients against public investors.

PIABA is not a referral service, but the "find a lawyer" page utilizes a convenient search tool to help you find potential counsel. By entering your zip code and the mileage around your zip code within which you would like to search, the tool provides you with a list of attorneys with offices within that distance, starting with those closest to you and working out from there. Each attorney listing includes the name, address, phone number, and e-mail address of the participating attorney, as well as any website he or she maintains.

PIABA maintains a list of attorneys who will handle small claims. You can obtain this list by using the "e-mail PIABA" option on the association's website.

In addition, you can contact one of the law school securities arbitration clinics, most of which are in the New York City area. These clinics provide assistance by students and professors for investors filing small claims, or those who cannot afford an attorney. They include:

- Brooklyn Law School Securities Arbitration Clinic; (718) 780-7994
- Fordham University School of Law Securities Arbitration Clinic; (212) 636-7231
- Pace University School of Law/John Jay Legal Services Securities Arbitration Clinic; (914) 422-4333
- State University of New York at Buffalo School of Law Legal Assistance Program; (716) 645-2167

TERMINOLOGY

ARBITRATION: A method by which a conflict between two or more parties is resolved by impartial people—arbitrators—who are knowledgeable in the area(s) of controversy.

CLAIM: A demand for money or other relief.

CLAIMANT: A party (person or organization) making a claim.

ELIGIBILITY RULES: The NASD Code of Arbitration states that no claim shall be eligible for submission to arbitration where six years have elapsed since the occurrence of the event giving rise to the controversy.

FILING: Delivery to the director of arbitration of the appropriate self-regulatory organization (NASD or NYSE) of the statement of claim or other pleadings, to be kept on file as a matter of record and reference.

MEDIATION: An informal, voluntary process used in securities industry disputes (and other disputes) in which a mediator helps negotiate a mutually acceptable resolution between parties to a dispute. Unlike arbitration or litigation, mediation does not impose a solution. If the parties cannot negotiate an acceptable settlement, they may still arbitrate and/or litigate their dispute.

PARTY: A person or organization making or responding to a claim in an arbitration proceeding.

RESPONDENT: The person or organization against whom a claim is made.

10

Whom Do You Sue?

Sometimes you can run but you can't hide. The Oppenheimer Funds company in November 2001 agreed to pay two investors a total of about $150,000 they had been awarded by an NASD arbitration tribunal decision against MultiSource Services Inc., an Oppenheimer subsidiary that cleared stock trades for other brokers.

The two claimants had gone after MultiSource after failing to collect a $1.5 million NASD arbitration award against the Denver-based boiler-room brokerage firm Sauceda & Granville Securities.

The two claimants, both from Indiana, had purchased shares in the same company, SureQuest Systems, a Texas-based company that supplied dietary management software to the health care and food service industries. The two had responded to telephone solicitations made in 1997 by S&G brokers, who the claimants allege promised the stock would rise to $12 a share; instead, it dropped to pennies a share after their purchase. Together, they bought about $450,000 of the stock. The shares turned out to be not registered with the SEC and illegally sold.

In 1998, the NASD revoked S&G's membership because the company did not maintain the minimum level of capital required. Also that year, the Indiana Securities Division fined the firm for selling unregistered securities and for using abusive, high-pressure tactics in its telephone sales.

MultiSource said it did not know what was going on at S&G. But in a written opinion against MultiSource, the NASD arbitration panel found that the company "was or should have been aware of various red flags in its dealings with [S&G]," including S&G's concentration of transactions in thinly traded stocks and its weak capitalization.

Indiana Securities Commissioner Brad Scolnik told *The Indianapolis Star* that "many of these clearing firms were conducting a large volume of business for firms that were . . . the subject of regulator actions."

There are a host of potential respondents to claims involving brokers and brokerage firms. For the most part, you have one consideration when choosing whom to name: If you are successful in obtaining an award from the arbitration panel, will the named respondent(s) be able to pay?

In addition, you may have a viable action against investment professionals other than brokers for your market losses, most notably a registered investment advisor (RIA).

The Complaint Against the Broker and/or Brokerage Firm

As I mentioned in the last chapter, it is important that your claim clearly state the facts that occurred that led you to make the claim, and the particular respondent(s) against whom the claim is made. Depending on the circumstances, you may wish to file claims against any or all of the following parties within the brokerage firm:

- The brokerage firm
- Your broker
- The branch manager and/or other supervisor
- The firm's owners, principals, or other "controlling persons"
- The "clearing broker" firm that cleared trades for your firm

THE BROKERAGE FIRM

Always name the brokerage firm as a respondent.

Frequently, you may be able to assert claims against the firm that are not available against any other respondent, such as the failure to supervise the broker. Obviously, if you have a claim against the firm, as distinguished from the broker, it is necessary to name the firm as a respondent.

Even if this is not the case, the brokerage firm generally has liability for the conduct of its brokers, who are acting within the scope of their authority and engaging in the business of generating commission income for their employer. Even in some cases of "selling away," where the broker is acting outside of his or her scope of authority, arbitration panels and courts have found that firms have a duty to learn about and put an end to such behavior or be held liable for the broker's actions.

Naming the brokerage firm is routine in securities arbitration because it permits claimants to obtain the discovery of relevant documents from the firm and, more importantly, may make the firm liable for the payment of any award issued by the tribunal. Since large brokerage firms have the ability to pay, they are often the only party named in an arbitration claim from which you can actually receive payment. For these reasons, naming the brokerage firm as a respondent is a no-brainer.

YOUR BROKER

The question of whether or not to name the individual broker in an arbitration claim is one securities arbitration lawyers love to argue about.

Some lawyers think you should never name the broker. They believe arbitrators are more likely to rule for you as an investor if you are seen as seeking compensation from a large, faceless firm rather than from an individual with a family to feed. Sometimes the broker really doesn't have the financial ability to pay an award.

Obviously, if the loss was caused by some kind of back-office failure, the broker really isn't a party to the issue at all.

Also, if the broker no longer works at the firm, or has even left the industry, he or she might be willing to become a friendly witness for your case. Many people have left the industry because they do not like industry practices, and many others have left one particular firm because they were unhappy about such practices as being forced to sell "house" products that were not competitive or appropriate for their clients.

In addition, if a broker is named as a respondent, he or she has a right to have separate counsel for the arbitration hearing and to be present during the entire hearing. This poses two problems for you. First, the "opposition" has two attorneys who can cross-examine every witness, including you, and who are entitled to make opening and closing statements. Second, the broker is forced to take an adversarial position against you, something he or she may not have done if not named.

If the broker is not named, you can still call him or her as a witness for your case (which I always do) and try to drive a wedge between the broker and the firm through your questioning of the reasons for the broker's behavior. This can be difficult to do if you name the broker because, as a practical matter, the broker and the brokerage firm will usually be represented by the same law firm, and they will try to present a united front to the tribunal.

Finally, naming the broker as a respondent has sometimes led to the anomalous (and, in my view, indefensible) holding by the tribunal that the broker, but not the brokerage firm, is solely liable for the alleged misconduct. Since the broker does not have the deep pockets of the brokerage firm, a successful claimant may find that he or she has obtained a favorable award without the ability to collect from anyone.

There is one circumstance when, in my opinion, you should name the broker as a respondent: when you anticipate a problem in collecting the award.

The U.S. General Accounting Office (GAO) issued a report in June 2000 that highlighted the problem of unpaid awards. In the report (available at www.gao.gov/new.items/gg00115.pdf), the GAO found that 500 out of 845 investors who received awards in 1998 had either not been paid or had received partial payment. It appears that obtaining an award is but the first step in the minefield of recovering your losses from your broker.

Therefore, if the brokerage firm is small and thinly capitalized, it is wise to name the broker, among others, as a respondent so you have an additional party from whom you can try to collect an award. Of course, with the benefit of hindsight, it would be better not to do business with such a firm in the first place.

If collection is not a problem, I see no benefit in naming the broker as an individual respondent, and it is not my practice to do so.

A 1996 survey by the *Securities Arbitration Commentator* newsletter found that five firms accounted for 58 percent of all claims initiated by customers: Smith Barney, Prudential, Merrill Lynch, Dean Witter, and PaineWebber.

This is not surprising, and does not reflect adversely on these firms, since they are among the largest and best-known firms with the largest number of retail customer accounts.

The survey also found that among these major firms, customers prevailed in the highest percentage of claims against PaineWebber (61 percent, with successful customers receiving an average of 48 percent of the amount of the claim). Customers prevailed in the lowest percentage of claims against Merrill Lynch (45 percent, with successful customers receiving an average of 38 percent of the amount of the claim).

However, it is difficult to evaluate these statistics because there is no data indicating the number of claims settled by each firm, or the percent of the amount claimed paid out in settlements.

THE BRANCH MANAGER OR OTHER SUPERVISOR

It is possible to name individuals other than the broker, as well as the firm itself, as respondents to the charge of failure to supervise. Individuals who might be named respondents of such a claim include the branch manager, the branch's compliance officer, or even a remote supervisor such as a district or regional manager.

For example, in 1999, a Securities and Exchange Commission administrative law judge ruled that a Detroit metropolitan area manager for a major brokerage firm could indeed be disciplined for failure to supervise a broker who worked out of a smaller suburban branch that had its own full-time branch manager. The judge found that both the broker and the small-office branch manager worked "under the control of" the metropolitan manager. The metropolitan manager was barred from serving as a supervisor for a broker-dealer for six months and fined $20,000.

Notwithstanding the ability to name these individuals as respondents, applying the same standards I discussed with regard to naming the individual broker as a respondent, I generally do not name the branch manager or other supervisor as a respondent unless I anticipate a collection problem.

Counterclaims, Cross Claims, and Third-Party Claims

Sometimes when you file an arbitration claim, you start the ball rolling on a process that is more complex than what you had wished. This happens when one of the respondents files a counterclaim, cross claim, or third-party claim.

A counterclaim is a claim filed by a respondent against the claimant (you). A counterclaim is most often filed by the brokerage firm and usually asserts an unpaid debit balance in your account. Brokerage firms that pursue a "scorched earth" policy of defending claims against them can be more creative in coming up with counterclaims intended to intimidate their former customers. These counterclaims usually revolve around "abuse of process," with the additional request for reimbursement of attorney fees and costs.

A cross claim is a claim by one respondent against another respondent named in the claim. When both the broker and firm are named in the claim, either party can file a cross claim against the other. This claim is often made by one party asking the other for indemnification of an action. However, usually the broker and brokerage firm enter into an agreement preserving their rights against each other so they can present a united front defending against the claims before the tribunal.

A third-party claim is filed by a respondent against a party not named in your claim. Brokerage firms usually file third-party claims against an unnamed broker to bring the broker into the claim and try to argue that the broker acted outside his or her scope of employment, and that the firm has no liability in a supervisory, agent, or controlling person capacity.

THE FIRM'S OWNERS, PRINCIPALS, OR OTHER "CONTROLLING PERSONS"

The naming of "controlling persons" in an arbitration claim is almost always done as a way to find a party able to pay a judgment in cases of small "fly-by-night" brokerage firms. Section 20 of the Securities Exchange Act of 1934 states that a person who:

> . . . directly or indirectly controls any person liable under any provision of this chapter or any rule or regulation thereunder shall also be liable jointly and severally with and to the same extent as such controlled person . . . unless the controlling person acted in good faith and did not directly or indirectly induce the act or acts constituting the violation or cause of action.

In his article "Pruning the Judicial Oak: Developing a Coherent Application of Common Law Agency and Controlling Person Liability in Securities Cases" in the June 1993 issue of the *Columbia Law Review,* James L. Burns writes that the securities statutes create three classes of defendants (respondents):

> . . . primary violators, who are liable for their own violation of a substantive provision of the securities laws; principals, who are secondarily liable based on common law agency principles; and "controlling persons," who are made secondarily liable by the Securities Acts. . . .
> The controlling person provisions were intended to reach those individuals who would not be liable under agency law, such as officers,

directors, or shareholders, who either directed the violation of or reck-lessly allowed others to violate the securities law.

During the 1980s and 1990s, an enormous number of small brokerage firms came into existence. Many of them were boiler-room operations, a number of which engaged in illegal market manipulations of small-capital-ization stocks, so-called "pump-and-dump" operations. A number of these firms were associated with organized crime figures.

Beginning in the mid-1990s and continuing for about five years, investiga-tions by the Securities and Exchange Commission, the United States Attorneys for the Southern and Eastern Districts of New York, and the Manhattan District Attorney led to indictments against numerous firms and dozens of brokers, supervisors, and principals of the most notorious firms. (See Chapter 3 for a detailed discussion of pump-and-dump frauds.)

While the large, well-established brokerage firms were increasingly be-coming public corporations in order to attract investor money and grow their companies, these small firms were always closely held by small groups of owners. Many times, the owners siphoned large amounts of money out of their firm's corporate shell and into their own private accounts.

When investors succeeded in arbitration claims against brokers, supervi-sors, and the firms themselves, they found that no one, especially the firm, had any money with which to pay the award. (I'll discuss in detail how to make sure you get paid in Chapter 12.)

The use of controlling person legal theory has allowed investors to "pierce the corporate veil" of these small boiler-room firms and seek judg-ment personally from the firms' owners and other principals. However, it is important to note that "controlling person" liability is only available when you have a claim that a violation of the federal securities laws occurred, not when you are claiming a violation of the rules and regulations of the SRO.

THE CLEARING BROKER

Another element that characterized the small boiler-room firms of the 1980s and 1990s was that they did not have any back-office operations to clear trades. For these activities, the firms hired "clearing firms" on an outsourcing basis. Clearing firms were usually large, well-known firms; often these outsourced clearing relationships were managed through a subsidiary of the major firm.

The growth of clearing firms was a lesson in symbiosis.

Large firms have the expertise and staff to perform back-office activities, including maintaining records; trade processing; and receipt, custody, and delivery of securities and funds. In addition, clearing firms often provide the credit to finance customers' margin accounts for a smaller, less well-capitalized "introducing broker," the brokerage firm that has the relationship with the customer and "introduces" the customer to the clearing broker.

These large firms often have excess capacity in their computer systems and can hire additional personnel at a relatively low cost, since these activities can be undertaken anywhere. Clearing for small firms became a cash-cow operation through the 1990s.

For the small firm, clearing through a major firm had many advantages.

First, they did not have to undertake the start-up costs of a clearing operation.

Second, and more important, they could use the cachet of a large firm's name and reputation as an additional hook to get investors to open brokerage accounts. They often used the term "affiliated with" or "associated with" when describing their relationship with the major firm.

When you sign a new-account form with a brokerage firm that uses another firm to clear trades, you establish a relationship with the clearing firm as well. In fact, in many cases, the account-opening form you sign is with the clearing broker, which buttresses your belief that you are dealing with a well-established, reputable company when you are really the customer of the introducing broker.

The issue is how much responsibility the clearing broker has to make sure the introducing broker acts in accordance with securities laws and the rules and regulations of the SEC, the exchanges, and the NASD (formerly the National Association of Securities Dealers).

One notorious case has made going after the clearing broker a legitimate avenue in cases against boiler-room firms, many of which are now defunct.

In April of 2000, Richard Harriton, a senior managing director of Bear Stearns & Co., Inc., a New York Stock Exchange (NYSE) member firm, entered into a settlement (formally called a consent decree) with the Securities and Exchange Commission in which he neither admitted nor denied guilt, but agreed to cease and desist from violating the Securities Act of 1933 and the Securities Exchange Act of 1934, and accepted remedial sanctions. The following narrative is based on the SEC complaint and the offer of settlement.

In 1992, Andrew Bressman and others established A.R. Baron & Co., a small broker-dealer firm, with the intent of underwriting securities of small companies. After their initial public offerings, Baron continued to make a market in these securities, trading them on the over-the-counter markets.

Baron was a classic boiler room, engaging in high-pressure sales tactics to induce investors to buy these "house" stocks. There was never a real market for any of these stocks; Baron manipulated the market and the securities' prices. Buyers bought the stock out of Baron's inventory, and when they sold at any profit, they did so at the expense of other Baron customers, since Baron's principals maintained a "no net selling" policy under which no broker could allow a customer to sell a stock unless there was an accompanying "crossing order" from another customer to buy the other customer's position. (Crossing orders and collecting a commission on both sides of the buy-sell transaction is in itself a violation of NASD rules.)

To generate additional demand and maintain an appearance of liquidity in the market for Baron house stocks, brokers frequently made unauthorized purchases for customers. They covered this activity by claiming trading errors, or by getting the customer to accept the unauthorized purchase through high-pressure sales tactics, or by manipulating the price higher by the time the customer became aware of the unauthorized trade.

Baron also "parked" stock in the accounts of customers who were willing to hold it, or in accounts at other brokerage firms held by individuals closely associated with the frauds.

Together, the unauthorized trading and parking created an appearance that Baron had more assets than it did by reducing the amount of inventory in its trading account and increasing its cash balance. Baron brokers often moved stock out of its inventory through parking and unauthorized trading near the close of business so it could end each day appearing to be in compliance with requirements that it maintain a certain level of cash on deposit with its clearing broker, and in compliance with the SEC's net capital rule. Many times Baron would move the stock back into its inventory early the next morning.

Over time, more than 80 percent of "purchases" made after 3:45 p.m. (15 minutes before the stock markets close) were never paid for. This left Baron's clearing broker on the hook, since it was responsible for extending payment for the purchase of the securities. However, it was only a few days after each of these fraudulent trades, when no payment had been made for the shares, that the clearing broker would be able to "sell out" the position and recoup some of the money it had paid out.

By February of 1995, the clearing broker used by Baron, Adler Coleman, had gone bankrupt and been liquidated. In July 1995, Bear Stearns Securities Corp., a major Wall Street brokerage firm, began clearing for Baron. Bear Stearns's clearing department head, Richard Harriton, agreed over his management colleagues' objections to clear for Baron. Harriton forced Baron to keep $5 million on deposit with Bear Stearns and to agree not to have more than $12 million in customer transactions not yet paid for at any time.

Within two months of beginning the clearing relationship, Bear Stearns employees noticed clear signs of parking and unauthorized trading. Harriton assured his colleagues that Bear Stearns would end its clearing arrangement with Baron. On August 30, 1995, the NASD told Bressman that Baron was not in compliance with the net capital requirement rule and would have to close if he could not raise $3.5 million. Harriton intervened with the NASD when it refused to recognize capital Bressman raised over the Labor Day weekend without original signed loan documents.

Over the next nine months, although he and his employees had suspicions that Baron was continuing to engage in unauthorized trading and market manipulation of a number of stocks, Harriton arranged for Bear Stearns to maintain its clearing relationship with Baron.

On May 29, 1996, the SEC issued a cease-and-desist order against Baron to halt fraudulent practices. Less than a month later, on June 27, Baron told the NASD that it had insufficient net capital and had gone out of business. Baron was liquidated a few weeks later under provisions of the Securities Investor Protection Act of 1970. The SEC revoked Baron's broker-dealer license. In December 1997, Bressman pleaded guilty to enterprise corruption and grand larceny, just some of the charges in a 174-count indictment in a New York state court.

Unfortunately, since there was no real market for the stocks sold by Baron, investors were left unable to get from Baron any of the money they had been swindled out of.

But on April 20, 2000, a new avenue opened up for defrauded investors. On that day, Richard Harriton of Bear Stearns agreed to a settlement with the SEC. The SEC found that Harriton had willfully aided and abetted Baron in its fraudulent violation of a number of portions of the Securities Act of 1933 and the Securities Exchange Act of 1934. (Bear Stearns itself had agreed to SEC sanctions in the same matter in August 1999.)

Harriton was barred from the securities business for two years and fined $1 million. (Bear Stearns was also fined by the SEC.)

In his article "Barring Baron at the Gate: An Argument for Expanding the Liability of Securities Clearing Brokers for the Fraud of Introducing Brokers" in the October 1999 issue of the *New York University Law Review*, John M. Bellwoar writes:

> *Introducing broker fraud is a serious problem. . . . Recent cases of introducing broker fraud of tens and even hundreds of millions of dollars show that the current liability regime is ineffective. . . . Boiler room introducing firms go in and out of business with regularity. . . . The introducing brokers make money, the firms that clear the trades for them make money, and the only people who lose money are the defrauded investors . . . [who] find themselves with no viable legal recourse after they become aware of the fraud. . . .*
>
> *The type of liability that should be imposed on clearing brokers is "gatekeeper liability," which is "liability imposed on private parties who are able to disrupt misconduct by withholding their cooperation from the wrongdoers." . . . Introducing brokers require the services of clearing brokers in order to trade securities; if clearing brokers withhold their services from an introducing broker who wants to engage in misconduct, then the introducing broker would be unable to engage in that misconduct.*

Nevertheless, while pursuing the clearing broker may be the only option for customers defrauded by boiler-room firms employing pump-and-dump stock manipulations that have subsequently gone out of business, obtaining an award against them remains an uphill battle.

As a general matter, under the law as it is presently interpreted, clearing brokers are not liable for the conduct of introducing brokers, even when the introducing broker engages in fraudulent activities, and even when the clearing broker continued to provide clearing services after it knew or should have known of the introducing broker's fraudulent scheme.

In order to recover from the clearing broker, the customer of the introducing broker must prove that the clearing broker's activities went beyond those of performing routine clearing services and that it became actively and directly involved in the introducing broker's fraudulent conduct. That is a very difficult burden for most claimants to meet.

For this reason, most claims against clearing brokers fail (as was the case with the claim I made on behalf of my client Fred, discussed in detail in Chapter 3). However, the law in this area is evolving rapidly, and there are indications—like the story at the beginning of this chapter—that the dam preventing claims against clearing brokers may be cracking.

Going After the Analysts

In July 2001, Merrill Lynch became the first brokerage firm to settle an arbitration claim contending that an investor had been induced to become overly concentrated in Internet stocks due to the cries of "buy" from superstar analysts.

Merrill agreed to pay $400,000 to Debasis Kanjilal to settle an $800,000 claim. Kanjilal charged Merrill Lynch with failing to disclose a material conflict of interest (that the analyst was recommending a stock the firm had an underwriting relationship with), as well as violation of NYSE Rule 405, which requires a broker or analyst to have a "reasonable basis" for making a recommendation.

Kanjilal contended that his broker used a research report by Henry Blodget, the firm's Internet analyst, to persuade him to hold the stock even as it was plummeting during the Internet-stock meltdown.

A few weeks later, Morgan Stanley's Internet analyst, Mary Meeker, was named a co-defendant in two class-action lawsuits in federal court by shareholders of Amazon.com and eBay who bought the stock between August 1, 1998, and January 22, 2001, and claimed that Meeker recommended the stocks "not based on objective analysis, but rather on her desire to attract and retain" the companies' investment banking business.

A federal judge dismissed the counts in the suits involving Meeker in early 2003 but did not dismiss the suits entirely against Morgan Stanley at that time.

Another group of investors in August filed suit in federal court against six major securities firms, alleging they committed fraud by not disclosing that they required analysts to recommend stocks of corporate clients as a way of keeping the companies' investment banking fees. The six firms named were Morgan Stanley, Merrill Lynch, Credit Suisse First Boston, Goldman Sachs, Salomon Smith Barney, and Robertson Stephens. The other case against

Morgan Stanley was joined to this one, and all were dismissed in the spring of 2003, mainly on the grounds that the investors who filed the suit were professional investors—part of the Wall Street inside crowd—and did not truly represent individual investors who may have been hurt.

Despite the success of the Kanjilal arbitration decision, most securities lawyers were not optimistic about the prospects of holding analysts liable for their recommendations, either in court or through the arbitration process. However, that all changed in the spring of 2002.

On April 8, 2002, New York State Attorney General Eliot Spitzer obtained an order from the State Supreme Court requiring Merrill Lynch to disclose in its research reports whether the company being reported on is an investment banking client or prospective investment banking client. Spitzer called much of the advice provided by Merrill and Blodget during the Internet boom days "tainted" by conflicts. This opened the floodgates to what would eventually become known as the "global settlement" between 10 of the largest brokerage firm/investment banks on one hand and the New York Attorney General, the state securities regulators in the other 49 states (either the attorney general or the secretary of state), the federal Securities and Exchange Commission, the NYSE, and the NASD on the other.

The firms were accused of misleading retail brokerage customers in order to enrich themselves through investment banking services offered to corporate clients. As part of the evidence Spitzer presented to a judge in his request for the original order against Merrill Lynch, he released e-mail communications between Merrill analysts, including one arguing that the idea they were independent of the investment bankers was "a big lie."

Immediately after Spitzer's agreement with Merrill Lynch was announced in early June of 2002, two other brokerage firms, Salomon Smith Barney, a division of Citigroup, and Goldman Sachs, jumped into the fray, announcing that they would change their firms' policies to mirror the changes Merrill Lynch had agreed to make as part of the agreement. By the end of the fall, all 10 firms had agreed to these changes, which included:

■ Paying total penalties of $1.4 billion, divided among the 10 firms in accordance with their size and the volume of initial public offering (IPO) business they had done in the late 1990s through 2001. Some of this money was to be paid in the form of fines to the SEC and the states; part was to be paid in the form of payments to the states for investor education; and part was to be put in a restitution fund for investors hurt by these actions.

■ Decoupling research from investment banking. No longer is the investment banking management supposed to have a say in analyst compensation; neither can they promise companies good analyst reports in exchange for IPO business.

■ Agreeing to stricter supervision and outside oversight of the analysts' work.

The language of the agreement was not finalized and accepted by a judge until mid-year 2003. Much of the wrangling focused on whether the payments would be categorized as penalties or something else. The companies wanted to be able to seek money back from the insurance companies with which they had taken out policies to cover restitution and other payments to clear up securities violations; fines and other penalties explicitly are not covered by that insurance. The firms also wanted to be able to deduct the payments from their taxable income, thereby having taxpayers pick up some of the tab for their egregious violations of business ethics.

What neither the agreement between Merrill Lynch and the New York attorney general nor the global settlement did, and what many of us who represent individual investors against brokers and brokerage firms hoped these settlements would do, was force these firms to admit publicly that the conflict of interest in the research area directly hurt retail investors, who so often depended on the advice of brokers who were utilizing research by the firm's analysts to make recommendations.

In fact, a couple of days after the agreement with Merrill Lynch was announced in June 2002, the *New York Times* reported that Merrill managers were squeezing brokers to try to head off legal challenges by their clients. Merrill's then-chairman and CEO David Komansky talked with brokers the day after the settlement was announced and urged them to talk to their clients and explain the policy changes Merrill had made. A Merrill spokesman told the *New York Times* that analysts "do not make specific recommendations to specific clients. That's the job of a financial advisor. It's ultimately between the advisor and the client." Of course, as we saw in the case of Chung Wu, the broker in the Houston office of PaineWebber who sent an e-mail to his clients in August 2001 suggesting they reduce their holdings of Enron (see Chapter 2), brokers who go against their firm's analysts' recommendations risk being fired for doing so.

And in 2003, after an arbitration panel found for an investor and specifically noted the analysts' conflict of interest in its written decision, Morgan Stanley went to court to have the reference to the analysts' conflict stricken from the decision so as not to allow it to create precedent in future arbitration hearings.

Although many "analyst arbitrations" have been filed, as of the end of 2005 the vast majority have been won by the brokerage firms, which are defending them vigorously. The primary hurdle that investors may find difficult to overcome is proving that they relied on the conflicted analyst reports in making their decision to invest. Therefore, unless you purchased one of the securities for which a conflicted analyst report was issued from the brokerage firm that issued the report, and can establish that you either received a copy of the report or that the report was discussed with you by your broker and that you relied on it in making your decision to purchase the security, it is unlikely you will be able to prevail at arbitration against the analyst. This does not mean that you may not have very valid claims on issues such as suitability of the investment for your portfolio; but that claim will be against the broker and firm, not against the analyst.

Nevertheless, it seems clear that the conduct of brokerage firms in preparing and disseminating misleading, conflicted analyst reports is a violation of the fiduciary duty that brokers have (or should have) to their clients. Certainly this conduct does not comport with the duty to act "in the utmost good faith" toward clients. On a more fundamental level, it represents a disturbing departure from the most minimal business ethics that the investing public should expect from large corporate entities that spend millions of marketing dollars annually to convince the investing public that they are "trusted advisors."

Investment Advisors

You don't feel comfortable giving a stockbroker discretion to make trades in your investment account. That's good.

But you don't feel comfortable making your own stock picks, either. So you give your money to an investment advisor to invest for you. That may or may not be so good. Investment advisors may be as tempted to rip off their clients as are brokers.

An investment advisor is a professional money manager who is registered with the SEC as a registered investment advisor (RIA). Investment advisors generally are given discretion to manage a client's investment portfolio and are generally paid as a percentage of the assets under management rather than on a commission basis. This is a similar arrangement to a "wrap account" at a brokerage firm, although investment advisors generally charge less than brokerage firms. Investment advisors seldom take on clients with less than $100,000 in investment assets (some will not take on a client with less than $1 million), and usually charge 1 percent of the account's value for accounts with less than $1 million in assets, and a fraction of 1 percent for accounts with over $1 million in assets.

Here's just a few ways they defraud clients, as described in SEC case press releases and case documents about regulatory actions taken by the SEC:

■ The SEC determined that an investment advisor violated his fiduciary duties to clients by purchasing for them or recommending to them the purchase of $2.2 million in high-risk, unregistered debenture securities issued by his advisory company's parent company.

■ A grand jury indicted an investment advisory company president for violating the Investment Advisors Act of 1940 by making false claims that client funds would be invested in safe, nonspeculative securities; principal would remain at low risk; returns would be between 7 and 11 percent annually; and confirmations and statements would be accurate.

■ A number of advisors were charged with misappropriating client funds through borrowing from clients and lying about the nature of how the borrowed funds would be used (funds were used to buy cars, rent apartments, and even buy $1 million-plus houses); forging client endorsements on checks made out from brokerage accounts to clients; paying personal expenses with client fund assets; and "borrowing" from hedge funds established as limited partnerships for clients.

One investment advisor misappropriated $475,000 from client accounts through forging endorsements on checks, and borrowed over $1 million from many of the same clients, claiming he needed to make payments to his ex-wife. After the SEC initiated proceedings asking for a cease-and-desist order, it found out through an employee of the advisory company that the advisor was taking money from a hedge fund managed by an unregistered advisory company he also owned. A federal district court judge issued a restraining order against the continued looting of the hedge fund.

■ Advisors overcharged clients through "soft-dollar" commission schemes and misappropriating soft-dollar commissions. Soft-dollar practices are arrangements under which an investment advisor obtains from a broker-dealer products or services other than securities transaction executions in exchange for directing trading activities for clients through that broker-dealer. Typically, these "credits" are used to purchase research, either from the broker-dealer conducting the transactions or from another research company.

In one particular case, an investment advisor made an agreement with a brokerage firm to receive $1 in soft-dollar credits for every $1.75 in commissions generated. The advisor set the commission rate to his clients at $0.30 per share (six times higher than the average institutional commission rate), then churned one client's account such that over $900,000 in soft-dollar credits were generated over a four-year period.

The advisor established a dummy corporation and had the dummy corporation charge the soft-dollar credit account at the brokerage firm with "consulting" fees in order to siphon the soft-dollar money back into his own pocket.

In July 2001, the SEC issued an order stopping the fraud and ordering $1,120,007 in disgorgement payments from the advisory firm.

■ Some advisors engaged in cherry picking (a cousin to frontrunning). In one such scheme, which ran from March 2000 through July 2001 (a very difficult time to make money in the stock market), one investment advisor earned a whopping 5,487 percent (that's five thousand, four hundred eighty-seven percent) on his own account—growing it from about $263,000 to about $6.5 million, while his clients collectively lost $57 million.

The advisor would call in buy orders to a broker at the start of the market day and wait until the end of the day to direct where the orders went. Profitable purchases were sold and the proceeds placed in his personal account, while losing purchases were held and placed in client accounts. The SEC obtained an order in October 2000 against the advisor, stopping him from the fraudulent practice, and a federal grand jury indicted him in July 2001. In November 2001, he stood trial in federal court on a charge that during that time he received millions of dollars in brokerage-house kickbacks, and was convicted in early 2002. In June 2002, he was convicted of criminal charges in the cherry-picking case as well.

If you decide to use an investment advisor, you should be sure that the advisor subscribes to the investment principles I have described in earlier chapters. Investment advisors have no greater ability to time the market or to select undervalued stocks than brokers or any other person. Be sure your investment advisor focuses on asset allocation, broad asset-class diversification, and investments in low-transaction-cost, passively managed mutual funds or comparable investment vehicles like Exchange Traded Funds and the new inflation-protection debt securities, TIPS and I Bonds.

Your investment advisor should charge a fixed fee based upon the value of your assets. He or she should not receive any commissions on any investments made in your account. You should ask your investment advisor to aggregate his or her fee and the expense ratio of the investments selected for your account. This number should be in the range of .75-1.25 percent. If it is more than that, you should be concerned. Remember, the one factor that correlates positively with good returns is low transaction costs and professional fees. This is just as true when dealing with investment advisors as with brokers.

DOING DUE DILIGENCE ON AN INVESTMENT ADVISOR

Investment advisors must be registered with the states in which they do business or with the SEC. In 2001, the SEC initiated an Investment Advisor Public Disclosure website, which provides clients and prospective clients with the registration documents filed by the more than 9,000 registered investment advisors. The site includes each advisor's fees and services offered, as well as any disciplinary actions against the advisor, advisory company, or employees during the previous 10 years.

Prior to doing business with an investment advisor, you should check out the information by finding the site through www.sec.gov.

HOW CAN YOU GET MONEY BACK FROM
AN INVESTMENT ADVISOR?

Many investment advisors do not provide for mandatory arbitration in their contracts, and their clients are therefore not required to submit to the arbitration process. If there is no arbitration clause, you probably will need to pursue any claim against an investment advisor through litigation in court.

Claims against investment advisors typically involve allegations of breach of contract, breach of fiduciary duty, and negligence. The viability of these claims depends on the wording of the agreement between the investor and the advisor, and also on the particular state law governing the relationship.

Many of the same issues that determine the outcome of an action against a broker or brokerage firm govern the conduct of investment advisors. For example, if a portfolio recommended by a broker was deemed not to be suitable for an investor, the same portfolio purchased by an investment advisor would also be deemed not to be suitable. This is true even if the portfolio made money.

In fact, many investment advisors have clauses in their contracts that they must track the market within a certain range. In one case, Merrill Lynch agreed to pay the giant Anglo-Dutch consumer goods firm Unilever a reported $105 to $110 million in 2001 for failing to meet its contracted targets. The case was filed in 1998.

In a seven-week trial that preceded the settlement, Unilever said that Merrill had failed in its risk controls and inadequately diversified, thus failing to provide adequate downside protection in the portfolio. The contract called for Merrill to try to beat the benchmark index of British stocks by 1 percent, and never fall more than 3 percent below the index for four consecutive quarters.

As a general rule, investment advisors who have discretionary authority are held to a higher standard of trust than those who do not, and will be held accountable for conduct that violates their fiduciary duty to their clients. This is significant, since many investment advisors, as a matter of normal practice, have discretionary authority over their clients' portfolios.

(Full disclosure: I am a principal in Academic Wealth Management, LLP, a registered investment advisor. Academic Wealth Management is authorized to recommend funds managed by Dimensional Fund Advisors to its clients.)

TERMINOLOGY

ASSOCIATED PERSON: A person engaged in the investment banking or securities business who is directly or indirectly controlled by an NASD member, whether or not registered or exempt from registration with the NASD. This includes sole proprietors, partners, officers, directors, or branch managers of any NASD member firm.

CLEARING BROKER: A brokerage firm that provides "back-office" activities for other brokerage firms; services include maintenance of books and records, trade processing, receipt of securities and cash, and maintenance of account statements.

CONTROLLING PERSON: An individual who serves as an officer, director, owner, or principal of a firm and incurs secondary liability for frauds and violations committed by brokers and others.

INTRODUCING BROKER: A brokerage firm that does not perform its own clearing activities, but is still responsible to its customers for taking and executing orders and recommending suitable investments.

11

Filings, Discovery, Motions, Negotiations, and Settlements

Sometimes you can win, even if you have already won once before.

In June 2001, an NASD arbitration tribunal awarded an investor $58,000 she had paid in commissions, as well as attorney's fees, after she alleged that her $1 million-plus brokerage account had been illegally churned. This despite the fact that during the 11-month period in question, the account actually gained $300,000 in value.

The tribunal ruled that the firm, Reliance Capital, Inc., and the woman's broker excessively traded the account for the purpose of generating commissions. The account, which had an average balance of about $1 million, was turned over more than 7.0 times in less than a year.

While Reliance argued that it shouldn't be penalized because it made money for its client, the investor's attorney, James Eccleston, presented evidence that during the time period in question, alternative investments such as a growth-stock mutual fund would have had equal or better returns without being subject to the commission costs the investor had borne. "It's simply irrelevant that an account was profitable despite being churned," Eccleston stated in a Business Wire press release.

A large proportion of arbitration claims never go before a tribunal. Many settle before the hearing begins. Many settle at the last minute, just before the hearing. In some instances, the investor simply gives up, unable to deal with the stress of an adversarial proceeding or the burden of complying with demands for discovery. The process of getting a claim from filing to a tribunal can be arduous. At every step of the way, the brokerage firm buries a complaining customer under a blizzard of legal paperwork, hoping to wear the customer down. They try to get you to see that you are, after all is said and done, responsible for your own losses.

The "pre-hearing" phase of an arbitration claim falls into six parts:

- Filings and Answers
- Tribunal Selection
- Discovery
- Motions
- Negotiations
- Settlement (when it happens)

Filings and Answers

When you file a Statement of Claim with either the NASD or the New York Stock Exchange (NYSE)—or the American Arbitration Association (AAA)—you put into motion a formal, choreographed process through which the claim moves.

Each respondent has 20 business days for an NYSE claim and 45 calendar days for an NASD claim during which he, she, or it (for corporate entities such as brokerage firms) formulates a response to the Statement of Claim—known as the Answer—and files it with the director of arbitration for the self-regulating organization (SRO) with which you made the claim. This period can be extended by the SRO or by consent of both parties.

As part of its answer, each respondent may also file a counterclaim against you, a cross claim against another named respondent, or a third-party claim against an individual or entity not named by you as a respondent.

If a counterclaim is filed against you, you have 10 business days (NYSE) or 10 calendar days (NASD) after receipt in which to file your reply to the counterclaim.

Together, all of these statements regarding claims and responses are known as "filings." Any time you make a filing, you need to send five copies to the director of arbitration (for the file, the staff, and each arbitrator on a three-person panel) as well as a copy to every individual and entity who has become a party to the case.

Once this set of preliminary filings is completed, the process of discovery begins, and motions may be filed by any party involved in the claim. It is also at this time that the SRO begins the process of selecting the members of the tribunal who will hear the dispute.

Tribunal Selection*

There is nothing more important than the selection of the arbitrators who will hear your dispute. In NYSE arbitrations, one arbitrator hears claims under $25,000 and three arbitrators hear all claims over $25,000. The cutoff for one-arbitrator cases at the NASD is $50,000, although for cases between $25,000 and $50,000 either party can request a three-arbitrator tribunal.

In three-arbitrator cases before either SRO, two of the arbitrators are "public" arbitrators (not professionally affiliated with the securities industry) and one is a "nonpublic" or "industry" arbitrator, meaning that the person had or has an association with the securities industry. Whether any particular arbitrator is really public or nonpublic is a source of much controversy and discussion among securities lawyers. The truth is that in order to have the required expertise, most arbitrators have far more than an average knowledge and familiarity with the securities industry, either as former executives or brokers, or as attorneys or retired attorneys who do or did securities work.

While there are some differences between the SROs in the method of selecting arbitrators (e.g., the ability of one party to the dispute to "strike" a potential panelist is unlimited in NASD arbitrations and limited in NYSE arbitrations), the procedure is substantially the same.

Each party receives a list of proposed arbitrators, divided into public and nonpublic categories. The SROs also provide information on the background and experience of each arbitrator and information concerning previous awards by that arbitrator (or panels on which that arbitrator was a member). The parties strike from the lists those arbitrators they don't want, and rank the others in order of preference (separating rankings for public and nonpublic). The SRO then attempts to match up the parties' lists by order of preference and arbitrator availability.

Given the importance of who sits on a panel, considerable effort is expended by securities lawyers to determine whatever they can about prospective arbitrators. For example, it is possible to obtain copies of prior awards by each proposed arbitrator. Further investigation can be made by contacting attorneys who participated in hearings before that arbitrator.

There are four major problems with arbitration panels today:

1. As I noted earlier, the fact that at least one arbitrator is or was affiliated with the securities industry leads to the perception, if not the reality, of bias. In my view, claimants should be entitled to a tribunal of completely independent, impartial arbitrators. If the industry arbitrator is a strong presence, he or she can dominate the proceedings, furthering the impression—and even creating the reality—that the investor is simply not getting a fair hearing.

2. The investigative process, while helpful, may not really tell you all that much about the predilections and biases of a particular arbitrator. Essentially, you are "flying blind."

3. A study of panelists available to serve on these tribunals found that 89 percent of them were white men over 60. Women and minorities are poorly represented on panels, although I have been assured by both the NASD and the NYSE that they are aggressively trying to add more diversity to their panels. Until they do, however, claimants will be deprived of tribunals that are really impartial and representative of their communities.

4. Serving on these panels is a much sought-after assignment for retired men, who wish to supplement their retirement income and who enjoy the prestige of acting as judges of these disputes. This desire for continued appointments makes them unlikely to ruffle the feathers of the securities industry, the lawyers representing the securities industry, or the directors of arbitration for the NASD and the NYSE. As a consequence of these factors, there is a clear pro-industry bias that makes it very difficult for investors to get a fair hearing.

Discovery

Discovery is the process through which each party to a legal proceeding (in this case an arbitration) gets to request documents from the other party or parties about the transactions or arrangements that are at issue in the case.

One of the goals of arbitration is to streamline the discovery process from what it would be in a typical civil case filed in a federal or state court. However, beginning in 1987, when arbitration became the way nearly all disputes between investors and brokers and brokerage firms were resolved, the discovery process almost immediately began metastasizing to such a degree that by the mid-1990s it looked nearly identical to the process in court, which is cumbersome and time-consuming, and to the nonlawyer often seems just plain out of control.

At each step of the way, lawyers often argued with the arbitrators about why each document requested by the other party should not be produced, increasing costs and causing delays.

In an effort to get the discovery process for securities arbitration back under control, the NASD in 1999 produced a Discovery Guide (see Appendix A at the end of the book) that sets forth categories of documents that are "presumptively discoverable."

The guide, which can be found at www.nasdr.com, has 14 document lists. List 1 is all the documents that must be produced by a broker or firm in all cases, while list 2 is all of the documents that must be produced by the investor making a claim against a broker and/or firm.

The other 12 lists cover documents that must be produced by the claimant or respondent for specific claims:

    3 & 4: churning
    5 & 6: failure to supervise
    7 & 8: misrepresentation/omission
    9 & 10: negligence/breach of fiduciary duty
    11 & 12: unauthorized trading
    13 & 14: unsuitability

In theory, all documents must be produced by the parties within 30 days after the answer is filed. In practice, this is rarely done.

DOCUMENTS YOU NEED TO PRODUCE

The documents that you must provide in any case include portions of your personal and business tax returns, financial statements, and statements of other brokerage accounts you hold with other firms. You can expect the lawyers for the brokerage firm (and any other party you name or who is subsequently named) to scrutinize these documents carefully in an effort to find something to defeat your claim, or to intimidate or embarrass you so you will lose your desire to pursue your claim.

The NASD Discovery Guide lists the following 13 documents that are to be produced by a customer filing a claim in all cases. (Reprinted with permission of National Association of Securities Dealers Dispute Resolution [NASD-DR].)

1. All customer and customer-related business (including partnership or corporate) federal income tax returns, limited to pages 1 and 2 of Form 1040, Schedules B, D, and E, or the equivalent of any other type of return, for the three years prior to the first transaction at issue in the Statement of Claim through the date the Statement of Claim was filed.

2. Financial statements or similar statements of the customer's assets, liabilities, and/or net worth for the period(s) covering the three years prior to the first transaction at issue in the Statement of Claim through the date the Statement of Claim was filed.

3. Copies of all documents the customer received from the firm/ Associated Person(s) and from any entities in which the customer invested through the firm/Associated Person(s), including monthly statements, opening account forms, confirmations, prospectuses, annual and periodic reports, and correspondences.

4. Account statements and confirmations for accounts maintained at securities firms other than the respondent firm for the three years prior to the first transaction at issue in the Statement of Claim through the date the Statement of Claim was filed.

5. All agreements, forms, information, or documents related to the account(s) at issue signed by or provided by the customer to the firm/ Associated Person(s).

6. All account analyses and reconciliations prepared by or for the customer related to the account(s) at issue.

7. All notes, including entries in diaries or calendars, related to the account(s) at issue.

8. All recordings and notes of telephone calls or conversations about the customer's account(s) at issue that occurred between the Associated Person(s) related to the account(s) at issue.

9. All correspondence between the customer (and any person acting on behalf of the customer) and the firm/Associated Person(s) related to the account(s) at issue.

10. Previously prepared written statements by persons with knowledge of the facts and circumstances related to the account(s) at issue,

including those by accountants, tax advisors, financial planners, other Associated Person(s), and any other third party.

11. All prior complaints by or on behalf of the customer involving securities matters and the firm's/Associated Person(s)' response(s).

12. Complaints/Statements of Claim and Answers filed in all civil actions involving securities matters and securities arbitration proceedings in which the customer has been a party, and all final decisions and awards in these matters.

13. All documents showing action taken by the customer to limit losses in the transaction(s) at issue.

I find it more than just a little ironic that when you file a dispute, the brokerage firm can ferret through your personal financial information; yet when you open a new account with the firm, many times the broker does not even ask you for the most basic financial information, which presumably is necessary for him or her to determine which investments are suitable for you.

WHAT ARE YOU LOOKING FOR IN DISCOVERY?

There is a lot of potentially useful information for your case among the documents that are presumptively discoverable in all cases, and in cases specific to your particular claim. Among the most important items are:

■ Documents related to any disciplinary action taken against the broker or other arbitrations the broker has been involved in. These documents include within them not only the results of any arbitrations in which the broker has been a party, but also any sanctions against the broker by the Securities and Exchange Commission (SEC), any SRO (the exchanges and the NASD all have the ability to fine brokers or suspend or revoke their right to work for an exchange or NASD member), or any state licensing, regulatory, or law-enforcement body. There are also documents in this category that show customer complaints about the broker to the firm and results of any internal audits of the broker's records.

These can all be important if trying to prove a pattern of particular misdeeds by the broker. They are also helpful in trying to show that the firm did not supervise the broker appropriately, given his or her history of misdeeds.

■ Portions of the firm's training materials and compliance manuals having to do with the particular claim being made. From this you can see if any of the firm's policies or procedures were violated by the conduct at issue in your case.

■ Information about the broker's compensation, including commissions he or she generated and the basis for the broker's compensation. If you are trying to show, for instance, that the broker recommended an unsuitable investment, you can possibly glean from the compensation reports that the broker sold the same investment to a number of customers in a short period of time and also determine if there was any sort of incentive provided to brokers to sell that particular investment. If such were the case, you could make the argument that the broker was looking to earn the incentive rather than to assist his or her client to maximize return and/or minimize risk.

■ Materials prepared by the broker, or prepared by others and subsequently used by the broker, regarding the particular investment product. These might include analyst research, prospectuses and other offering materials, or "crib sheets" and other sales assistance tools. These materials can help you determine whether the broker truly understood the product's risk characteristics and could make a determination if it was suitable for his or her clients. This material could also help you tie conflicts of interest within the firm's research organization and the firm's investment banking operations to particular recommendations.

■ Although not presumptively discoverable, a number of attorneys are acquiring through the discovery process the broker's telephone records and using sophisticated techniques to mine those records, especially in cases of unauthorized trading and in cases where the defense contends that the broker was directed by the investor to purchase the allegedly unsuitable securities for his or her account. Determining whether a telephone call was "outbound" or "inbound" can help you determine whether a particular transaction was solicited by the broker or unsolicited. If a number of "unsolicited" transactions occur immediately following "outbound" telephone calls from the broker to the investor, one can question whether the investor really directed those transactions, or if the investor made them on the basis of a broker recommendation and the broker mismarked the trade confirmation, a violation of NASD and exchange rules and possibly a fraud under SEC Rule 10(b)-5.

DOES YOUR BROKER OWE YOU MONEY?

Frequently, a review of the "presumptively discoverable" documents can lead to further inquiries, which may result in the claim being settled. In one case, my clients claimed that a well-known brokerage firm had mismanaged their pension account by placing it in unsuitable, speculative securities.

When I became aware of the fact that the broker who had handled my clients' account had been fired, I asked the firm to produce a record of his personal trading for his own account. An examination of those documents revealed that he bought thinly traded stocks for his own account shortly before placing large orders of the same stocks for my clients and others—an activity called frontrunning that I described in detail in Chapter 3.

Further analysis showed that he sold his holdings shortly after making the purchases for his clients, reaping significant profits from this practice. Once my expert had prepared a spreadsheet demonstrating this practice, the case was promptly settled.

The importance of discovery, and careful follow-up of documents obtained in discovery, cannot be overemphasized.

Motions

One of the virtues of arbitration for investors is that "motions" are limited. A motion is a legal request by a party in a dispute for the ruling individual (in this case, usually the chairman appointed to the arbitration panel) to compel the other party in the dispute to either do something or refrain from doing something.

The seemingly endless filing of motions in civil court cases is one reason the process takes so long.

Previously, motions were strongly discouraged in arbitration proceedings. But recently that has changed and more motions are being filed, usually by respondents, in an effort to dispose of claims without a hearing.

The major type of motion confronted in securities arbitrations (other than a motion to compel the production of documents) is a "motion to dismiss," which essentially asserts that even if all of the statements in the claim are true, there is no basis for the claim.

These motions are appropriate, for example, where a claim is filed outside of the time window set by the SRO or where the SRO does not have jurisdiction. However, motions to dismiss are now being used by respondents to attack claims for many different reasons, causing significant cost and delay in proceedings that were intended to be efficient and cost-effective.

As a result of these and other tactics, securities arbitration, to many practitioners, is becoming more and more like court litigation.

Negotiations

Most claims can be settled without a formal arbitration hearing if both parties act in good faith. And, in general, that is often the case, at least after some preliminary posturing. Negotiation is, in some ways, like a mating ritual, and both sides have to get their behavioral displays out of the way before they can sit down and seriously hash out the issues at hand.

You should never refuse to negotiate a claim. And, if you are using an attorney, you and your attorney should have a serious discussion about negotiating strategy before he or she enters into discussions with the respondent(s) to your claim. That way the attorney knows exactly what he or she can do to settle the claim, without having to come back to you after each negotiating discussion.

In any negotiation, you should:

- Know what your "bottom line" is; that is, at what dollar value you will be willing to settle the case.
- Know what you are willing to "give up" in order for the deal to get done.
- Have patience.

YOUR BOTTOM LINE

You will very rarely, if ever, receive the total amount of your stated claim through a process of negotiation. Therefore, you have to decide up front what your bottom-line number will be.

One fact is very important to remember here: the U.S. General Accounting Office (GAO) study that showed that about 60 percent of investors are successful in arbitration hearings, and that on average, tribunals award about 60 percent of the total claim. The success rate of investors in arbitration decisions has declined to 43 percent in recent years, and fewer cases are being settled by brokerage firms, who have developed a siege mentality.

Once an investor understands the mathematics of probability and risk (Chapter 6), it seems to me that he or she should be pretty satisfied with a negotiated settlement for 60 percent of the amount of damages stated in the claim, and perhaps even less, given the biased nature of arbitration tribunals.

HOW MUCH WILL YOU GIVE UP?

Negotiating is not a zero-sum game; it is not necessarily a case where one party wins and the other party loses. Negotiations can provide a situation where each side gives a little and gains a little.

One way a negotiation can fall apart is if you don't know how much you are willing to "pay"—to give up—in order to reach a negotiated settlement.

Many people who file a securities arbitration claim are seeking some kind of revenge. They would love to see the broker and/or firm publicly humiliated. In order to reach a negotiated settlement, you need to put that out of your mind and focus on the benefit of the settlement versus the risk of arbitration. This is especially important since one part of most negotiated settlements is a nondisclosure agreement, which bars the parties from discussing the claim or the amount paid in the settlement.

PATIENCE

Patience is perhaps the biggest virtue in negotiations.

Most negotiated settlements in securities arbitration claims do not come early in the process. It is important that, even if you get increasingly frustrated with the process as it drags on—which happens to almost every client of mine—you do not lose sight of your bottom line or what you are willing to give up in order to achieve a settlement.

The truth is that in the legal profession, as in so many others, there is a set of rituals that need to be carried out before any outcome can be attained.

Settlements

Somewhere over two-thirds of the claims I initiate for clients are settled either before or during arbitration. They are usually settled for between 50 and 60 percent of the amount of the claim.

MEDIATION USUALLY LEADS TO SETTLEMENT

Mediation settles most claims. Mediators have a way of getting investors to understand that they will not get everything they want, and getting brokerage firms to understand that they can save themselves money, time, and potentially bad publicity by settling.

I don't know what it is, but it seems that once parties agree to mediation, they have decided emotionally that they are ready to settle. No matter how badly the mediation seems to be going, at the end of the day everyone just sort of says, "What's the bottom line to get this deal done?"

For instance, a few years ago, I was in a one-day mediation session. At the beginning of the session, I made a request for $500,000 in damages for my client (less than the full amount of the claim). The attorney for the brokerage firm countered with an offer of $100,000.

All day long, I showed the mediator and the attorney the kind of evidence I would use at the hearing. The attorney kept increasing her offer by $5,000 or $10,000 at a time. By mid-afternoon, she was up to about $150,000.

At about 3:00, the mediator decided to meet with the other attorney individually, then came to me and said, "She needs to leave soon to catch a plane. She wants to make a last and best offer." I said, "Fine, but tell her it has to start with the number four."

We settled the case less than an hour later for $425,000.

SETTLEMENT OFTEN HAPPENS AT THE LAST MINUTE

Some settlements occur as a result of damaging, or at least embarrassing, information that comes out during the discovery process. But most settlements occur either immediately prior to the arbitration hearing or during the hearing itself, simply because that is the right time for the brokerage house to settle.

My sense is that to brokerage houses, claims for arbitration are simply a part of doing business. When to settle is a simple economic decision: the longer they can hold on to the client's money (however they came by it), the longer they can invest it profitably (perhaps even in index funds).

As long as their annual legal fees for all of the claims in the pipeline are less than the investment income being generated by the money that is at issue in the claims, the brokerage house has little incentive to settle.

During the discovery phase, the brokerage house's legal costs are not large. They involve the time necessary to respond to filings and document-production requests.

But when the case goes to a hearing, the legal fees can begin to pile up. A three-day hearing (average time) with two lawyers and two paralegals from a large law firm, billing anywhere from $150 per hour for a paralegal to $500 or more per hour for a partner, can cost the firm more than $30,000. Then there are the experts, and the expenses around bringing the lawyers, experts, witnesses, and respondent(s) to the arbitration tribunal's site (which could be across the country).

Some brokerage firms do use in-house counsel exclusively to handle arbitration claims, which reduces their expenses considerably and reduces the impact of legal fees as an incentive to settle. However, in all cases, once the issue gets to an adjudicating body, no one ever knows which way the decision will go. By offering to settle at the last minute, the brokerage firm is at the same time reducing its risk and hoping that you will have cold feet about a formal hearing.

It can take months to get a brokerage firm to acknowledge an offer to settle, but once the settlement dam has been broken, cases often settle in a matter of hours.

TERMINOLOGY

ANSWER: A respondent's response to a claim.

DISCOVERY: The process through which each party in a legal proceeding gets to request documents from the other party or parties about the transactions or arrangements that are at issue in the case.

MOTION TO DISMISS: A formal request for the arbitrators to determine that even if all of the statements in the claim are true, there is no basis for the claim.

NASD DISCOVERY GUIDE: A document prepared by the NASD in 1999 listing all the documents that are "presumptively discoverable" and must be turned over by one party to the other for various types of securities arbitration claims.

TRIBUNAL: The arbitrator or arbitrators selected to hear a claim make up a tribunal.

12 Arbitration Proceedings and Decisions

Getting a brokerage firm to pay an award can be a complex and even harrowing experience. Sometimes you have to pull out all the stops. It helps to have an aggressive lawyer and strong state consumer protection laws.

Take the case of Arthur Leider. An 84-year-old retired metallurgist from Joshua Tree, California, Leider in March 2002 won an NASD arbitration award for over $800,000 against a bond broker, Mark Augusta. Augusta had worked for the Solana Beach office of the Minneapolis bond brokerage firm Miller & Schroeder.

Leider was just one of 25 claimants who won arbitration awards against Miller & Schroeder for claims involving the firm's sales of "tax-free municipal" bonds of Heritage Health Care of America. Heritage had received state backing of its bonds, saying it would use the money to rehabilitate medical facilities for use by Alzheimer's patients.

Miller & Schroeder sold $144 million of Heritage bonds, earning $6.6 million in commissions. Heritage subsequently defaulted on the bonds. After failing to pay an arbitration award to another California investor, Miller & Schroeder's license was suspended by the NASD. The firm was subsequently sold to another brokerage firm, which bought M&S's assets but not its liabilities. There were no assets in the shell with which to pay arbitration awards.

So Leider's attorney, Bradd Milove, filed another claim against the broker. As one of the charges, Milove charged Augusta with violating California's rigorous consumer protection laws that protect the elderly from fraudulent sales practices.

Milove has also filed suit against the brokerage firms (M&S and the firm that bought it) in state court, on behalf of all the investors in Heritage bonds, including those who have won arbitrations but failed to receive payment.

A securities arbitration hearing is war. It is intellectually and physically taxing for everyone in the hearing room.

In a hearing, remember four rules about arbitrators:

1. They want to appear to be fair and impartial, although frequently they are neither.
2. They don't like being manipulated.
3. They do like to be entertained.
4. They regard incivility and hostility as reflecting negatively on that person, or his or her client.

I always try to keep opening and closing presentations brief—no more than 15 minutes each—and keep questioning of witnesses short and to the point.

I don't introduce a lot of documents, believing that if you bury the arbitrators in too much paper, they won't be able to find the important pieces.

I usually call only three or four witnesses.

It is not unusual for me to call the broker, instead of my client, as the first witness. I do this for a number of reasons.

First, the atmosphere is very tense at the beginning of an arbitration hearing, and I want to give my client time to get used to the environment. More importantly, I want to elicit the broker's testimony without giving him or her the advantage of tailoring testimony to my client's prior testimony.

By letting my client first hear the broker's testimony, he or she is better able to rebut that testimony and make a more effective presentation to the tribunal.

I do not ask hostile questions of the broker (or of anyone else testifying). I ask questions in a respectful manner. I don't argue with the broker's answers. I find that hostility engenders more hostility and diminishes the effectiveness of a presentation in the tribunal's eyes.

I always tell my clients, "If your tone, attitude, or what you are saying would be offensive in a social situation, it will be offensive to the members of the tribunal."

Kindness and respect, coupled with an almost compulsive preparation and perseverance, are the hallmarks of successful securities arbitration. Conversely, when faced with hostility, I do not respond in kind, because I know that it serves no purpose and is in reality counterproductive.

Silently I hope that the broker and/or brokerage firm executives will be hostile and overzealous in their advocacy. I want the contrast between these people and my client to be as stark and dramatic as possible.

When it comes time for my client to testify—I usually call my client as my second witness—I have him or her simply tell the story the way he or she told it to me a year or so earlier when we first met. I don't play a violin, or ask for my client to embellish the story. Real stories are powerful, and when told honestly an audience (the arbitrators) can intuit the truth.

Naturally, I prepare my client thoroughly for the hearing. We go over relevant documents and review the facts that led to his or her losses. I emphasize the need to be honest and sincere, and to be truthful at all costs. I remind the client that, although he or she will be sitting across the table from me while being examined, it is important—in a non-contrived way—to make eye contact with the tribunal members during key points in the testimony (both on direct and cross-examination).

Sometimes I videotape my client prior to the hearing and ask the client to observe his or her mannerisms. It can be an eye-opening experience. By and large, most claimants, with this kind of preparation, are calm and relaxed during direct examination and relatively unrattled by cross-examination.

My third witness is usually the branch manager or compliance officer in the broker's office. This gives me the chance to introduce evidence to back up the failure-to-supervise and breach-of-fiduciary-duty claims I have made against the firm. Sometimes I can use evidence obtained through document discovery (like the firm's compliance manual) to show conduct by my client's broker that violated the firm's own guidelines, which should not have escaped the attention of brokerage firm executives and supervisors.

My fourth and final witness is the expert I use to analyze my client's portfolio(s). The easy part of his testimony relates to his calculations of profit and loss, turnover ratio, and cost-equity ratio. These are mathematical calculations that don't lend themselves to dispute.

The far more challenging testimony relates to the concepts discussed in Chapters 6 and 7: Modern Portfolio Theory, standard deviation, beta, proper diversification within a portfolio, and the effect of asset allocation on portfolio return. These concepts are not well understood by most arbitrators who make up tribunals, by the brokerage firm executives and brokers, or by the firm's counsel.

Many attorneys for brokerage firms have a tendency to belittle these concepts in an effort to persuade tribunal members that these are theories put forth by pointy-headed academic types and have no application in the real world of making money.

In one recent arbitration, the brokerage firm's attorney, in exasperation, asked, "Does Mr. Solin think that brokers have an obligation to recommend index funds to their clients?" as if index funds were a radical and ill-conceived notion.

If all goes well, my case takes a day or two to present, including the cross-examination of all of my witnesses by the respondent(s)' attorney(s).

Being Cross-Examined

Most attorneys would rather have a sympathetic client with a weak case than an off-putting client with a strong case. Being cross-examined can be a very humbling experience, and it can bring out the worst in many people.

Preparation is the key to being an effective witness who can withstand cross-examination. You should be thoroughly familiar with the transactions, conversations, or other events. You can assume that the brokerage firm attorney has spent hours going over every document produced by you in discovery. He or she has also carefully debriefed your broker for evidence of any incriminating conversations you two have had, or incriminating information about you.

I find that the typical cross-examination of a claimant in a securities case follows a set pattern. Assuming my direct examination took 30 minutes, the cross-examination will last anywhere from two to four hours. Defense counsel usually has a large, loose-leaf notebook with the cross-examination written out. He or she reads the questions to the witness. It seems endless, often repetitive, and it is very boring. But it can also wear the witness down over time.

I instruct my clients to treat opposing counsel with the same civility and respect that I do; to answer questions directly; to avoid the temptation to "score points" or to argue with counsel. Since it is not uncommon for counsel to be hostile and aggressive, we discuss strategies for coping with this kind of conduct.

I owe my most effective tip to a psychiatrist I used as an expert in one case to establish that my client suffered emotional distress as well as financial damages because of his broker's actions. The psychiatrist testified extensively, and during cross-examination had to deal with all kinds of aberrant behavior by opposing counsel.

He told me later that he never made eye contact with the counsel. Instead, he would focus his gaze on the bridge of the lawyer's nose when it was necessary to look in his or her direction at all; and he would look directly at the tribunal members when his responses were of particular importance.

Finally, I try to reduce the stress by telling my clients to treat this experience like an adventure, and to be proud of the fact that they are standing up for their rights against a large, powerful institution. The experience should be almost enjoyable and something they will look back on with pride.

When clients are prepared in this way, some of them actually look forward to being cross-examined. I have had some clients express disappointment that opposing counsel was not more abusive and hostile. They were ready for the challenge.

The Broker and/or Brokerage House's Case

Once the brokerage firm decides to take a case to a hearing, it has determined that it has a reasonable prospect of winning. Otherwise, it would have settled the case. You can expect counsel for the brokerage firm to be well prepared to mount a very serious defense to your claims.

While the nature of the defense varies depending on the claims at issue, the central theme tends to be the same: You knew what was going on in your account; it was what you wanted at the time; you wanted to take risks; you were happy when your account was doing well; this is just sour grapes.

These arguments are made with great force and indignation when the client is "sophisticated"—loosely defined as someone with a reasonable education and some investing experience. Even if you are not at all sophisticated, the brokerage firm may allege that you had family members who should have advised you that your portfolio was too risky. While it remains my view that this defense is intellectually and ethically bankrupt, it can be very effective.

I find these arguments offensive because, if the broker has failed to properly allocate your portfolio, or has recommended a portfolio that is too volatile for your risk tolerance, or engaged in other improper activity, I don't understand why he or she should not be held accountable for this misconduct, whether or not you went along with the strategy and whether or not your son or daughter has a Ph.D. in finance. After all, you go to a brokerage firm because it purports to have expertise in portfolio management among other things.

You should be entitled to rely on the advice given to you by these professionals, the same way you rely on advice given by your doctor or accountant. If a doctor prescribes the wrong medication to a person trained as an emergency medical technician, the doctor cannot claim as a defense that the EMT "should have known that there was an error" and brought it to the doctor's attention. That is ludicrous. As one former client of mine said, "When I had my wisdom teeth pulled, I didn't read a book on oral surgery. I assumed the surgeon knew what he was doing."

Nevertheless, you can expect the broker ("your" former broker and former "trusted advisor") to defend him- or herself vigorously at your expense. He or she will explain how many of the stocks in your portfolio were actually your idea to buy; how you wanted aggressive growth because your friends were making a killing in the market and you felt left behind; and how he or she carefully explained the risks you were undertaking.

The branch office manager or the compliance officer will explain to the tribunal members how he or she monitors accounts daily, and saw nothing amiss in your trading.

Counsel for the brokerage firm will constantly repeat the refrain that "just because you had losses doesn't mean you have a claim" and "don't blame the broker for a down market."

However, you are unlikely to hear any evidence that your standard deviation and/or your beta were consistent with your risk tolerance. I have still never had a case where a broker calculated either of these critical measurements of risk. I even had one broker testify that he did not believe that standard deviation accurately measured risk! However, when I asked him how he measured risk, he was unable to come up with any alternative.

Calculating Damages

If the respondent is found by the tribunal to have committed the misdeed(s) alleged in the claim, the claimant is provided with monetary compensation, called damages. Attorneys who work for investors can compute the damages they ask for in many different ways, using a few different methodologies and in some cases utilizing state laws to their advantage.

Arbitrators can determine damages they award in many different ways as well (they do not have to use the computation method suggested by the claimant or his or her attorney). There is a difference between actual damages and market-adjusted damages. And arbitrators have the ability to add punitive damages against brokers and/or brokerage firms, although this is rarely done. Arbitrators can also add to damages an assessment for attorney's fees and arbitration proceeding fees.

Assuming the arbitrators conclude that your claim is valid, they generally seek through the award to "make customers whole" by putting you back in the same relative economic position you were in before the broker carried out the misdeeds.

Among the various ways you, your lawyer, or the arbitration tribunal may calculate damages are:

- Out-of-pocket method
- Benefit-of-the-bargain method
- Well-managed account method
- Disgorgement method
- Recision method

OUT-OF-POCKET
The out-of-pocket method calculates net out-of-pocket losses by adding all realized profits and losses through securities bought and sold, adding unrealized gains and losses (securities bought but not sold), interest and dividends on investments held, and expenses incurred such as margin debt. It also takes into account any additional deposits or withdrawals made by the client during the time period being analyzed.

This method focuses on an investor's actual losses, and does not take into account any "opportunity costs," potential gains from more prudent investments that could have been made.

BENEFIT-OF-THE-BARGAIN
The benefit-of-the-bargain gives the investor the benefit of any misrepresentation made by the broker by calculating how much the investment would have been worth if everything the broker said were true. It is often difficult to determine what the "bargained for" value of a particular investment was, and therefore this method is not frequently used by arbitration tribunals when setting damage awards. However, if you can establish that your broker promised

you a specific return on your investment (e.g., "We should double your money in a year"), you may be able to use this calculation.

WELL-MANAGED ACCOUNT

The well-managed account method calculates the difference between the portfolio's actual performance and what the portfolio would have earned if it had been appropriately managed.

Some attorneys use a related calculation called "market-adjusted damages" to remove the subjectivity of what "well-managed" means and substitute an objective measure of market performance. You can either calculate return against a model portfolio or against market indexes. The same cash inflows and outflows are taken into account when comparing portfolio results.

DISGORGEMENT

The disgorgement method is sometimes used in churning or excessive trading cases, where the amount of excess commissions a broker has run up can be easily calculated. The broker is forced to disgorge the ill-gotten gains. Disgorgement is more frequently used by a regulatory authority such as the Securities and Exchange Commission (SEC) or NASD Regulation when it finds a broker, brokerage firm, or investment advisor guilty of violating federal securities laws or NASD regulations. In that case, the disgorgement is a payment to the government or to NASD Regulation, which goes to offset the cost of investigating and prosecuting the offense.

RECISION

The recision method is a way of calculating the investor's position had the fraud not taken place, and returning the investor to that position. Recision is often used in cases of unregistered brokers or brokers who sell unregistered securities or securities that have no liquid market and no way for the investor to sell the security. The respondent is forced to return the investor's money and take back the illiquid security.

In most of my cases, I have my expert calculate both out-of-pocket damages and market-adjusted damages, and select the higher of the two figures.

We run two kinds of market-adjusted damage calculations. The first analysis takes the asset classes in the actual account and compares them to a similarly allocated account. As our proxy index for the domestic equity portion of the portfolio, we use the Center for Research in Security Prices (CRSP) 1-10

All Equity Universe Index. For foreign stocks, we use the Morgan Stanley Europe, Australia, Far East (EAFE) Index. As a proxy for the fixed income portion we use the Lehman Intermediate Government Bond 1-10 Index, and for the cash portion of the portfolio, we use the three-month U.S. Treasury bill. We have access to a number of other market indexes that we can use when appropriate, for municipal bonds, real estate, and other asset classes.

We compare the performance of the actual portfolio to these proxies and claim the difference as the damages.

In addition, we also calculate what the account's performance would have been if it had been invested in an asset allocation consistent with Modern Portfolio Theory. For example, in the last few years my typical client has a portfolio invested almost 100 percent in stocks, usually with a tilt toward technology stocks. We look at the client's age and financial situation and conclude, for example, that it would have been much more appropriate if he or she had been invested in a static 60 percent diversified equity to 40 percent fixed-income asset allocation. We then calculate how an account allocated in that manner would have performed, and compare those results to the actual account performance.

Finally, state law may provide attractive options for increasing the amount of the damages that can be recovered. Some states have statutes that provide for double or even triple damages, plus attorney's fees, under some circumstances. Other states provide for different measures to calculate damages, like permitting you to "rescind" all of your purchases and sales, then add a statutory rate of interest on the amount of your investment. These statutes can materially increase the amount of any potential award. Therefore, it is important to consider the effect of these statutes in formulating a damage claim.

The Award

Arbitration decisions are written. They are usually issued 30 to 60 days after the hearing. They are simple and not discursive. The object is to state which party the ruling is for, and if it is for the claimant, the amount of damages awarded. A majority of the tribunal members is required to rule for one party or the other. It is unusual for there to be any stated dissent from a tribunal's decision.

In my experience, even when investors prevail, the amount they are awarded is less than they deserve. I believe that arbitrators are very concerned about serving on future panels and they know that awards that are perceived as generous by the NASD, the New York Stock Exchange (NYSE), or the securities defense bar may compromise their selection in the future. Consequently, as a practical matter, investors should anticipate that, if they prevail, the best they can expect is their out-of-pocket losses, and frequently the award will be for less than this amount.

APPEALS

If the brokerage house or the claimant loses the arbitration hearing, the losing party can appeal the decision to a state or federal court. Appeals, however, are unusual, although they are becoming more common. Appeals are expensive and the possibility of success is very small. Under NASD rules, brokerage firms have 30 days after losing a tribunal hearing within which to either appeal or pay the award.

The primary grounds a brokerage firm has for an appeal are "evident partiality of the arbitrators" and "manifest disregard" for the facts.

In terms of partiality, it's pretty hard for a brokerage firm to prove partiality toward complainants in a system skewed toward the brokerage industry, with one arbitrator coming from the industry and even the two "public" arbitrators often having a background in the industry. Manifest disregard appeals have to demonstrate that no rational tribunal could have reached the result the particular tribunal did based upon the facts of the claim. It is a very difficult standard to meet.

Brokerage firms sometimes use another tactic when they lose before a tribunal: intimidation.

I had a case against a large brokerage firm where we prevailed at the tribunal. The lawyers for the firm were outraged at this outcome, which they believed was unfair and not warranted by the evidence. They sent a lengthy letter to the NASD (for transmission to the tribunal members) setting forth all of the reasons the decision was wrong. They told the tribunal that unless it reversed itself, they intended to appeal the decision and they were confident they would win the appeal.

As you can imagine, my client was upset about the possibility of an appeal. Even though appeals rarely succeed, some do and there is always significant delay, cost, and uncertainty. We discussed whether we should approach the brokerage firm and settle for a discount from the award amount. We decided not to, but to wait and see if the firm would actually appeal.

On the thirtieth day after the award, at 5 p.m., the brokerage firm delivered a check to my office.

Getting Paid

Just because you have been wronged does not mean that an arbitration tribunal will see it that way.

And just because an arbitration tribunal agrees that you were wronged, and assesses damages against the broker or brokerage firm, doesn't mean you will actually be able to collect the award.

When an arbitration tribunal hands down a judgment against a major brokerage firm, like Merrill Lynch, Salomon Smith Barney, PaineWebber, or the like, the check usually arrives within a few weeks (under NASD and NYSE rules, payments of awards are to be made within 30 days).

But many of the most egregious violations of securities laws are perpetrated by brokers at small, fly-by-night boiler-room firms. And, according to a June 2000 U.S. General Accounting Office (GAO, since renamed the Government Accountability Office) study,

> . . . an estimated 61 percent (+/–7 percentage points) of investors who won arbitration awards in 1998 either were not paid or received only partial payment.
>
> Our estimates showed that these investors did not receive nearly 80 percent of the $161 million that they were awarded (i.e., they only received 20 percent of money awarded). Nearly all of the unpaid awards involved arbitration cases decided in NASD's arbitration forum.
>
> Better follow-up on award payments, however, will not address the primary nonpayment problem, because most broker-dealers that failed to pay the awards were no longer in business.

The reasons most of the unpaid awards came from NASD cases is that boiler-room firms, while NASD members, were not NYSE member firms. Claims heard by the NYSE are usually against major firms with strong capitalization. Nonpayment of an arbitration award would lead to the firm's membership being revoked.

This is why it is so important when exploring a possible arbitration filing against small, thinly capitalized firms to consider naming the brokerage firm's controlling persons and filing a claim against the brokerage firm's clearing firm if there is a basis for doing so. A better option is not to deal with those kinds of brokerage firms in the first place.

Tax Status of Awards

There are two related tax issues that are important for you to consider in connection with securities arbitration matters.

Presumably you would not be filing a claim if you did not suffer a loss (although it is technically possible to make a claim even with an account that gained value but should have gained more if managed prudently). But assuming you had a loss, you have probably deducted at least part of that loss against other kinds of investment gains on your tax returns.

If you have previously taken a loss, any award you receive in a subsequent tax year will be taxed at ordinary income-tax rates in the year in which you receive the award, up to the amount you have previously deducted. You should take this tax liability into account when calculating the net financial benefit to you of a successful claim.

An additional issue surrounding previously deducted losses is that attorneys for the brokerage firm may ask you about these deductions during the tribunal, accusing you of trying to rip off the brokerage house for an award after you have already claimed the deduction. They will argue in their presentation to the tribunal that any award should be reduced by the deduction you have already taken. I warned you that many brokerage firms instruct their attorneys to pull out all the stops in order to defeat, or at least minimize, your claim.

Fortunately, this argument has been soundly rejected by arbitration tribunals and by the courts, including the U.S. Supreme Court in its 1986 decision in the *Randall v. Loftsgaarden* case.

Tax Status of Attorney Fees

The second tax issue can be far more troubling. This issue concerns the deductibility of the fees you will pay to your attorney under your contingent-fee agreement.

Claimants receiving awards who have entered into contingent-fee agreements with their attorneys rarely receive a check for the entire amount of the award. These claimants typically receive a check from their attorney for the amount of the award less the attorney's fee.

In a pair of cases decide by the U.S. Supreme Court in 2005, the Court ruled that the contingent-fee portion of lawsuit settlements and awards is taxable to the client, even if the money goes directly to the attorney.

As a practical matter, this means that you will be required to report as taxable income and pay tax on money you never receive, even though the fees you pay to your lawyer are not fully deductible.

As a consequence of these decisions, you will be left only with the ability to deduct these fees as miscellaneous itemized deductions.

There are several disadvantages to deducting legal fees as miscellaneous itemized deductions. In the first place, miscellaneous itemized deductions are allowed only to the extent that they exceed 2 percent of a taxpayer's adjusted gross income. Second, even if a taxpayer has legal fees that exceed 2 percent of his or her adjusted gross income, the taxpayer's total itemized deductions will be subject to the phaseout provisions and further reduced if his or her adjusted gross income exceeds a specific dollar amount ($150,500 in 2006). In such a case, the amount of itemized deductions allowed is reduced by the lesser of 3 percent of the excess adjusted gross income or 80 percent of the itemized deductions allowable for the tax year. The limit on itemized deductions, however, is due to be phased out starting in tax year 2006 and eliminated completely in 2009.

All taxpayers are also subject to an "alternative minimum tax" (AMT), the complexities of which are far beyond the scope of this book. It is sufficient for our purposes to note that a taxpayer's miscellaneous itemized deductions are not allowed as a deduction in computing a taxpayer's AMT. The combined effect of the limitations on miscellaneous itemized deductions and the applicability of the AMT may totally nullify, or very significantly reduce, your ability to take deductions for the legal fees you pay your lawyer.

Therefore, prior to making a claim and prior to entering into a contingent-fee agreement with an attorney, it is prudent to consult your accountant or a tax attorney to calculate the tax consequences of winning an award and paying a fee.

Is It Worth Even Filing a Claim?

This is, to use the phrase from the old television game show, the $64,000 question.

Before you file a claim against a broker and/or brokerage firm for your market losses, you need to do a careful cost-benefit analysis. To do this, you need to understand the basic concepts of risk and probability I discussed in

Chapter 6, and understand your own tolerance for stress and uncertainty. In some instances, even if you lost a lot of money and you feel you have a legitimate claim, it is simply best for your physical and emotional well-being to walk away and try to pick up the pieces in some other way.

Here's the calculation you need to do. I'll use a hypothetical case of a $500,000 investment loss, and consider a "worst-case scenario" and stay away from trying to calculate the AMT.

> 1. As I have previously stated, current statistics show that about 40 percent of all claimants receive awards, which average about 60 percent of the claim. To use gross probability calculations, this means you have a 2 in 5 chance of receiving a $300,000 award.
>
> 2. More and more lawyers are charging 40 percent of an award received from a tribunal. This means you would pay your lawyer a fee of $120,000, reducing your net award to $180,000.
>
> 3. Assume you have about $5,000 in out-of-pocket expenses, reducing your net to $175,000.
>
> 4. Assume you have previously deducted all of your losses against other income. This means the entire $300,000 (minus out-of-pocket expenses) is taxed at the top federal income tax rate of about 35 percent, at 2005 rates (about $105,000).

This means that after paying your attorney, costs, and federal income taxes, your net income from the award would be about $75,000.

The bottom line is that you have a 2 in 5 probability of receiving a net award of, on average, between 15 and 23 percent of your claim.

Is it really worth going through the process for such an "expected" outcome? This is a question only you can answer.

The Final Word

It is not surprising that millions of Americans continue to place trust and confidence in brokers and brokerage firms. The securities industry spends hundreds of millions of dollars a year on marketing, in a successful effort to convince many investors that they can trust and rely on brokers and that brokers provide a valuable and meaningful service that investors simply can't do without.

I have tried to demonstrate that the conflicts inherent in the broker/client relationship make it very difficult, if not impossible, for brokers to resist lining their own pockets at the expense of their clients. The recent appalling conduct of the securities industry, culminating in the global settlement regarding analysts and now the mutual fund scandal, has deeply shaken investor confidence in brokers, as well it should.

However, all of this begs a much more fundamental issue: Why use brokers?

Most are not trained in basic principles of finance. Most do not understand the importance of asset allocation and diversification within asset classes. And almost all of them engage in stock picking, market timing, or the selection of actively managed mutual funds or managed accounts—strategies that all of the credible data has established add cost and subtract value over the long term.

It is my view that brokers are emperors with no clothes, selling overpriced services that are often too risky and unsuitable for the risk tolerance and investment objectives of their clients. Even worse, the performance of the portfolios recommended by brokers is almost certain to underperform a properly diversified portfolio, using index or passively managed funds, over the long term.

So, what's an investor to do?

As I explain in my new book, *The Smartest Investment Book You'll Ever Read* (Perigee Books, 2006), the vast majority of investors would be far better served avoiding brokers altogether. Instead, these investors should invest in an appropriate mix of index-based mutual funds purchased directly from fund managers such as Vanguard, Fidelity, or T. Rowe Price, or exchange traded funds (ETFs) such as iShares. Remember that low transaction costs are a significant determinant of positive returns.

Those investors who require the services of an advisor should consider fee-based financial advisors. These advisors receive a fixed fee based on the portfolio's value. Unlike brokers, they have no incentive to churn accounts and generate commissions.

Smaller investors who require advice should use a financial advisor who charges an hourly fee (fee only). These advisors should be able to recommend an appropriate asset allocation, with broad diversification within asset classes, that these investors can then implement themselves by buying no-load index funds directly from a mutual fund company.

One limitation of Vanguard is that it does not presently offer passively managed international small-cap and international value funds. For larger portfolios that need exposure to these asset classes, the undisputed leader in passively managed index funds with both domestic and international stock and bond exposure is Dimensional Fund Advisors (DFA), based in Santa Monica, California (www.dfaus.com). DFA offers larger investors the flexibility to optimally tilt asset-class exposure toward value and small-cap equities that, over long holding periods, have been shown to outperform the broader equity market.

DFA funds are only available through selected fee-based investment advisors. One such firm is Academic Wealth Management (www.academic wealth.com), a firm in which I am a principal.

When interviewing fee-based or hourly-fee-only advisors, you should be wary of advisors who do not at least consider Vanguard or DFA as the best option for most investors. In addition, advisors who do not subscribe to the following basic principles of portfolio management should be avoided:

1. Low transaction costs should be a primary objective.
2. Active managers add little value.
3. Passively managed funds should be a major part of any portfolio.

Finally, please remember this: If you want to avoid becoming a victim of stockbrokers and the cozy mandatory arbitration system that is the price of admission in order to deal with them, simply avoid using them. You don't need them and you will most likely be better off without them.

Glossary

ANNUALIZED TURNOVER: The percentage of a securities portfolio's value that has been turned over each year. A "low" turnover is below about 0.5 times per year, while a "high" turnover is above about 1.2 times per year (based on a study of mutual fund styles). A turnover of more than 2.0 times a year is a possible indication of churning.

ANSWER: A respondent's response to a claim.

ARBITRATION: A method by which a conflict between two or more parties is resolved by impartial people—arbitrators—who are knowledgeable in the area(s) of controversy.

ASSET ALLOCATION: The mix of investments among the various classes of financial assets, typically stocks, bonds, and cash equivalents. The goal is to create an "efficient" portfolio that provides the highest return for a given amount of risk, and reduces the risk by placing portions of the portfolio in asset classes that move up or down in value in inverse relation to one another.

ASSOCIATED PERSON: A person engaged in the investment banking or securities business who is directly or indirectly controlled by an NASD member, whether or not registered or exempt from registration with NASD. This includes sole proprietors, partners, officers, directors, or branch managers of any NASD member firm.

AWARD: A decision by an arbitration tribunal that resolves an arbitration between a customer and the brokerage firm, and perhaps other respondents.

BEST EXECUTION: Brokers and firms are required under the rules of the NASD and the various stock exchanges to seek the best possible execution for their customer of any order to buy or sell a security.

BETA: A measure of an investment's sensitivity to market movements. By definition, the beta of the entire stock market is 1.0. A security or portfolio with a beta of less than 1.0 is less volatile than the market, while a security or portfolio with a beta of greater than 1.0 is more volatile. Typically, the S&P 500 is used as the benchmark index and proxy for "the market," against which individual stocks or mutual funds measure their beta.

BOILER ROOM: Sometimes called a "chop shop." A brokerage firm that uses high-pressure telephone sales techniques to get investors to buy stocks. Boiler rooms often engage in manipulating the price—and sometimes even the market—in thinly traded stock, unauthorized trading, churning, and other fraudulent practices.

CHURNING: Excessive trading in a securities portfolio in order to continually generate commissions for the broker and brokerage firm.

CLAIM: A demand for money or other relief.

CLAIMANT: The party making the claim.

CLEARING BROKER: A brokerage firm that provides "back-office" activities for other brokerage firms; services include maintenance of books and records, trade processing, receipt of securities and cash, and maintenance of account statements.

COMMISSION: A payment received by the sales agent for selling an investment product. Commissions are split between the broker and the brokerage firm.

CONTROLLING PERSON: Every individual who, directly or indirectly, controls any other individual liable for violating federal securities laws. In securities arbitration matters, "controlling persons" are frequently the officers or shareholders of the brokerage firm that employs the broker involved in the disputed transactions. "Controlling persons" may be held liable to the same extent the broker is, unless the controlling person acted in good faith and did not directly or indirectly induce the act or acts that constituted the violation or cause of action.

COST-EQUITY RATIO: Sometimes called the "break-even" ratio, cost-equity tells what portion of the portfolio's value is being spent on transaction costs and margin interest. Cost-equity shows how much a portfolio would have to generate in investment returns in order to cover the costs. A cost-equity ratio above 3 percent may be considered excessive and indicate churning.

COUNTERCLAIM: A claim filed by a respondent against the claimant.

CROSS CLAIM: A claim filed by one respondent against another respondent named in the same claim.

DAMAGES: The amount of money being requested or awarded. Damages can include compensatory damages (to make up for money lost or reimbursement for poor investment returns); punitive damages (as a punishment for extremely bad behavior by a broker or firm); attorney's fees for the claimant's attorney; and reimbursement of filing fees and the portion of hearing fees paid by the claimant.

DISCOVERY: The process through which each party in a legal proceeding gets to request documents from the other party or parties about the transactions or arrangement that are at issue in the case.

DIVERSIFICATION: The process by which an investor can eliminate or reduce certain risks by spreading investments across asset classes and among many securities within each asset class.

EFFICIENT FRONTIER: The two-dimensional graph that shows the highest potential return from a diversified portfolio for any desired level of risk an investor is willing to assume.

EFFICIENT MARKET: The efficient market concept posits that all information about a security is available to all interested parties, and that the market price for the security factors in all of that information. Hence, the "true value" of a security is, in fact, the market price.

ELIGIBILITY RULES: The NASD Code of Arbitration states that no claim is eligible for submission to arbitration where six years have elapsed from the occurrence of the event giving rise to the controversy. The NYSE has a similar eligibility rule. State statutes may require that claims be brought within a shorter time period.

FAILURE TO SUPERVISE: A claim that is made against the firm for which a broker worked, or against individuals in the administration of the branch in which the broker worked. It charges that the individuals and institution responsible for overseeing the broker's behavior and performance were negligent in their supervision, which allowed the broker to commit a fraud or violation of NASD or exchange rules and cause harm to an investor.

FIDUCIARY: An individual or organization that has a special relationship with and duty toward another individual or organization to act "in the highest good faith" and "with integrity." In many states, brokers are deemed to have a fiduciary relationship with their clients.

FILING: Delivery to the director of arbitration of the appropriate self-regulatory organization (NASD or NYSE) of the Statement of Claim or other pleadings, to be kept on file as a matter of record and reference.

FINANCIAL SUICIDE: An investor is said to be committing financial suicide if he or she engages in trading that is contrary to his or her risk tolerance and investment objectives. Whether or not a broker may be held liable in "economic suicide" cases may depend upon the nature and extent of the broker's involvement in the trades at issue.

FRAUD: Obtaining money from another party through an act of lying, cheating, deceit, or misrepresentation. Securities fraud involves use of a deliberate "manipulative or deceptive device" including misstatement of "material fact," or failure to disclose a "material fact" in connection with the purchase or sale of a security.

FRONTRUNNING: An illegal activity in which a broker, brokerage firm, or investment advisor takes a position in a security in advance of an action that he or she knows his or her brokerage firm (or advisory company), or a client, will take that will cause the security's price to move in a predictable fashion.

INDEX FUND: A stock mutual fund that holds all or substantially all of the securities that make up a particular market index. Index funds are sometimes called "passive funds" because they do not seek to improve investment returns over the index's expected return through any kind of trading strategy.

INITIAL PUBLIC OFFERING (IPO): The first sale of stock in a company to the general public.

INTRODUCING BROKER: A brokerage firm that does not perform its own clearing activities but is still responsible to its customers for taking and executing orders, and for recommending suitable investments.

"KNOW-YOUR-CUSTOMER" RULE: The New York Stock Exchange (NYSE) rule that requires brokers to know their clients' investment objectives and financial condition before making any investment recommendations. The NASD has a similar rule, as do the other exchanges.

LOAD: The sales charge for a mutual fund. The load can be charged either as a "front-end load" when shares in the fund are purchased, or as a "back-end load," usually referred to as a "contingent deferred sales charge" (CDCS), when shares in the fund are sold.

MARGIN ACCOUNT: A type of brokerage account that allows an investor to use the value of the securities held in the account as collateral against a cash loan; this loan can then be used to purchase additional securities.

MARGIN CALL: When the ratio of equity to the total of equity plus margin debt falls below a particular level, the brokerage firm requires the investor to bring the ratio back up (issues a margin call). The margin call can be met either by putting more cash (or more securities) into the account, or by selling some of the securities in the account.

MARKUP: The amount a brokerage firm charges above the market price for securities it makes a market in.

MEDIATION: An informal, voluntary process used in securities industry disputes (and other disputes) in which a mediator helps negotiate a mutually acceptable resolution between parties to a dispute. Unlike arbitration or litigation, mediation does not impose a solution. If the parties cannot agree on an acceptable settlement, they may still arbitrate and/or litigate their dispute.

MISREPRESENTATION & OMISSION: A category of frauds under the antifraud section of the Securities Exchange Act of 1934 under which a broker induces an investor to either purchase or sell a security through misrepresenting a "material fact" that, had it not been misrepresented, might have caused the investor to act differently; or omitting a "material fact" that, had it been disclosed, might have caused the investor to act differently.

MODERN PORTFOLIO THEORY (MPT): The underlying theory from which portfolio management concepts are derived: that investors seek to maximize investment returns while simultaneously minimizing investment risk.

MOTION TO DISMISS: A formal request for arbitrators to determine that even if all of the statements in the claim are true, there is no basis for the claim.

NASD DISCOVERY GUIDE: A document prepared by the NASD (Appendix B in this book) listing all of the documents that are "presumptively discoverable" and must be turned over by one party to the other in various types of securities arbitration claims.

NASD RULES OF FAIR PRACTICE: The NASD rules that govern how brokers and brokerage firms are supposed to deal with their clients.

NASDAQ: A computerized trading system for trading listed stocks; Nasdaq takes the place of an open-call-out stock exchange.

ONLINE SUITABILITY: The concept that, even when investors trade online with no interaction with a broker, the brokerage firm has some responsibility to know the customer's objectives and financial condition, and to not allow the investor to make investments that are incompatible with those objectives and conditions, and thus are unsuitable. This is very much an evolving legal area.

PARTY: A person or organization making or responding to a claim in an arbitration proceeding.

PAYMENT FOR ORDER FLOW: A system where a brokerage firm that makes the market in a particular stock with multiple market makers pays back some of the markup it earns to the brokerage firm that sent the order to it. Payment for order flow sometimes conflicts with a firm's duty to provide its customers with the best execution possible.

PENNY STOCK: A stock that trades for under $1 per share. Penny stocks are highly risky. They often do not trade on an exchange, but rather on the "pink sheets" or the "over-the-counter" broker-to-broker marketplace. The Securities and Exchange Commission (SEC) has special regulations regarding to whom penny stocks may be sold.

PUMP-AND-DUMP: A classic stock fraud in which a boiler-room firm or group of boiler-room firms manipulate the market and price of a thinly traded stock by selling to a small, closed circle of public investors (pumping the stock). Insiders in the stock sell out their positions in the security at the top of the market (dumping the stock), causing the price to begin to collapse, which usually sends the stock into a free fall.

RESPONDENT: The person or organization against whom a claim is made.

RISK: A measure of the probability of potential outcomes, and of the potential change in portfolio value, as a result of differences in the economic environment between now and some point in the future.

RISK PREMIUM: The excess investment return above the risk-free return an investor hopes to obtain in exchange for taking on a degree of investment risk.

RISK-FREE RETURN: The investment return available from a risk-free security, usually considered to be the rate paid on short-term U.S. Treasury bills.

R-SQUARED: A measure of how closely the return characteristics of a security or portfolio match those of a particular market index. Typically, the S&P 500 is used as the benchmark. An R-squared value of 100 means the security has a perfect correlation with the benchmark index. In order to properly understand the meaning of an investment's beta, you need to know how closely it correlates to its comparative index by measuring its R-squared.

S&P 500: The Standard & Poor's company's index of 500 of the largest American corporations, as measured by market capitalization (stock price × number of shares outstanding = market capitalization).

SCIENTER: A legal term that means intent. Scienter is a very important concept when making a claim of securities fraud; in order to have committed a fraud, the broker or firm must have acted either with scienter or with reckless disregard for the investor's interest.

SECTION 10(B) & RULE 10(B)-5: Section 10(b) of the Securities Exchange Act of 1934 prohibits securities fraud in connection with the sale or purchase of securities to the public. Securities and Exchange Commission Rule 10(b)-5 expands on Section 10(b). Many securities arbitration cases cite this section and rule in one or more of the charges against the broker and/or brokerage firm.

SELF-REGULATING ORGANIZATIONS (SROS): Organizations that regulate their members' actions outside the legal system. An SRO can establish policies and procedures that sanction members or adjudicate disputes without using the courts. The national securities and commodities exchanges (NYSE, AMEX, CBOE) and the NASD are all SROs.

SELLING AWAY: Selling away occurs when a broker sells securities or other investments outside the scope of his or her work for the brokerage firm he or she works for (a violation of NASD Rule 3040).

SHARPE RATIO: A measure of an investment's risk-adjusted return, using the investment's return minus the risk-free return as the numerator and the investment's standard deviation as the denominator.

SHINGLE THEORY: The legal theory that holds that the brokerage firm and individual broker, by "hanging out a shingle" as a licensed professional, implies a level of professionalism and ethical dealing with clients.

SOLICITED/UNSOLICITED ORDER: A solicited order is a securities transaction that results from a broker's recommendations, either directly or indirectly. An unsolicited order is one that results from an investor's request.

SOPHISTICATED INVESTOR: Under SEC guidelines, an investor is defined as "sophisticated" if he or she meets certain income and net-worth requirements. Being classified as a "sophisticated" investor allows the investor to purchase unregulated securities, such as private placements of stock and limited partnerships.

SPREAD: The difference between the bid and ask price on a security being offered for sale in the marketplace. The bid-ask spread provides an automatic profit for the firm making a market in the security, which compensates for the market maker being required to maintain an orderly market by buying from any seller or selling to any buyer.

STANDARD DEVIATION: A statistical calculation that measures the "dispersion" of all individual data points in a set around and away from the mean (average). In the world of investments, standard deviation is a proxy for the "volatility" of a security; a security's expected return over a given time period (e.g., annually) falls within one standard deviation above or below the mean approximately two-thirds of the time, and within two standard deviations approximately 95 percent of the time.

STOP-LOSS ORDER: An order placed to sell a security at a particular price. If the order is placed at a price below which you bought the security, you automatically stop the loss on the investment at a particular place. If the order is placed above the price at which you bought the security but below the price at the time the order is placed, you automatically lock in a profit.

SUBPOENA: An order issued by a court, investigating authority, arbitration panel, or other authorized party that compels an individual to provide sworn testimony or to provide documents for the purpose of the investigation or adjudication.

SUITABILITY (UNSUITABILITY): The legal theory under which an investor can recover compensatory damages in an account where the broker recommended and encouraged the purchase of securities that are inappropriate for the investor, given the investor's risk tolerance, financial conditions, and investment objectives.

THIRD-PARTY CLAIM: A claim filed by a respondent against a party not named in the claim (usually filed by a brokerage firm against a broker not named in the investor's claim).

TRIBUNAL: The arbitrator or arbitrators selected to hear a claim make up the arbitration tribunal.

UNAUTHORIZED TRADING: When a broker buys or sells securities without the investor's consent. Unauthorized trading typically (but not always) occurs in accounts where the investor has not given the broker discretion to engage in trading for the account without his or her permission.

WRAP ACCOUNT: A managed account held by a brokerage firm. Instead of commissions being charged on each transaction, an annual fee is charged (usually 1 to 2 percent of the account's value).

ORGANIZATIONS:

The following organizations have websites that contain a great deal of very useful information for investors:

American Arbitration Association: www.adr.org

American Stock Exchange: www.amex.com

Chicago Board Options Exchange: www.cboe.com

National Association of Investors Corporation: www.better-investing.org

National Association of Securities Dealers: www.nasd.com

New York Stock Exchange: www.nyse.com

Public Investor Arbitration Bar Association: www.piaba.org

Securities and Exchange Commission: www.sec.gov

Securities Industry Association: www.sia.com

Securities Investor Protection Corporation: www.sipc.org

Bibliography

BOOKS

Allen, John Lawrence. *Investor Beware: How to Protect Your Money from Wall Street's Dirty Tricks*. New York: Wiley, 1993.

Anonymous and Timothy Harper. *License to Steal: The Secret World of Wall Street Brokers and the Systematic Plundering of the American Investor*. New York: HarperBusiness, 1999.

Asensio, Manuel P., with Jack Barth. *Sold Short: Uncovering Deception in the Markets*. New York: Wiley, 2001.

Association for Investment Management & Research. *Standards of Practice Handbook*. Charlottesville, VA: AIMR, 1999.

Bernstein, William. *The Intelligent Asset Allocator: How to Build Your Portfolio to Maximize Returns and Minimize Risks*. New York: McGraw-Hill, 2001.

Blitzer, David M. *Outpacing the Pros: Using Indexes to Beat Wall Street's Savviest Money Managers*. New York: McGraw-Hill, 2001.

Bogle, John C. *John Bogle on Investing: The First 50 Years*. New York: McGraw-Hill, 2001.

Cadsby, Ted. *The Power of Index Funds: Canada's Best-Kept Investment Secret*. Toronto: Stoddard, 1999.

Dembo, Ron S., and Andrew Freeman. *The Rules of Risk: A Guide for Investors*. New York: Wiley, 1998.

Dempsey, Mark. *Robbing You Blind: Protecting Your Money from Wall Street's Hidden Costs and Half-Truths*. New York: Morrow, 2000.

Eichenwald, Kurt. *Serpent on the Rock*. New York: HarperBusiness, 1995.

Evans, Richard E. *The Index Fund Solution: A Step-by-Step Investor's Guide*. New York: Fireside, 1999.

Fabozzi, Frank J., ed. *Selected Topics in Equity Portfolio Management*. New Hope, PA: Fabozzi Associates, 1998.

Fridson, Martin S. *Investment Illusions: A Savvy Wall Street Pro Explodes Popular Misconceptions About the Markets*. New York: Wiley, 1993.

Gibson, Roger C. *Asset Allocation: Balancing Financial Risk, Third Edition*. New York: McGraw-Hill, 2000.

Grinold, Richard C., and Ronald N. Kahn. *Active Portfolio Management: A Quantitative Approach for Producing Superior Returns and Controlling Risk, Second Edition*. New York: McGraw-Hill, 2000.

Kantor, Sanford S., Joel H. Bernstein, David W. Kennedy, and editors of Consumer Reports Books. *Stand Up to Your Stockbroker: Your Rights as an Investor*. Yonkers, NY: Consumer Reports Books, 1991.

Lederman, Jess, and Robert A. Klein, eds. *Global Asset Allocation: Techniques for Optimizing Portfolio Management*. New York: Wiley, 1994.

Little, Kenneth E. *Bear-Proof Investing: Protecting Your Financial Future in a Bear Market and Taking Advantage of an Emerging Bull Market*. Indianapolis: Alpha Books, 2002.

Lowenstein, Roger. *When Genius Failed: The Rise and Fall of Long-Term Capital Management*. New York: Random House, 2000.

Malkiel, Burton G. *A Random Walk Down Wall Street, Fourth Edition*. New York: W.W. Norton, 1985.

Robbins, David E. *Securities Arbitration Procedure Manual, Fourth Edition*. New York: Matthew Bender, 2000.

Schwed, Fred Jr. *Where Are the Customers' Yachts? or A Good Hard Look at Wall Street*. New York: Wiley, 1995. (A Wiley Investment Classic, original publication 1940, Simon & Schuster.)

Sincere, Michael. *101 Investment Lessons from the Wizards of Wall Street: The Pros' Secrets for Running with the Bulls Without Losing Your Shirt*. Franklin Lakes, NJ: Career Press, 1999.

Stoneman, Tracy Pride, and Douglas J. Schulz. *Brokerage Fraud: What Wall Street Doesn't Want You to Know*. Chicago: Dearborn, 2002.

Swedroe, Larry E. *The Only Guide to a Winning Investment Strategy You'll Ever Need: Index Funds and Beyond—The Way Smart Money Invests Today.* New York: Dutton, 1998.

Swedrow, Larry E. *What Wall Street Doesn't Want You to Know: How You Can Build Real Wealth Investing in Index Funds.* New York: St. Martin's, 2001.

Trader X. *Dancing with Lions: One Man's Odyssey Through the Chicago Markets, Trading, and Self-Discovery.* Speculative Holdings Inc. 1999.

Williams, Ellie. *The McGraw-Hill Investor's Desk Reference.* New York: McGraw-Hill, 2001.

Yanis, Edward. *Dancing with Bears.* San Jose, CA: Writers Club Press, 2000.

LAW REVIEW ARTICLES

Anderson, Seth C., and Donald A. Winslow, "Defining Suitability," *Kentucky Law Journal,* 1993 (81 Ky. L.J. 105).

Bellwoar, John M., "Bar Baron at the Gate: An Argument for Expanding the Liability of Securities Clearing Brokers for the Fraud of Introducing Brokers," *New York University Law Review,* October 1999 (74 N.Y.U.L. Rev. 1014).

Burns, James L., "Pruning the Judicial Oak: Developing a Coherent Application of Common Law Agency and Controlling Person Liability in Securities Cases," *Columbia Law Review,* June 1993 (93 Colum. L. Rev. 1185).

Campbell, Douglas, "Symposium: Effective Resolution of Disputes in the New Millennium: Perceptions, Myths, and the Law: Comment Alternative Dispute Resolution: 'Waiver of Trial' Clause Mandating Arbitration of Securities Disputes Should Require Application of State Law," *St. Mary's Law Journal,* 2000 (31 St. Mary's L.J. 1039).

Charrier, Aaron C., "Taxing Contingency Fees: Examining the Alternative Minimum Tax and Common Law Tax Principles," *Drake Law Review,* 2002 (50 Drake L. Rev. 315).

Feldman, Stephen D., "Exclusion of Contingent Attorneys' Fees from Gross Income," *University of Chicago Law Review,* Fall 2001 (68 U. Chi. L. Rev. 1309).

Freeman, John P., "Mutual Fund Advisory Fees: The Cost of Conflicts of Interest," *The Journal of Corporate Law,* University of Iowa, 2001 (26 Iowa J. Corp. L. 609).

Horan, Stephen M., and Bruce D. Johnson, "Portfolio Management, Private Information, and Soft-Dollar Brokerage: Agency Theory and Evidence," Draft article, 1999.

Hu, Henry T. C., "Illiteracy and Intervention: Wholesale Derivatives, Retail Mutual Funds, and the Matter of Asset Class," *Georgetown Law Journal,* July 1996 (84 Geo. L.J. 2319).

Karmel, Roberta S., "Is the Shingle Theory Dead?" *Washington & Lee Law Review,* Fall 1995 (52 Wash & Lee L. Rev. 1271).

Langbvein, John H., and Richard A. Posner, "Market Funds and Trust-Investment Law," paper for delivery, 1996, American Bar Foundation.

Libin, Nancy C., and James S. Wrona, "The Securities Industry and the Internet: A Suitable Match?" *Columbia Business Law Review,* 2001 (2001 Colum. Bus. L. Rev. 601).

Rapp, Robert N., "Rethinking Risky Investments for That Little Old Lady: A Realistic Role for Modern Portfolio Theory in Assessing Suitability Obligations of Stockbrokers," *Ohio Northern Law Review,* 1998 (24 Ohio N.U.L. Rev. 189).

Root, Stuart D., "Suitability—The Sophisticated Investor—And Modern Portfolio Management," *Columbia Business Law Review,* 1991 (1991 Colum. Bus. L. Rev. 287).

Steinberg, Marc I., "Symposium: Securities Arbitration: A Decade After McMahon: Securities Arbitration: Better for Investors Than the Courts?" *Brooklyn Law Review*, Winter 1996 (62 B.L. Rev. 1503).

Stout, Lynn A., "Are Stock Markets Costly Casinos? Disagreement, Market Failure, and Securities Regulation," *Virginia Law Review,* 1995 (81 Va. L. Rev. 611).

Wonnell, Christopher T., "The Structure of a General Theory of Nondisclosure," *Case Western Reserve Law Review,* 1991 (41 Case W. Res. L. R. 329).

NASD Discovery Guide

The Discovery Guide

For NASD arbitrations, the Discovery Guide supplements the section in the Securities Industry Conference on Arbitration (SICA) publication entitled *The Arbitrator's Manual*, and captioned "Prehearing Conference," regarding public customer cases.

I. The Need for New Discovery Procedures

Discovery disputes have become more numerous and time consuming. The same discovery issues repeatedly arise. To minimize discovery disruptions, NASD Dispute Resolution, Inc., has developed two initiatives to standardize the discovery process: early appointment of arbitrators to conduct an initial prehearing conference and document production lists (Document Production Lists).

No requirement under the Discovery Guide supersedes any record-retention requirement of any federal or state law or regulation or any rule of a self-regulatory organization.

The Discovery Guide and Document Production Lists are designed for customer disputes with firms and Associated Person(s).[1] The Discovery Guide also discusses additional discovery requests, information requests, depositions, admissibility of evidence, and sanctions. The Discovery Guide, including the Document Production Lists, will function as a guide for the parties and the arbitrators; it is not intended to remove flexibility from arbitrators or parties in a given case. For instance, arbitrators can order the production of documents not provided for by the Document Production Lists or alter the production schedule described in the Discovery Guide. Further, nothing in the Discovery Guide precludes the parties from voluntarily agreeing to an exchange of documents in a manner different from that set forth in the Discovery Guide. In fact, NASD Dispute Resolution encourages the parties to agree to the voluntary exchange of documents and information and to stipulate to various matters. The fact that an item appears on a Document Production List does not shift the burden of establishing or defending any aspect of a claim.

II. Document Production Lists

NASD Dispute Resolution will provide the parties with Document Production Lists (attached to the Discovery Guide) at the time it serves the statement of claim in customer cases. The arbitrators and the parties should consider the documents described in Document Production Lists 1 and 2 presumptively discoverable. Absent a written objection, documents on Document Production Lists 1 and 2 shall be exchanged by the parties within the time frames set forth below.

The arbitrators and parties also should consider the additional documents identified in Document Production Lists 3 through 14, respectively, discoverable, as indicated, for cases alleging the following causes of action: churning, failure to supervise, misrepresentation/omission, negligence/breach of fiduciary duty, unauthorized trading, and unsuitability. For the general document production and for each of these causes of action, there are separate Document Production Lists for firms/Associated Person(s), and for customers.

NASD Rule 10321 provides that the parties shall cooperate to the fullest extent practicable in the voluntary exchange of documents and information to expedite the arbitration process. As noted, nothing in the Discovery Guide precludes parties from voluntarily agreeing to an exchange of documents in a manner different from that set forth in the Discovery Guide.

---

1 NASD Dispute Resolution may develop separate Document Production Lists for intra-industry disputes.

A. Time Frames for Document Production and Objections

The parties should produce all required documents listed in the applicable Document Production Lists not later than 30 days[2] from the date the answer is due or filed, whichever is earlier. If a party redacts any portion of a document prior to production, the redacted pages (or ranges of pages) shall be labeled "redacted." A party may object to the production of any document, which would include an objection based upon an established privilege such as the attorney-client privilege. If any party objects to the production of any document listed in the relevant Document Production Lists, the party must file written objections with NASD Dispute Resolution and serve all parties not later than 30 days following the date the answer is due or filed, whichever is earlier. Objections should set forth the reasons the party objects to producing the documents. An objection to the production of a document or a category of documents is not an acceptable reason to delay the production of any document not covered by the objection. A response to an objection should be served on all parties within 10 days from service of the written objections. Objections and responses should be filed with NASD Dispute Resolution at the time they are served on the parties. The arbitrator(s) shall then determine whether the objecting party has overcome the presumption based upon sufficient reason(s).

B. Confidentiality[3]

If a party objects to document production on grounds of privacy or confidentiality, the arbitrator(s) or one of the parties may suggest a stipulation between the parties that the document(s) in question will not be disclosed or used in any manner outside of the arbitration of the particular case, or the arbitrator(s) may issue a confidentiality order. The arbitrator(s) shall not issue an order or use a confidentiality agreement to require parties to produce documents otherwise subject to an established privilege. Objections to the production of documents, based on an established privilege, should be raised in accordance with the time frame for objections set forth above.

C. Affirmation in the Event that there Are No Responsive Documents or Information

If a party responds that no responsive information or documents exist, the customer or the appropriate person in the brokerage firm who has personal knowledge (i.e., the person who has conducted a physical search), upon the request of the requesting party, must: 1) state in writing that he/she conducted a good faith search for the requested information or documents; 2) describe the extent of the search; and 3) state that, based on the search, no such information or documents exist.

---

2 All time periods referenced herein are calendar days.

3 Section II.B. is also applicable to additional discovery requests and information requests (see Sections IV. and V.).

III. The Initial Prehearing Conference

To maximize the efficient administration of a case by the arbitration panel,[4] the NASD Dispute Resolution staff will schedule an initial prehearing conference in which the arbitrator(s) usually participates.[5] The initial prehearing conference gives the arbitrator(s) and the parties an opportunity to organize the management of the case, set a discovery cut-off date,[6] identify dispositive or other potential motions, schedule hearing dates, determine whether mediation is desirable, and resolve any other preliminary issues.[7] During the initial prehearing conference, the arbitrator(s) and the parties should schedule hearing dates for the earliest available time, consistent with the parties' need to prepare adequately for the hearing.

Prior to the initial prehearing conference, each arbitrator should become familiar with the claims and defenses asserted in the pleadings filed by the parties. At the initial prehearing conference, the arbitrator(s) should order time limits for discovery that will allow the scheduling of hearing dates within a reasonable time and address all outstanding discovery disputes. If the exchange of properly requested documents has not occurred, the arbitrator(s) should order the production of all required documents, including those outlined in the Document Production Lists (see section II above), within 30 days following the conference.

IV. Additional Discovery Requests

The parties may request documents in addition to those identified in the Document Production Lists pursuant to Rule 10321(b). Unless a longer period is allowed by the requesting party, requests should be satisfied or objected to within 30 days from the date of service of the document request. A response to an objection should be served on all parties within 10 days from service of the written objections. Requests, objections, and responses should be filed with NASD Dispute Resolution at the time they are served on the parties.

A party may move to compel production of documents when the adverse party (a) refuses to produce such documents or (b) offers only to produce alternative documents that are unacceptable to the requesting party. NASD Dispute Resolution will provide the Chairperson of the panel with the motion, opposition, and reply, along with the underlying discovery documents the parties have attached to their pleadings. The Chairperson should determine whether to decide the matter on the papers or to convene a prehearing conference (usually via telephone). In considering motions to compel, particularly where non-production is based upon an argument asserting an established privilege, such as the attorney-client privilege, the arbitrator(s) should always give consideration to the arguments set forth by both sides, particularly as to the relevancy of the documents or information. The arbitrator(s) should carefully consider such motions, regardless of whether the item requested is on any of the Document Production Lists. If in doubt, the arbitrator(s) should ask the requesting party what specific documents it is trying to obtain and what it seeks to prove with the documents.

---

4 The panel consists of three arbitrators in most cases. Claims between $25,000 and $50,000 may proceed with a single arbitrator. Claims under $25,000 are decided by a single arbitrator, generally on the pleadings.

5 In some instances, the parties may opt out of the initial prehearing conference. To opt out, parties must supply the following information to NASD Dispute Resolution by the specified deadline:

1) a minimum of four sets of mutually agreeable hearing dates;
2) a discovery cut-off date;
3) a list of all anticipated motions with the motion due dates, opposition due dates, and reply due dates provided;
4) a minimum of four dates and times for any proposed prehearing conferences to hear motions; and
5) a determination whether briefs will be submitted and, if so, the due date for submission.

6 NASD Dispute Resolution recommends that the panel set a cut-off date during the initial prehearing conference for service of discovery requests, giving due consideration to time frames that permit timely resolution of objections and disputes prior to the scheduled exchange of hearing exhibits pursuant to the NASD Code of Arbitration Procedure.

7 The arbitrators should direct one of the parties to prepare and forward to NASD Dispute Resolution, within 48 hours, a written order memorializing the results of the prehearing conference, approved as to form and content by the other parties. When motions are heard at the initial prehearing conference, the panel may order the parties to submit the order with a stipulation as to form and content from all parties.

V. Information Requests

Like requests for documents, parties may serve requests for information pursuant to Rule 10321(b). Requests for information are generally limited to identification of individuals, entities, and time periods related to the dispute; such requests should be reasonable in number and not require exhaustive answers or fact finding. Standard interrogatories, as utilized in state and federal courts, are generally not permitted in arbitration.

Unless a longer period is allowed by the requesting party, information requests should be satisfied or objected to within 30 days from the date of service of the requests. A response to an objection should be served on all parties within 10 days from service of the written objections. Requests, objections, and responses should be filed with NASD Dispute Resolution at the time they are served on the parties.

A party may move to compel responses to requests for information that the adverse party refuses to provide. NASD Dispute Resolution will provide the Chairperson of the panel with the motion, opposition, and reply, along with the underlying discovery documents the parties have attached to their pleadings. The Chairperson should determine whether to decide the matter on the papers or to convene a prehearing conference (usually via telephone).

VI. Depositions

Depositions are strongly discouraged in arbitration. Upon request of a party, the arbitrator(s) may permit depositions, but only under very limited circumstances, such as: 1) to preserve the testimony of ill or dying witnesses; 2) to accommodate essential witnesses who are unable or unwilling to travel long distances for a hearing and may not otherwise be required to participate in the hearing; 3) to expedite large or complex cases; and 4) to address unusual situations where the arbitrator(s) determines that circumstances warrant departure from the general rule. Balanced against the authority of the arbitrator(s) to permit depositions, however, is the traditional reservation about the overuse of depositions in arbitration.

VII. Admissibility

Production of documents in discovery does NOT create a presumption that the documents are admissible at the hearing. A party may state objections to the introduction of any document as evidence at the hearing to the same extent that any other objection may be raised in arbitration.

VIII. Sanctions

The arbitration panel should issue sanctions if any party fails to produce documents or information required by a written order, unless the panel[8] finds that there is "substantial justification" for the failure to produce the documents or information. The panel has wide discretion to address noncompliance with discovery orders. For example, the panel may make an adverse inference against a party or assess adjournment fees, forum fees, costs and expenses, and/or attorneys' fees caused by noncompliance. In extraordinary cases, the panel may initiate a disciplinary referral against a registered entity or person who is a party or witness in the proceeding, or may, pursuant to Rule 10305(b), dismiss a claim, defense, or proceeding with prejudice as a sanction for intentional failure to comply with an order of the arbitrator(s) if lesser sanctions have proven ineffective.

---

8 As with other rulings, an arbitration panel's ruling need only be by majority vote; it need not be unanimous.

LIST 1

Documents To Be Produced In All Customer Cases[9]

Firm/Associated Person(s)

1) All agreements with the customer, including, but not limited to, account opening documents, cash, margin, and option agreements, trading authorizations, powers of attorney, or discretionary authorization agreements, and new account forms.

2) All account statements for the customer's account(s) during the time period and/or relating to the transaction(s) at issue.

3) All confirmations for the customer's transaction(s) at issue. As an alternative, the firm/Associated Person(s) should ascertain from the claimant and produce those confirmations that are at issue and are not within claimant's possession, custody, or control.

4) All "holding (posting) pages" for the customer's account(s) at issue or, if not available, any electronic equivalent.

5) All correspondence between the customer and the firm/Associated Person(s) relating to the transaction(s) at issue.

6) All notes by the firm/Associated Person(s) or on his/her behalf, including entries in any diary or calendar, relating to the customer's account(s) at issue.

7) All recordings and notes of telephone calls or conversations about the customer's account(s) at issue that occurred between the Associated Person(s) and the customer (and any person purporting to act on behalf of the customer), and/or between the firm and the Associated Person(s).

8) All Forms RE-3, U-4, and U-5, including all amendments, all customer complaints identified in such forms, and all customer complaints of a similar nature against the Associated Person(s) handling the account(s) at issue.

9) All sections of the firm's Compliance Manual(s) related to the claims alleged in the statement of claim, including any separate or supplemental manuals governing the duties and responsibilities of the Associated Person(s) and supervisors, any bulletins (or similar notices) issued by the compliance department, and the entire table of contents and index to each such Manual.

10) All analyses and reconciliations of the customer's account(s) during the time period and/or relating to the transaction(s) at issue.

11) All records of the firm/Associated Person(s) relating to the customer's account(s) at issue, such as, but not limited to, internal reviews and exception and activity reports, which reference the customer's account(s) at issue.

12) Records of disciplinary action taken against the Associated Person(s) by any regulator or employer for all sales practices or conduct similar to the conduct alleged to be at issue.

---

9 Only named parties must produce documents pursuant to the guidelines set forth herein. However, non-parties may be required to produce documents pursuant to a subpoena or an arbitration panel order to direct the production of documents (see Rule 10322). In addition, the arbitration Chairperson may use the Document Production Lists as guidance for discovery issues involving non-parties.

LIST 2
Documents To Be Produced In All Customer Cases

Customer

1) All customer and customer-owned business (including partnership or corporate) federal income tax returns, limited to pages 1 and 2 of Form 1040, Schedules B, D, and E, or the equivalent for any other type of return, for the three years prior to the first transaction at issue in the Statement of Claim through the date the Statement of Claim was filed.

2) Financial statements or similar statements of the customer's assets, liabilities, and/or net worth for the period(s) covering the three years prior to the first transaction at issue in the Statement of Claim through the date the Statement of Claim was filed.

3) Copies of all documents the customer received from the firm/Associated Person(s) and from any entities in which the customer invested through the firm/Associated Person(s), including monthly statements, opening account forms, confirmations, prospectuses, annual and periodic reports, and correspondence.

4) Account statements and confirmations for accounts maintained at securities firms other than the respondent firm for the three years prior to the first transaction at issue in the Statement of Claim through the date the Statement of Claim was filed.

5) All agreements, forms, information, or documents relating to the account(s) at issue signed by or provided by the customer to the firm/Associated Person(s).

6) All account analyses and reconciliations prepared by or for the customer relating to the account(s) at issue.

7) All notes, including entries in diaries or calendars, relating to the account(s) at issue.

8) All recordings and notes of telephone calls or conversations about the customer's account(s) at issue that occurred between the Associated Person(s) and the customer (and any person purporting to act on behalf of the customer).

9) All correspondence between the customer (and any person acting on behalf of the customer) and the firm/Associated Person(s) relating to the account(s) at issue.

10) Previously prepared written statements by persons with knowledge of the facts and circumstances related to the account(s) at issue, including those by accountants, tax advisors, financial planners, other Associated Person(s), and any other third party.

11) All prior complaints by or on behalf of the customer involving securities matters and the firm's/Associated Person(s') response(s).

12) Complaints/Statements of Claim and Answers filed in all civil actions involving securities matters and securities arbitration proceedings in which the customer has been a party, and all final decisions and Awards entered in these matters.

13) All documents showing action taken by the customer to limit losses in the transaction(s) at issue.

LIST 3

Churning

Firm/Associated Person(s)

1) All commission runs relating to the customer's account(s) at issue or, in the alternative, a consolidated commission report relating to the customer's account(s) at issue.

2) All documents reflecting compensation of any kind, including commissions, from all sources generated by the Associated Person(s) assigned to the customer's account(s) for the two months preceding through the two months following the transaction(s) at issue, or up to 12 months, whichever is longer. The firm may redact all information identifying customers who are not parties to the action, except that the firm/Associated Person(s) shall provide at least the last four digits of the non-party customer account number for each transaction.

3) Documents sufficient to describe or set forth the basis upon which the Associated Person(s) was compensated during the years in which the transaction(s) or occurrence(s) in question occurred, including: a) any bonus or incentive program; and b) all compensation and commission schedules showing compensation received or to be received based upon volume, type of product sold, nature of trade (e.g., agency v. principal), etc.

LIST 4
Churning

Customer

No additional documents identified.

LIST 5
Failure To Supervise

Firm/Associated Person(s)

1) All commission runs and other reports showing compensation of any kind relating to the customer's account(s) at issue or, in the alternative, a consolidated commission report relating to the customer's account(s) at issue.

2) All exception reports and supervisory activity reviews relating to the Associated Person(s) and/or the customer's account(s) that were generated not earlier than one year before or not later than one year after the transaction(s) at issue, and all other documents reflecting supervision of the Associated Person(s) and the customer's account(s) at issue.

3) Those portions of internal audit reports at the branch in which the customer maintained his/her account(s) that: (a) focused on the Associated Person(s) or the transaction(s) at issue; and (b) were generated not earlier than one year before or not later than one year after the transaction(s) at issue and discussed alleged improper behavior in the branch against other individuals similar to the improper conduct alleged in the Statement of Claim.

4) Those portions of examination reports or similar reports following an examination or an inspection conducted by a state or federal agency or a self-regulatory organization that focused on the Associated Person(s) or the transaction(s) at issue or that discussed alleged improper behavior in the branch against other individuals similar to the improper conduct alleged in the Statement of Claim.

LIST 6
Failure To Supervise

Customer

No additional documents identified.

LIST 7
Misrepresentation/Omissions

Firm/Associated Person(s)

Copies of all materials prepared or used by the firm/Associated Person(s) relating to the transactions or products at issue, including research reports, prospectuses, and other offering documents, including documents intended or identified as being "for internal use only," and worksheets or notes indicating the Associated Person(s) reviewed or read such documents. As an alternative, the firm/Associated Person(s) may produce a list of such documents that contains sufficient detail for the claimant to identify each document listed. Upon further request by a party, the firm/Associated Person(s) must provide any documents identified on the list.

LIST 8
Misrepresentation/Omissions

Customer

1) Documents sufficient to show the customer's ownership in or control over any business entity, including general and limited partnerships and closely held corporations.

2) Copy of the customer's resume.

3) Documents sufficient to show the customer's complete educational and employment background or, in the alternative, a description of the customer's educational and employment background if not set forth in a resume produced under item 2.

LIST 9
Negligence/Breach Of Fiduciary Duty

Firm/Associated Person(s)

Copies of all materials prepared or used by the firm/Associated Person(s) relating to the transactions or products at issue, including research reports, prospectuses, and other offering documents, including documents intended or identified as being "for internal use only," and worksheets or notes indicating the Associated Person(s) reviewed or read such documents. As an alternative, the firm/Associated Person(s) may produce a list of such documents that contains sufficient detail for the claimant to identify each document listed. Upon further request by a party, the firm/Associated Person(s) must provide any documents identified on the list.

LIST 10
Negligence/Breach Of Fiduciary Duty

Customer

1) Documents sufficient to show the customer's ownership in or control over any business entity, including general and limited partnerships and closely held corporations.

2) Copy of the customer's resume.

3) Documents sufficient to show the customer's complete educational and employment background or, in the alternative, a description of the customer's educational and employment background if not set forth in a resume produced under item 2.

LIST 11
Unauthorized Trading

Firm/Associated Person(s)

1) Order tickets for the customer's transaction(s) at issue.

2) Copies of all telephone records, including telephone logs, evidencing telephone contact between the customer and the firm/Associated Person(s).

3) All documents relied upon by the firm/Associated Person(s) to establish that the customer authorized the transaction(s) at issue.

LIST 12
Unauthorized Trading

Customer

1) Copies of all telephone records, including telephone logs, evidencing telephone contact between the customer and the firm/Associated Person(s).

2) All documents relied upon by the customer to show that the transaction(s) at issue was made without his/her knowledge or consent.

LIST 13
Unsuitability

Firm/Associated Person(s)

1) Copies of all materials prepared, used, or reviewed by the firm/Associated Person(s) related to the transactions or products at issue, including but not limited to research reports, prospectuses, other offering documents, including documents intended or identified as being "for internal use only," and worksheets or notes indicating the Associated Person(s) reviewed or read such documents. As an alternative, the firm/Associated Person(s) may produce a list of such documents. Upon further request by a party, the firm/Associated Person(s) must provide any documents identified on the list.

2) Documents sufficient to describe or set forth the basis upon which the Associated Person(s) was compensated in any manner during the years in which the transaction(s) or occurrence(s) in question occurred, including, but not limited to: a) any bonus or incentive program; and b) all compensation and commission schedules showing compensation received or to be received based upon volume, type of product sold, nature of trade (e.g., agency v. principal), etc.

LIST 14
Unsuitability

Customer

1) Documents sufficient to show the customer's ownership in or control over any business entity, including general and limited partnerships and closely held corporations.

2) Written documents relied upon by the customer in making the investment decision(s) at issue.

3) Copy of the customer's resume.

4) Documents sufficient to show the customer's complete educational and employment background or, in the alternative, a description of the customer's educational and employment background if not set forth in a resume produced under item 3.

Investment Policy Statement

INVESTMENT POLICY STATEMENT

For: Investor
Date: Today's Date

INVESTMENT POLICY STATEMENT
Rev. 04/00
REM McGladrey Investment Policy Statement 4-00

INVESTMENT POLICY DISCUSSION

WHAT IS AN INVESTMENT POLICY?

An investment policy outlines and prescribes a prudent and acceptable individualized investment philosophy, and sets out the investment advisory procedures and long-term goals for the investor.

THE NEED FOR A WRITTEN POLICY

Requirements to which company retirement plans were subject originally created the need for written investment policies. We have found the process so useful that we have expanded the concept and now make use of written investment policies for all of our clients.

A written investment policy allows our clients to clearly establish their investment time horizon and goals, their tolerance for risk (as measured by historic volatility) and the prudence and diversification standards that they want the investment process to maintain.

INTRODUCTION

The purpose of this Investment Policy Statement (IPS) is to establish a clear understanding between #1 Investor ("Investor") and RSM McGladrey, Inc. ("Advisor") as to the investment objectives and policies applicable to the Investor's investment portfolio. This Investment Policy Statement will:

- Establish reasonable expectations, objectives and guidelines for the investment of the Investor's assets.

- Set forth an investment structure detailing permitted asset classes and the desired allocation among asset classes.

- Encourage effective communication between Advisor and the Investor.

- Create the framework for a well-diversified asset mix that can be expected to generate acceptable long-term returns commensurate with the level of risk suitable to the Investor.

- Serve as a reference over time to provide long-term discipline for an established investment plan.

- Describe constraints that Investor chooses to place on the investment strategy.

This IPS is not a contract but will provide the framework within which the Investment Advisor will exercise discretion on Investor's behalf. This IPS is intended to be a summary of an investment philosophy that provides guidance for the Investor and Advisor.

INVESTMENT OBJECTIVES

The Investor's objectives for the investment assets of the accounts, set forth in Exhibit A, is #3 Primary Investment Objectives, accompanied by a #8 Risk Level level of risk. The Investor has no expected immediate need of the assets in this account and is willing to accept short-term volatility in order to achieve higher expected rates of return over the long run. The Investor's performance objective is to equal or exceed #4 Performance Objectives. However, no guarantees can be given about future performance and nothing contained in this IPS shall be construed as offering such a guarantee.

Comments:

_____
_____
_____

LIQUIDITY AND INCOME NEEDS

The Investor has determined that sufficient disposable income and liquidity is available from other sources so that the Investor does not need to maintain cash balances among these assets, except for investment reasons, including payment of investment advisory fees or as dictated below. The Investor's income need from the investment portfolio is $#5 Income Needs per year to be distributed #5 Income Needs and to be achieved on a total return basis (i.e. interest, dividends and capital appreciation). The size of the required annual distribution relative to the size of the account may necessitate a withdrawal of principal (assets as they were valued on 12/31 of the prior year) depending on capital market performance. Diminution of portfolio value due to prolonged periods of poor market performance may require an alteration of this investment policy.

Comments:

_____
_____
_____

TIME HORIZON

For the purpose of planning, the investor's time horizon for these investments is to be #6 Investment Time Horizon years. Capital values do fluctuate and the Investor recognizes that the possibility of capital loss does exist. Historical asset class return data suggests the shorter the holding period the greater the risk of the investor's objective not being achieved.

Comments:

_____

_____

_____

RISK TOLERANCE

The Investor recognizes that seeking increased returns generally involves accepting greater volatility and risk. In determining Investor's own risk tolerance, Investor acknowledges that since January 1,1973 a portfolio with the approximate asset allocation being implemented under this IPS experienced the following:

Worst single calendar year decline in value	Worst 3-year total return	% of calendar quarters with negative returns	# of occurrences of 2 consecutive negative quarters	# of occurrences of 3 consecutive negative quarters
#7a	#7b	#7c	#7d	#7e

Investor understands that similar results in the future are possible, and is prepared to tolerate such short-term performance in order to meet Investor's longer-term objectives.

The Portfolio will be managed in a manner that seeks to minimize principal fluctuations within realistic market expectations consistent with the chosen asset allocation over the established horizon and is consistent with the stated objectives. Financial research has demonstrated that risk is best minimized by holding assets over time and through diversification of assets, including international investments. Investor recognizes, however, that performance results cannot be guaranteed and historical performance is not indicative of future performance.

ASSET ALLOCATION

Academic research suggests that the decision on how to allocate total assets among various asset classes will have far greater impact upon portfolio performance than security selection and market timing. After reviewing the long-term performance and risk

INVESTMENT POLICY STATEMENT
Rev. 04/00
REM McGladrey Investment Policy Statement 4-00

characteristics of various asset classes and balancing the risks and rewards of market behavior, the following asset classes were selected to achieve the objectives of the Investor's Portfolio, as stated above, subject to any constraints listed below:

ASSET CLASS	% OF PORTFOLIO		
Domestic	Min	Target	Max
U.S. Large Cap	0.0	0.0	0.0
U.S. Large Cap Value	0.0	0.0	0.0
U.S. Small Cap	0.0	0.0	0.0
U.S. Small Cap Value	0.0	0.0	0.0
Real Estate	0.0	0.0	0.0
TOTAL DOMESTIC EQUITIES	-5.0	0.0	5.0
International			
International Large Cap Value	0.0	0.0	0.0
International Small Cap	0.0	0.0	0.0
International Small Cap Value	0.0	0.0	0.0
Emerging Markets Large	0.0	0.0	0.0
Emerging Markets Value	0.0	0.0	0.0
TOTAL INTERNATIONAL EQUITIES	-5.0	0.0	5.0
TOTAL EQUITY	-5.0	0.0	5.0
Fixed Income			
Short-Term Fixed Income/Cash - U.S.	0.0	0.0	0.0
- Global	0.0	0.0	0.0
Intermediate Fixed Income	0.0	0.0	0.0
Global Fixed Income	0.0	0.0	0.0
TOTAL FIXED INCOME	-5.0	0.0	5.0
		0.0	

Other assets considered in determining this allocation:

_____
_____
_____

Investment constraints and/or preferences:

_____
_____
_____

INVESTMENT STRATEGY AND REVIEW

DIVERSIFICATION

Investment of the funds shall be limited, in general, to the following categories:

1. Cash and cash equivalents, including money market funds and bank certificates of deposit
2. Bonds (investment grade or better corporate, U.S. government, municipal, or foreign government)
3. Stocks (U.S. and foreign-based companies)
4. Real Estate (REIT'S)

INVESTMENT ADVICE

Generally, Advisor will assist client implement their asset allocation through passively managed asset class mutual funds, actively managed mutual funds, separate account managers, or any combination of the above. Advisor strongly believes that passively managed asset class mutual funds should be considered if appropriate. These funds are employed to capture the return behavior of an entire asset class. This approach is based upon the major tenets of Modern Portfolio Theory which states that markets are "efficient" and that investors' returns are determined principally by asset allocation decisions, not market timing or selection of specific securities. Advisor does not rely on economic forecasts, employ strategies which shift allocations between stocks, bonds and cash or search for "undiscovered" stocks. Asset classes with historically demonstrated low correlation and different risk/return profiles are combined together in an attempt to both lower the volatility of the overall portfolio and enhance returns.

PORTFOLIO REVIEW AND REBALANCING PROCEDURES

From time to time, market conditions may cause the Portfolio's investment in various asset classes to vary from the established allocation guidelines established by this IPS. Each asset class in which the Portfolio is invested shall be reviewed on a quarterly basis by Advisor and may, with Investor's approval, be rebalanced back to the recommended weighting when appropriate. Except, however, rebalancing will be advised if either the weighting of an individual asset class varies by 25%, plus or minus, of its recommended weighting, or if the total equity and/or fixed income components vary by 500 basis points, plus or minus, from that components' recommended weighting. When necessary and/or available, cash flows will be deployed in a manner consistent with rebalancing the asset allocation. In the absence of cash flows, the advisor may effect transactions to rebalance the portfolio. Income tax considerations will be reviewed where appropriate in determining rebalancing activity.

INVESTMENT POLICY STATEMENT
Rev. 04/00
REM McGladrey Investment Policy Statement 4-00

ADJUSTMENT IN THE TARGET ALLOCATION

The approved asset allocation set out above indicates an initial target allocation for each asset class. From time to time, based on the Investor's changing economic or life circumstances or new academic research, it may be desirable to make changes in the target allocation. Such changes should not, however, be made due to expectations of the relative performance of individual asset classes. The Investor must approve any proposed changes in the form of a written amendment to this IPS.

INVESTMENT STRATEGY PERFORMANCE

The Investor recognizes that asset class investment performance is cyclical and, therefore, the Investor may experience periods of time in which investment objectives are not met. In addition, unless there are extenuating circumstances, patience will often prove appropriate when performance has been disappointing for a particular asset class, or the overall portfolio.

For the overall portfolio, the Investor should allow a five-year time period or longer for achieving the stated investment return objectives. Shorter time frames contradict the principles of long-term investing. Under no circumstances, however, can results be guaranteed.

DUTIES AND RESPONSIBILITIES

The Investor should always be cognizant that they have the ultimate responsibility for the investment of their own assets. The Advisor shall assist Investor to discharge this responsibility with the care, skill, prudence and diligence under the circumstances then prevailing, that a prudent person, acting in a like capacity and familiar with such matters, would use in such conduct with like aims.

Advisor is responsible for assisting the Investor in making an appropriate asset allocation decision based on the particular needs, objectives, and risk profile of the Investor, implementing such decisions, reporting portfolio performance to the Investor and rebalancing the portfolio, as necessary.

Advisor is a Registered Investment Advisor and shall act as the investment advisor to the Investor, pursuant to the Investment Advisory Agreement between the Investor and Advisor.

The Investor should provide Advisor with all relevant information on financial condition, net worth, and risk tolerances and shall notify Advisor promptly of any changes to this information. Failure to disclose all such relevant information will limit advisor's ability to provide prudent investment advice. The Investor's duties, rights, and responsibilities are set forth in the attached Investment Advisory Agreement.

INVESTMENT POLICY STATEMENT
Rev. 04/00
REM McGladrey Investment Policy Statement 4-00

ADOPTION

Adopted by the below signed Investor this _____ day of
_____, 20 _____.

NAME AND TITLE

_____
     (printed name)

_____
     (signature)

_____
     (printed name)

_____
     (signature)

EXHIBIT A
INVESTMENT ACCOUNTS COVERED BY THIS IPS

Account Title   Account Number

_____

_____

_____

_____

All accounts listed above will be treated as one aggregate portfolio. This should provide the most efficient method (i.e. reduced cost and income tax consequences) for designing and managing the portfolio. In doing so, each account may have different asset class representation and each account's growth may vary over time. This should not detract from the overall investment policy.

INVESTMENT POLICY STATEMENT
Rev. 04/00
REM McGladrey Investment Policy Statement 4-00

INVESTMENT POLICY AMENDMENT NUMBER

_____   _____

Client Signature   Date   Advisor Signature   Date

ASSET CLASS	% OF PORTFOLIO		
	Min	Target	Max
Domestic			
U.S. Large Cap	0	0	0
U.S. Large Cap Value	0	0	0
U.S. Small Cap	0	0	0
U.S. Small Cap Value	0	0	0
Real Estate	0	0	0
TOTAL DOMESTIC EQUITIES	-5	0	5
International			
International Large Cap	0	0	0
International Large Cap Value	0	0	0
International Small Cap	0	0	0
International Small Cap Value	0	0	0
Emerging Markets	0	0	0
TOTAL INTERNATIONAL EQUITIES	-5	0	5
TOTAL EQUITY	-5	0	5
Fixed Income			
Short-Term Fixed Income/Cash - U.S.	0	0	0
- Global	0	0	0
Intermediate Fixed Income	0	0	0
Global Fixed Income	0	0	0
TOTAL FIXED INCOME	-5	0	5
		0	

Other assets considered in determining this allocation:

Reason(s) for this amendment:

Account Name(s):   Account Number(s):

INVESTMENT POLICY STATEMENT
Rev. 04/00
REM McGladrey Investment Policy Statement 4-00

Copyrights and Permissions

Publisher's Note

This publication contains the opinions and ideas of its author. It is intended to provide helpful and informative material on the subject matter covered. It is sold with the understanding that the author and publisher are not engaged in rendering professional services in the book. If the reader requires personal assistance or advice, a competent professional should be consulted.

The author and publisher specifically disclaim any responsibility for any liability, loss, or risk, personal or otherwise, which is incurred as a consequence, directly or indirectly, of the use and application of any of the contents of this book.

Trademarks: All terms mentioned in this book that are known to be or are suspected of being trademarks or service marks have been appropriately capitalized. Perigee Books cannot attest to the accuracy of this information. Use of a term in this book should not be regarded as affecting the validity of any trademark or service mark.

Legal disclaimer: This book provides general information that is intended, but not guaranteed, to be correct and up-to-date. The information is not presented as a source of tax or legal advice. You should not rely on statements or representations made within the book or by any externally referenced sources. If you need tax or legal advice upon which you intend to rely in the course of your business or legal affairs, consult a competent, independent accountant or attorney.

The contents of this book should not be taken as financial advice, or as an offer to buy or sell any securities, fund, type of fund, or financial instruments. It should not be taken as an endorsement or recommendation of any particular company or individual, and no responsibility can be taken for inaccuracies, omissions, or errors. The information presented is not to be considered investment advice. The reader should consult a registered investment advisor or registered dealer prior to making any investment decision.

The author does not assume any responsibility for actions or nonactions taken by people who have read this book, and no one shall be entitled to a claim for detrimental reliance based upon any information provided or expressed herein. Your use of any information provided here does not constitute any type of contractual relationship between yourself and the provider(s) of this information. The author hereby disclaims all responsibility and liability for all use of any information provided in this book.

The materials here are not to be interpreted as establishing an attorney-client relationship between the reader and the author or his firm.

Although great effort has been expended to ensure that only the most meaningful resources are referenced in these pages, the author does not endorse, guarantee, or warranty the accuracy, reliability, or thoroughness of any referenced information, product, or service. Any opinions, advice, statements, services, offers, or other information or content expressed or made available by third parties are those of the author or publisher alone. Reference to other sources of information does not constitute a referral, endorsement, or recommendation of any product or service. The existence of any particular reference is simply intended to imply potential interest to the reader.

The views expressed herein are exclusively those of the author and do not represent the views of any other person or any organization with which the author may be associated.

Index

A

Academic Wealth Management, 207, 238
Adelphia, 141
A.G. Edwards
    case studies involving, 110–11
Alonso, Bruce, 95
American Arbitration Association (AAA), 172, 185
    website, 185
American Stock Exchange (ASE)
    rules of, 106
Ameritrade
    case studies involving, 113
analysts
    case studies involving, 71, 200–203
    filing a claim against, 199–203
    investment banking conflicts, 2, 9, 201–3
    IPO reports, 36–37
annuities, 128
appeals, 232–33
arbitration, 14–17, *see also* claims
    alternatives to, 16–17, 186
    awards, *see* awards
    costs of, 170
    cross-examination, 226–27
    definition of, 188
    mandatory, *see* mandatory arbitration
    pluses and minuses of, 16, 168
    pre-hearing phase proceedings, 224–36

statistics on, 3, 17, 177
    testifying, 225
    witnesses, 224–25
arbitrators, *see also* tribunals
    public and nonpublic, 211
    rules about, 224
asset allocation, 6, 121–24, 131–34, 138–39, 152–53
    definition of, 148
associated person, 208
attorneys
    costs of using, 177, 181
    deciding whether to hire, 176–77
    fees, 175–76
        tax status of, 234–36
    finding, 186–87
awards, 231–35
    attorney's portion of, 175–76
    getting paid, 233–34
    statistics about, 192
    tax status of, 234–36

B

Bank of America
    case studies involving, 99–100, 102
Bank One
    case studies involving, 99
Baron & Co.
    case studies involving, 196–99
Bear Stearns
    case studies involving, 196–99

definition of, 48, 77

case studies involving, 52,
53–54, 74–76, 110–11, 151,
167, 209

claimants, 184, 188

being cross-examined, 226–27

testifying, 225

claims

costs of filing, 175–76

counterclaims, 193, 210

cross claims, 193–94

deciding whether to pursue,
174, 235–36

definition of, 170, 188

filing, *see* filing a claim

negotiating, 218–20

parts of, 184–85

potential rewards of filing,
174–75

settling, 219–21

statistics about, 164, 183–84,
192

third-party claims, 193–94

clearing brokers

definition of, 208

filing claims against,
195–200

Clemente, Robert, 170–71

CNBC, 22, 29, 33

Cohn, Scott, 22, 29, 33

commissions, 27–31, 33

definition of, 44

deregulation of, 35

hidden, 30–31

trailing, in mutual funds, 31

compliance departments

problems with, 26–27, 43

conflicts of interest

between brokers and clients,
2, 7–10, 36–37, 40–41,
107

in mutual funds, 79–102

sell-side analysis, 36

with IPOs, 37–40

control, 48–50, 108–9

controlling persons, 60, 194–95

definition of, 208

correlation, 121, 131

cost-equity ratio, 43, 50, 51–52,
108, 135

case studies involving, 19, 52,
53

definition of, 77

costs, *see also* claims, costs of
filing; arbitration, costs of

effect on returns, 161

transaction, 13, 133, 134–35,
139, 143

annual management fees, 124,
134–35

Cutler, Stephen M., 102

D

damages

computation of, 174–75,
228–31

punitive, 175, 229

de Mere, Chevalier, 128

de Molvre, Abraham, 130

Dimensional Fund Advisors (DFA),
102, 138–39, 238

discovery, 210, 212–17, 222

disgorgement, 230

Dishman, Chris, 109

Regulation, *see* NASDR
rules of, 8, 26, 28–29, 32, 46,
    65, 66, 105–7
website, 185
NASDAQ
    operations of, 31–33
NASD Discovery Guide, 213–15,
    222
NASDR, 171
    website, 183
National Association of Investors
    Corporation (NAIC), 5
    investor survey, 5
negotiations, 218–19
New York Stock Exchange
    (NYSE)
    arbitration department, 17
    members of, 14
    rules of, 26, 105–7
    operations of, 32
    website, 183, 185
nonqualified stock options (NSOs),
    70–71

O

omissions, *see* misrepresentations
    and omissions
O'Neal, Edward S., 87, 90, 93, 98
online brokers
    case studies involving, 113
    disputes with, 12
    unsuitability, 112–14, 118
Oppenheimer Funds
    case studies involving, 189
options, 70–71
order failure, 11, 65–66
order flow, 32

Ostrowski, Robert, 79–80
overconcentration, 72–74, 109–10,
    157
over-leveraging, 11, 68–70

P

PaineWebber
    case studies involving, 38–39,
    62
parties, 184, 188
Pascal, Blaise, 128
penny stocks, 106, 118
pension fund managers, 159
Perusquia, Enrique, 62
PIABA, 164, 187
    website, 187
picking winners, *see* stock picking
portfolios
    active management of, 144–46
    construction of, 157, 238–39
    false beliefs about, 13–14
pre-hearing phase, 210–21
price manipulation, 11, 47, 57–61
private placements, 115
Prudential
    case studies involving, 61,
    79–80, 101
Prudent Investor Rule, 162–63
Public Investor Arbitration Bar
    Association, *see* PIABA
Public Citizen, 170
pump-and-dump schemes
    case studies of, 45–46
    definition of, 77–78
    logistics of, 59–60
Putnam
    case studies involving, 101